New Wave, New Hollywood

T0413897

ii

New Wave, New Hollywood

Reassessment, Recovery, and Legacy

Edited by
Nathan Abrams and Gregory Frame

BLOOMSBURY ACADEMIC

NEW YORK • LONDON • OXFORD • NEW DELHI • SYDNEY

BLOOMSBURY ACADEMIC
Bloomsbury Publishing Inc
1385 Broadway, New York, NY 10018, USA
50 Bedford Square, London, WC1B 3DP, UK
29 Earlsfort Terrace, Dublin 2, Ireland

BLOOMSBURY, BLOOMSBURY ACADEMIC and the Diana logo are trademarks of
Bloomsbury Publishing Plc

First published in the United States of America 2021
This paperback edition published 2023

Cover design: Eleanor Rose
Cover image: *The Graduate*, Anne Bancroft as Mrs. Robinson,
Dustin Hoffman as Ben Braddock, Dir. Mike Nichols, 1971 © Lawrence Turman /
Collection Christophel / ArenaPAL; www.arenapal.com

Library of Congress Cataloging-in-Publication Data
Names: Frame, Gregory, 1985– editor. | Abrams, Nathan, editor.
Title: New wave, new Hollywood : reassessment, recovery, and legacy /
edited by Gregory Frame and Nathan Abrams.
Description: New York : Bloomsbury Academic, 2021. |
Includes bibliographical references and index.
Identifiers: LCCN 2021013917 (print) | LCCN 2021013918 (ebook) |
ISBN 9781501360404 (hardback) | ISBN 9781501360398 (epub) |
ISBN 9781501360381 (pdf) | ISBN 9781501360374
Subjects: LCSH: New wave films—United States—History and criticism. |
Motion pictures—United States—History—20th century.
Classification: LCC PN1993.5.U6 N4855 2021 (print) | LCC PN1993.5.U6
(ebook) | DDC 791.430973—dc23
LC record available at https://lccn.loc.gov/2021013917
LC ebook record available at https://lccn.loc.gov/2021013918

ISBN: HB: 978-1-5013-6040-4
PB: 978-1-5013-7272-8
ePDF: 978-1-5013-6038-1
eBook: 978-1-5013-6039-8

Typeset by Newgen KnowledgeWorks Pvt. Ltd., Chennai, India

To find out more about our authors and books visit www.bloomsbury.com
and sign up for our newsletters.

Contents

List of Illustrations   vii

Acknowledgments   viii

1   Introduction   1
    Nathan Abrams and Gregory Frame

2   The Great Shift in Hollywood Cinema: Men, Women, and Genre
    Revisionism of the American New Wave   21
    Fjoralba Miraka

3   Formal Radicalism versus Radical Representation: Reassessing
    The French Connection (William Friedkin, 1971) and *Dirty Harry*
    (Don Siegel, 1971)   39
    Cary Edwards

4   A Wave of Their Own: How Jewish Filmmakers Invented the
    New Hollywood   59
    Vincent Brook

5   New Hollywood's "Zany Godards": A "Shirley" Serious Assessment
    of Zucker-Abrahams-Zucker   79
    Emilio Audissino

6   Design as Authorship: Polly Platt's New Hollywood Aesthetic   101
    Aaron Hunter

7   "The Ultimate Fusion of Commerce and Art": Waldo Salt and
    Screenwriting in the 1970s   121
    Oliver Gruner

8   Expanding the Past: Julie Dash and Zora Neale Hurston, African
    American Women Filmmakers of New Hollywood and Early Cinema   141
    Aimee Dixon Anthony

9   Lost in the Landscape: The Legacy of Barbara Loden's *Wanda*
     (1970) on the Contemporary American Independent Female
     Road Movie   161
     Aimee Mollaghan

10   The New Wave in the New Millennium: *Joker, Taxi Driver,*
     Nostalgia, and Trumpian Politics   179
     Karen A. Ritzenhoff and Hannah D'Orso

11   Indie Courtship: Pursuing the American New Wave   201
     Kim Wilkins

12   Afterword: New Wave, New Hollywood, New Research   221
     Peter Krämer

List of Contributors   243
Index   249

Illustrations

3.1 The clear separation between Doyle and Charnier (Doyle stands in the background) in *The French Connection* (1971) 50

3.2 Subjective alignment with Scorpio's scopophilic gaze in *Dirty Harry* (1971) 51

3.3 Callahan's scopophilic gaze in *Dirty Harry* (1971) 52

5.1 Dramatic perspiration in *Zero Hour!* (1957) and its intensification in *Airplane!* (1980) 88

5.2 ZAZ's audiovisual disjunction in *Top Secret!* (1984) 91

5.3 Peritextual jokes in the end credits of *The Naked Gun 2½: The Smell of Fear* (1991) 92

5.4 A ridiculously ample choice of "keys," *Police Squad!*, Episode Five (1982) 94

10.1 Travis Bickle in his cab in *Taxi Driver* (1976) 183

10.2 Arthur Fleck in the police car in *Joker* (2019) 184

10.3 Fog emerging from the sewers in *Taxi Driver* (1976) 185

10.4 The chaos and destruction at the end of *Joker* (2019) 185

10.5 Sophie puts a finger to her head in *Joker* (2019) 189

10.6 Arthur Fleck uses Bickle's classic hand gesture in *Joker* (2019) 189

10.7 The bank of televisions broadcasting Franklin's murder in *Joker* (2019) 191

10.8 Arthur Fleck admires the destruction he has wrought in *Joker* (2019) 196

Acknowledgments

We would like to thank Katie Gallof at Bloomsbury Publishing for her support for this project, which has been long in the making. With this in mind, we would also like to thank our contributors for their patience through the extended proposal stage and then delivering their chapters despite the disruptive effect the pandemic has had on all our lives. Their work makes an excellent contribution to our collective understanding of the New Wave and New Hollywood in relation to contemporary debates about film history, and film scholarship more widely.

We would also like to thank everyone who supported the initial conference commemorating the fiftieth anniversary of the New Wave in 2017: the British Association for American Studies who funded it in part through their small grants scheme supported by the US embassy; Nerys Boggan, from the College of Arts, Humanities and Business, who provided invaluable support in the organization and execution of the event; and Emyr Williams, cinema coordinator at Pontio Arts and Innovation Centre, who supported the event with screenings of *Bonnie and Clyde*, *2001: A Space Odyssey*, and *Apocalypse Now*. We also thank the many volunteers from our postgraduate community who helped us make the event such a success.

We would like to reserve special thanks to Peter Krämer not only for contributing his excellent afterword but also doing so in a manner that demonstrates how much more there is to say about the New Wave and New Hollywood. We hope this volume contributes to the beginning of a new conversation about the period.

1

Introduction

Nathan Abrams and Gregory Frame

When in the summer of 2016 we discussed holding a conference the following year to launch the new Centre for Film, Television and Screen Studies at Bangor University, the subject seemed obvious. The year 2017 would mark the fiftieth anniversary of the start of the American New Wave. The mythology of the New Wave or, if you prefer, "The Hollywood Renaissance" or "New Hollywood" has solidified around the idea that 1967 represented a radical and definitive break from that which came before. *The Graduate* (Mike Nichols, 1967) and *Bonnie and Clyde* (Arthur Penn, 1967) embodied something new in American cinema: rejecting the splashy, big-budget family entertainment that had dominated in the years following the Second World War, breaking the shackles of the stringent and moralistic Production Code, and finding inspiration from the stylistic swagger of European cinema, the young, maverick filmmakers of this "New Wave" aimed to deliver something different. More realistic, more alive to the politically turbulent times in which they were working, more experimental and challenging in terms of form, style, and narrative.

This is the story most commonly told of the American New Wave. It has been rehearsed and repeated by critics and scholars. Our absorption of this narrative of the New Wave reflects a certain historical naivete and, despite admiration for the films of the period, a level of ignorance regarding the debates that continue to rage about them. What was revealed through the development of the conference, the variety of papers that were delivered, and the subsequent assembly of this collection is that there remains a great deal, despite the plethora of writing about it, to be said about the New Wave (not least a debate about what would constitute an appropriate moniker). When did it start and end, for can it really be the case that it begins definitively with the release of *Bonnie and Clyde*, and is concluded by the spectacular failure of *Heaven's Gate* (Michael Cimino) in 1980? What would constitute an appropriate New Wave canon, given that the films that dominate discussion in this area are characterized by a rather narrow set of themes and aesthetic features? Relatedly, and most importantly, who gets to be a part of this story, and who gets to tell it? In this introduction, we seek to examine the parameters of this debate and illustrate how the chapters that follow seek to respond to, and challenge, the dominant discourse.

What, and When?

What is implied by the various names by which the New Wave goes? The term "New Wave" enables what was produced in the American cinema during this period to ally itself to the innovative films emerging out of a variety of other national contexts: most obviously, the films made in the United States owed a great deal to the French New Wave, though the very discourse of what constitutes a "wave" that is "new" demands some attention. New Hollywood is also a complex designation, as it often refers both to the idiosyncratic, challenging work of the late 1960s and early 1970s as well as to the more self-consciously popular and populist entertainment produced from the middle of the decade onward (as well as to the films a reconfigured corporate Hollywood produced through the 1980s and beyond). The Hollywood Renaissance, which has been employed by other prominent scholars in the area, could also be interpreted as reiterating the mythological construction of the films, most often associated with it being emblematic of a creative rebirth after a long period of aesthetically unchallenging, creatively moribund filmmaking. However, we will unpack here the various implications and usages of the different terms.

As all three terms have their benefits and drawbacks, it is tempting to pick one and stick with it. The recent scholarship examining the period is illuminating in its assessment of the current thinking in this aspect of the debate. Peter Krämer and Yannis Tzioumakis's volume addresses the problematics of the different terms and focuses particularly on the use of "new," a designation regularly employed by critics to describe American cinema from the late 1940s onward. Their argument raises significant issues about the appropriateness of any of the terms employed here: that innovation in postwar Hollywood was an ongoing process, and that it is impossible to say definitively that one film (or set of films) represented a definitive break with the past. As they suggest, "one has to be very cautious about making claims concerning fundamental breaks and turning points in American film history."[1] Their justification for the use of the term The Hollywood Renaissance derives principally from the famous *Time* magazine cover story in December 1967 that featured *Bonnie and Clyde* prominently and spoke of a new artistic flourishing in American filmmaking. Geoff King and David Cook have also used the term. For King, The Hollywood Renaissance is employed to differentiate the films and filmmakers from the earlier period (1967–74), before the success of *Jaws* (Steven Spielberg, 1975), the advent of the modern blockbuster, and the recovery and expansion of corporate Hollywood. For Cook, the term "Renaissance" is used to identify the period of auteurism's greatest flourishing in Hollywood, representing the creative apex for many of the directors most closely associated with it, followed by an overall decline. Krämer and Tzioumakis make a compelling case for the use of the term The Hollywood Renaissance to describe Hollywood in this period. Unlike King and Cook, they make clear that they are focused on a particular and rather small subset of American films in relation to it, and they leave the time frame under consideration open. They make an invaluable contribution to our understanding of the period through their close attention to the industrial conditions, production processes, and collaborative relationships between the creative personnel that produced some of the most important films of the time. Their departure from the ahistorical *auteurist* discourse that has dominated the study of Hollywood's "Renaissance" represents an important methodological step in the ongoing reevaluation and reappraisal of this period. However, this volume seeks a more expansive examination of the American cinema to incorporate consideration of the period's legacies and blind spots. Therefore, the term "Renaissance," wedded as it is to the analysis of the work of the films and filmmakers about which much has been said, is not the most appropriate one for us to use.

The New Hollywood, favored by Jonathan Kirshner and Jon Lewis in their recent volume, presents its own problems. Their justification for its use, however, is reasonable enough, built on the assessment that some of the films produced from 1967 until 1976 did represent a break with the past, citing not only *Bonnie and Clyde* but also the violence of *The Dirty Dozen* (Robert Aldrich, 1967), the temporally experimental *Point Blank* (John Boorman, 1967), and the youthful rebellion of *The Graduate*, as indicative of this newness. Their determination of 1976 as the end of New Hollywood draws on an analysis of wider political forces, particularly the end of the Vietnam War, the resignation of Richard Nixon, the election of Jimmy Carter, and the later conservative resurgence that resulted in Ronald Reagan's victory in 1980. Cinematically, the triumph of underdog *Rocky* (John G. Avildsen, 1976) at the 1977 Academy Awards against its apparently more prestigious, ambitious competitors *Taxi Driver* (Martin Scorsese, 1976), *Network* (Sidney Lumet, 1976), and *All the President's Men* (Alan J. Pakula, 1976) symbolized for them the relative decline of the New Wave and a shift in emphasis toward a New Hollywood centered on blockbusters and more conservative, traditional forms of entertainment.[2] J. Hoberman's contribution to the collection is illuminating in this regard, citing 1976 as an emblematic moment, which began with the release of *Taxi Driver*—"Hollywood's last great feel-bad movie" (this claim is rather grandiose, and very debatable)—and ending with the hugely successful debut of *Rocky*, "which created the template for the feel-good movies that would endure for the rest of the twentieth century and beyond."[3] There is a virtue in the neatness of this story. Though they acknowledge the potential slippages at either end of this period—the adaptation of the term "New Hollywood" to incorporate consideration of the modern blockbuster, and the continued growth of multinational media conglomerates in the early twenty-first century of which the old studios formed only a small part—Kirshner and Lewis remain attached to this somewhat definitive endpoint.

Because our collection is more interested in recovering those who have been marginalized and ignored by the plentiful studies of the period that have been conducted thus far, as well as exploring the long tail of the period's impact and influence, we do not consider the term to be that useful on its own. If New Hollywood is both the creative flourishing of auteurist cinema from 1967 to 1976 *and* the subsequent relentless growth and expansion of a revitalized, corporatized industry built on the financial logic of the blockbuster thereafter, where do the artists working at the margins fit in? And what of the spirit of creative innovation and politicized challenge that survived in American cinema after *Jaws* and *Star Wars* (George Lucas, 1977)?

It is, for this reason, this volume prefers to use both the terms New Wave and New Hollywood in its title and, for our contributors, they are employed interchangeably depending on the context about which they are writing. Some of the essays featured here are interested in critical reassessments of the films about which much has already been written, and would ordinarily fit straightforwardly under any of the three traditional designations. However, in looking at them from slightly different angles in their considerations of race, gender, and ethnicity, and emphasizing the involvement of important figures other than the director, they essentially challenge the received wisdom about much of this work. Similarly, in the focus on "genre" films that might otherwise fit easily within the "New Hollywood" designation, some chapters examine critically marginalized and neglected aspects of the period's output, which embodied the same kinds of aesthetic experimentation and innovation present in their more celebrated contemporary counterparts. The second part of the collection's mission, therefore, is to recover particular films, filmmakers, and creative artists from the margins of history—the screenwriters, production designers, and certain directors who have not received the level of attention they deserve. They were part of the New Wave in its initial flourishing, and many of them also continued to work in substantial and meaningful ways through the New Hollywood period.

Related to this, the final, and perhaps most significant, aspect of our purpose is to determine the legacy of the New Wave and New Hollywood. Here we move into a consideration of periodization, and what constitutes the appropriate time frame for analysis. It would seem the term one employs to describe the period—New Wave, New Hollywood, Hollywood Renaissance—is contingent on when one considers it to have begun and ended. The beginning seems obvious: *Time* magazine's cover story on December 8, 1967. This is this moment at which Kirshner and Lewis, and Krämer and Tzioumakis, begin their introductions, though the latter qualify this in relation to the important amendments made to the Production Code in 1966 and the "special arrangements" made for the release of *Who's Afraid of Virginia Woolf?* (Mike Nichols, 1966).[4] Jeff Menne's recent *Post-Fordist Cinema* offers a quite radical reconsideration of this aspect of the debate, arguing that many of the seeds that blossomed into the New Wave's biggest successes, such as *Bonnie and Clyde* and *The Graduate*, were planted a considerable time before 1967. Similarly, he argues that the rigid focus on aesthetic debates has "led critics to report its death arbitrarily and prematurely."[5] He bases his analysis around the year 1962, the year that saw both the publication of Milton Friedman's *Capitalism and Freedom*, which set in motion the long-term, fundamental restructuring of power relations between labor and capital, and Andrew Sarris's "Notes on the Auteur Theory in 1962," which played the crucial role of extracting Hollywood directors from their commercial surroundings, and made it possible to conceive of them as artists (and would become a vital means through which these films were produced and sold). His claim is very interesting and, again, has virtue in its neatness. However, Krämer makes a compelling case in an earlier essay that debates about authorship, and in particular, the valorization of the director, as well as the influence of European art cinema on Hollywood and the emergence of various types of "arty" American films, precedes even 1962, stretching back to 1945.[6] That said, Menne makes the important claim that his periodization (1962–75) is concerned primarily with the time it took to establish and entrench the New Hollywood, rather than a documentation of its entire existence. Therefore, the suggestion that the New Hollywood (or New Wave) existed *after* 1975 (or 1980) is beneficial to the conceptualization of this collection. While our collection does not share Menne's emphasis on the changes in production management and culture that ultimately birthed the New Hollywood, his approach nonetheless opens up the critical space to reconsider the before and after of the New Wave, New Hollywood, or "Hollywood Renaissance" in more expansive ways.

If the *mythos* of the New Wave suggests the period had an obvious beginning, it also has a manifest conclusion. Though Kirshner and Lewis cite the chaotic production of *Apocalypse Now* (Francis Ford Coppola, 1979), the shoot of which wildly overran along with its budget, as a precursor to this moment (though it was financially successful), the myth tells us it was the commercial disaster of *Heaven's Gate*, and the critical opprobrium leveled at it, that signaled the definitive endpoint of the kind of idiosyncratic, auteurist cinema that for a brief period had flourished within mainstream American filmmaking.

The truth is, as this collection reveals, not so simple. The rigid periodization (1967–80) is misleading, as a number of filmmakers with whom the New Wave and New Hollywood are most closely associated would continue to work in the subsequent decades (though admittedly many would do so in a diminished capacity). The most prolific of these, such as Steven Spielberg, Martin Scorsese, and Woody Allen, would make films throughout the subsequent years, enjoying significant directorial control as well as critical and commercial success. Spielberg has won two Academy Awards for Best Director since 1980, Scorsese has one, and Allen is still making films at a rate of about one per year. Mike Nichols and Brian De Palma worked frequently and made several important and successful films after the New Wave "ended," from *Silkwood* (Mike Nichols, 1983), *Working Girl* (Mike Nichols, 1988), and *Closer* (Mike Nichols, 2004), to *Blow Out* (Brian De Palma, 1981), *The Untouchables* (Brian De Palma, 1987), and *Mission: Impossible* (Brian De Palma, 1996). Robert Altman endured a lengthy spell of marginalization and stasis, before reemerging as a significant creative force with *The Player* (1992), *Short Cuts* (1993), and, later, *Gosford Park* (2003). After a significant hiatus, Terrence Malick emerged with *The Thin Red Line* (1998) and, later, *The Tree of Life* (2011). Though he worked very infrequently, Stanley Kubrick still produced two highly significant films after 1980—*Full Metal Jacket* (1987) and *Eyes Wide Shut* (1999). This is all to say that while for most New Wave directors, it was in the long 1970s that their movies mattered *most* (to adapt Kirshner and Lewis's phrase, itself borrowed from David Thomson), many of them nonetheless proved themselves capable of producing works that enjoyed significant critical attention and, in some cases, commercial success, in a radically altered industrial landscape.[7]

What this periodizing rigidity also ignores, and what is most pertinent to this collection, is the other filmmakers and artists who continued to work in various capacities to produce radical, challenging films in other contexts, often at the margins of production, through the Reagan era and beyond. How did the creative experimentation and innovation of the time survive in an era of convergence and corporatization (indeed, did it)? If what occurred in Hollywood was a New Wave in the same way that Hong Kong, Czechoslovakia, Brazil, the United Kingdom, France, India, Japan, and Germany enjoyed New Waves in their national cinemas at or around this time, what happened after that wave crested and broke, and how did what came after respond to and recall that which came before? How does the style and energy of the American New Wave persist today?

Related to this question of periodization is what constitutes an appropriate New Wave canon. As Krämer and Tzioumakis observe, the films that are often included in such discussions have some, if not all, of the following features: an increased "realism" in terms of style and subject matter; a left-leaning or liberal attitude to social issues; a self-consciousness in terms of form and style; young, rebellious male protagonists who lack the conventional qualities of Hollywood heroes; a looseness of narrative structure and downbeat endings; and, of course, more explicit depictions of sexuality and violence. This is certainly a comprehensive and effective definition of the American New Wave cinema that has enjoyed the most attention in critical circles. It is, however, also very limiting and exclusionary, not just in terms of the racial and gender politics of this (which we will address shortly), but in offering a very narrow framework through which to assess aesthetic and narrative experimentation in American cinema of the period. The "Hollywood Renaissance" canon, as Krämer and Tzioumakis refer to it, "constitutes only a small fraction of the output of the American film industry of the late 1960s and 1970s, a period during which African-American directors, for the first time, made inroads into Hollywood."[8]

This collection seeks, therefore, to write into the story of the American New Wave those films and filmmakers who have, for reasons ranging from a cultural elitism about genre pictures, to the rigid definition of the New Wave period, to the critical bias toward white male *auteur* directors, been otherwise excluded from it. While their films may not meet the definition of New Wave cinema outlined above, as our contributors demonstrate, their films nonetheless show a spirit of experimentation and innovation in terms of narrative and character construction, and aesthetic style, similar to their more critically deified counterparts. *Wanda* (Barbara Loden, 1970) has enjoyed a critical reappraisal and celebration in recent years, though despite this it remains relatively marginal in popular conceptions of New Wave cinema. More aesthetically conservative films like *Dirty Harry* (Don Siegel, 1971), featuring a director and star much more conventionally associated with the "old" Hollywood, have not traditionally been part of this story either. Comedy, aside from some attention paid to Allen and Mel Brooks, also finds no place in the above definition. Other filmmakers, who emerged in this period but did not enjoy their greatest critical and commercial successes until later, have been included in this collection on the basis that their work is part of the "long tail" of the New Wave (as we seek to engage with the complex legacy of the period).

Who Gets to Be Part of This Story?

According to Krämer and Tzioumakis, the literature about the American New Wave "deal[s] almost exclusively with films made by white, male directors born between the early 1920s and the late 1940s."[9] The discussion and analysis of the New Wave is suffused with an *auteurist* discourse that, inevitably, privileges the (mostly) white men who directed these films and excludes everybody else: screenwriters, producers, cinematographers, editors, production designers and managers, musicians, sound designers, costume designers, hair and makeup artists, and visual effects artists, not to mention the women and people of color who contributed to the films in the "canon" as it currently stands, as well as their own. The work that is currently being done in studies of this period is a welcome corrective to this, not just in terms of emphasizing the work of artists who did not necessarily sit in the director's chair but also to include women and people of color who have contributed to politically challenging, aesthetically innovative American filmmaking.

The preoccupation with New Wave directors is indicative of the fixation in Film Studies with the director more generally. It is not news to anybody that Andrew Sarris's import of the *auteur* theory to the United States in the early 1960s has had an enormous impact on both the academic study and industrial practice of film. However much the theory has been challenged, it retains a central position in the popular understanding and appreciation of cinema, and the director is still the figure on whom much industrial, critical, and analytical energy is expended (even if that energy is deployed to challenge their centrality and supremacy). It also remains the case that, thanks to the prominence of textual analysis and mise-en-scène criticism in Film Studies, it is the finished film that is most often the object of interrogation, and the visual and creative choices therein are often uncomplicatedly and uncritically attributed to the figure of the director.

Such ahistoricism has been frequently challenged in recent years through an archival approach that has sought to reveal the collaborative relationships between directors, screenwriters, actors, and other important creative influences. In this vein, Krämer and Tzioumakis have sought to challenge the dominance of this discourse by examining some of New Hollywood's most prominent films through close analyses of their productions. While our collection does not take this exact approach, it seeks in certain chapters to decenter the director as the only focus of our attention, including chapters that examine screenwriting and production design. In the instances in which the director is the focus, it is ordinarily those figures whose work has not often been considered part of the New Wave that command our attention, as we seek to recover important films, filmmakers, and other creative artists who have otherwise been marginalized and excluded in studies of this period.

The race and gender politics of this discourse are vital to address. Kirshner and Lewis issue something of a disclaimer in the introduction to their collection, in which they take into account the women and people of color who contributed to the New Hollywood, even if only one of the chapters in the book itself examine them in any detail (in Molly Haskell's examination of the stars of the "neo-woman's film"). In this short section, Kirshner and Lewis mention Barbara Loden and Claudia Weill, as well as the women who wrote, produced, and acted in the great pictures of the New Hollywood. There is also some discussion of Blaxploitation and its important role in providing opportunities to directors of color. However, as they freely acknowledge, their collection offers an opportunity to revisit a period of filmmaking they consider to have been a golden age, rather than revise what is known and understood of the period (or, indeed, to reassess its underlying problematics which, as revelations in recent years have indicated, were manifold).

Indeed, the anxiety about the term "retrospective," which implies a somewhat uncritical nostalgia for the past, is what drove us to reconsider the name of this collection. As two of the chapters demonstrate, there is considerable nostalgia for the spirit and style of the New Wave alive in contemporary cinema, a yearning Kirshner and Lewis are unashamed to admit of themselves (even the title of their collection betrays this). However, as our contributors suggest, such nostalgia for the New Wave is built on troublingly reactionary foundations, and some deeply problematic attitudes toward race, gender, and sexuality. The unchallenged position of the American New Wave in the cultural consciousness does rather elide many of these debates.

Much of the recent scholarship about the New Wave seeks to correct this. Maya Montañez Smukler's *Liberating Hollywood* represents an important intervention in this regard. Her work writes women filmmakers back into the story of American cinema of this period, demonstrating the ways in which the feminist movement of the 1970s had a tangible impact on the increasing number of women directing feature films in the US film industry in the period during which the New Wave is understood to have occurred (1967–80). Smukler is keen to emphasize the uncomfortable truths behind the myths of the American New Wave; namely, that it was a period of expansion and experimentation, where "doors once locked by tradition, unions or inertia are wide open."[10] It may have been true that the power of the studios had dramatically diminished, and with it, the significance of the old studio bosses, but it remained the case that being white and being male were still significant advantages in the decisions about who got to make movies. The failure of lawsuits filed by the Directors Guild of America against Warner Bros. and Columbia Pictures for discrimination demonstrated that there was "no reliable legal recourse against discrimination based on sex and race, specifically with regard to the position of director."[11] The continued and persistent problematics of auteurism and a preoccupation with the figure of the director is one of the areas for exploration in this collection, but it is important to note Smukler's overall intention: "to *expand* the existing historical narrative of the 1970s film industry and to then *integrate* within it the contribution of women directors during this period."[12]

While our collection is not as closely focused on the politics of sex and gender in the US film industry of the 1970s, the overwhelming preoccupation with male directors as the focus of scholarship of the American New Wave to date demands redress. It is for this reason too that we seek to include the work of the L.A. Rebellion in our consideration of New Wave cinema. The prominent collective of Black filmmakers at the University of California Los Angeles (UCLA), whose work spanned roughly the period traditionally identified as the "New Wave era" (late 1960s through to the mid-1980s), sought to challenge the ways in which Black people had been represented onscreen. They also looked to address institutional racism at UCLA and within the Hollywood film industry. As Allyson Nadia Field, Jan-Christopher Horak, and Jacqueline Najuma Stewart argue in the first edited collection addressing the origins, practices, and creative outputs of this filmmaking collective, "the L.A. Rebellion was rebelling for ways to make and circulate films free of the restrictions that the filmmakers believed made commercial 'official' cinemas corrupt and conservative in style and politics."[13] Interestingly, Field, Horak, and Stewart identify the wider revolutionary spirit alive in cinemas of all kinds in the introduction to their collection. The conventional narrative of the American New Wave is identified, whereby the challenges faced by Hollywood as a consequence of the breakup of the vertically integrated studios and the rise of television resulted in a period of upheaval and change. However, it is clear that while the L.A. Rebellion existed alongside these developments in Hollywood, it drew its inspiration from the wellspring of the "Third Cinema" of the postcolonial era and looked to experimental aesthetics, narrative, and character construction to realize an alternative depiction of the Black experience in the United States. Shaped by the civil rights movement, and moving away from the assimilationist strategies of conventional Hollywood cinema, the L.A. Rebellion's films shone a light on economic and structural oppression. Crucially, it is a political cinema that has been marginalized not just in New Wave discourse, but in Film Studies more generally. As Field, Horak, and Stewart suggest, the development of the archive at UCLA and the release of a DVD boxset in 2015 have begun the process of correcting this. Incorporating the histories of filmmakers from marginalized groups into a more inclusive and expansive consideration of the New Wave era in American cinema is one of the fundamental goals of this collection.

Who Gets to Tell It?

What struck us as we developed the conference program was how few women scholars sent in abstracts in response to our call for papers.[14] This has led to a long period of reflection on how exclusionary the discourse of the American New Wave is. Even the recent collections that have acknowledged the problem that American New Wave discourse is dominated by male voices nonetheless reinforce this: three of the contributors to Krämer and Tzioumakis's collection are women, while of the authors of the nine chapters in Kirshner and Lewis's recent volume, only two. Why? The dominant myth that the New Wave was all about young, male mavericks who shook up the Hollywood system no doubt plays its part in this, but it is also true that many of the films that feature most prominently in discussions of the New Wave are contemptuous of women if they are interested in them at all. The scholarly preoccupation with these films, and the tendency to ignore or explain away these deeply troubling aspects in favor of discourses about "art," and political and formal radicalism, suggests there exists an institutional, structural problem with sexism and misogyny within academia too—though this is unlikely to be news to anyone.

Our collection, by offering a more balanced number of contributions from men and women, is an attempt to correct this. In expanding what we think of as the "American New Wave"—looking outside the "canon" as it is currently constituted as well as beyond 1980 as a cutoff point—is one element. Another is considering the discourse itself, in terms of how and why women are denigrated, marginalized, and excluded in the films at present considered "canonical," and the manner in which white, male *auteurist* discourse has lingered, as a means to evaluate films considered to be stylistically and narratively innovative and challenging in American cinema.

However, one highly problematic aspect of designating the dominant discourse of the American New Wave as white and male is the fact that so many of the filmmakers most prominently associated with the period are Jewish. Jewishness has a complex relationship with whiteness, and some unpacking and clarification around these issues is therefore required. It is apparent that when people use the term "white" in a Western/American context what they are in fact referring to are White Anglo-Saxon Protestants (WASPs). While many Ashkenazi Jews might appear as "white," not least owing to success and privilege, for much of American history they have not been considered or treated as fully white. While there is an argument that Jews were gradually whitened, many of those Jews feel that this label is precarious and liable to being removed at any time, especially given the rise in antisemitism in Trump's America. With this in mind, one of our contributors (re)instates a consideration of Jewishness into the analysis of New Wave auteurs in order to break down this uncritical view of New Wave auteurs as monolithically white.

Reassessment, Recovery, and Legacy

It goes without saying that the American New Wave and New Hollywood have both been written about extensively by scholars. However, as we have shown in our introduction, this has, to a significant degree, rather fossilized what the period means in the cultural consciousness and has limited *what* is discussed under the auspices of New Wave and New Hollywood studies, as well as *how* it is discussed. To address this, we have divided our collection into three clear sections: reassessment, recovery, and legacy. In the first section, Reassessment, three chapters seek to challenge some of the preconceptions of the films of this period and provide new ways of analyzing them.

Fjoralba Miraka demonstrates how the films most prominently associated with the New Wave, in their focus on the travails of young, male protagonists, fundamentally realigned American cinema's melodramatic mode. While the women's films of the 1940s focused on women's experiences and struggles, Miraka identifies a "great shift" toward the drama of the male psyche in the films of the New Wave. In so doing, using the New Wave's problematic revision of the femme fatale as the backbone of her analysis, Miraka reveals how the films of the 1960s and 1970s marginalize and displace women. By looking at the archetype's adaptation and amendment in films as diverse as *The Graduate*, *Klute* (Alan J. Pakula, 1971), *Chinatown* (Roman Polanski, 1974), and *Taxi Driver*, she demonstrates the ways in which the films of the period policed their women into very conventional, unthreatening, and submissive ways of being.

Cary Edwards reassesses two police thrillers of the early 1970s, *The French Connection* (William Friedkin, 1971) and *Dirty Harry* (Don Siegel, 1971). Through close analysis of their reception, Edwards demonstrates how the former has become uncomplicatedly associated with the formal innovation and auteurism of New Wave, while the latter's reputation has been fixed as a reactionary product of the old Hollywood. However, through rigorous attention to the construction of character in *Dirty Harry*, and the ways in which the film invites its audience to align itself and identify with Harry Callahan (Clint Eastwood) or his antagonist, Scorpio (Andrew Robinson), Edwards reveals an altogether more ideologically complex, ambiguous film than its critics suggested on its initial release. In so doing, Edwards questions the binaries between "old" Hollywood and new, and not only invites consideration of Eastwood and Siegel in discussions of the New Wave but also questions the left-wing ideological bent of New Wave cinema more generally.

Vincent Brook presents an important reassessment of the filmmakers who both dominated the New Hollywood, as well as discussions of it thereafter. He identifies the fact that an overwhelming number of directors who produced some of the most important films of the period were Jewish and seeks to position their work as possessive of a specifically Jewish sensibility. Through close attention paid to the work of Arthur Penn, Mike Nichols, Stanley Kubrick, Sidney Lumet, and Woody Allen, Brook demonstrates how it is impossible to comprehend fully the New Hollywood without paying attention to how these directors, through their films, were expressing a form of cultural, secular Jewishness focused on progressive social change and cultural innovation. In so doing, Brook provides an invaluable and essential reassessment of films and filmmakers about which much has already been said, urging us to reconsider the New Wave through a new prism.

As indicated previously, studies of the New Wave have been dominated by an *auteurist* focus that has privileged the discussion of a rather narrow range of films telling stories of rebellious, young male protagonists in a realist style, directed by men and released in the period 1967 until (at the very latest) 1980. In the second section, "Recovery," we seek to expand our current understanding of the New Wave to add the contribution of film artists who were not directors to the overall achievements of the period, as well as incorporate directors who have not otherwise been considered as part of the discussion.

Emilio Audissino makes a compelling case to include the work of Jerry Zucker, Jim Abrahams, and David Zucker (ZAZ), who directed several parodic, spoof comedies, in our understanding of the New Wave. Jean-Luc Godard, the nouvelle vague, and European art cinema more widely have been commonly identified as sources of inspiration for the young filmmakers of the American New Wave period as it has been traditionally conceptualized. By contrast, Audissino makes the compelling case for how, in their generic deconstructionism, playfulness, and cinephilia, ZAZ's films are closer in spirit to Godard's parodic, style-centered approach than most American New Wave films which, despite the incorporation of some of the stylistic flourishes of the nouvelle vague such as jump cuts and handheld cameras, remained fairly closely wedded to conventional Hollywood style.

Aaron Hunter makes a clear and vivid argument for the expansion of our analysis and discussion of authorship in film to incorporate figures other than the director. Discussion of the New Wave has been hamstrung by a preoccupation with a very narrow band of male directors and, through his thorough investigation of the contributions of production designers to the aesthetics of several New Wave films, Hunter shows how we must consider the authorial role of artists working in other capacities in film production. Hunter's chapter also makes an important intervention in the recovery of Polly Platt's career as a production designer on many significant films. Hunter demonstrates explicitly how we must provide proper attribution to the artists who worked on a period of American cinema that continues to garner such significant attention. In so doing, we may manage to extricate ourselves from the lazy, uncritical, male-centric *auteurism* that has, until very recently, defined the study of the American New Wave.

In keeping with Hunter's intention to expand our discussion of authorship beyond the role of the director, Oliver Gruner's contribution to the collection pays careful attention to the screenwriter Waldo Salt. Using a close analysis of Salt's archive, Gruner's chapter demonstrates the significance of the screenwriter's politics in his New Wave-era work. Salt was blacklisted in 1951 though he reemerged to contribute to the screenplays of some of the films most commonly associated with the New Wave. Gruner's work shows how these films embody the countercultural spirit of the period, as well as demonstrating the extent to which Salt was thinking in terms of visual style and symbolism in his writing. In so doing, Gruner's contribution to this collection forms part of a wider conversation in which the screenwriter may move from a marginalized position in discussions of film authorship to, perhaps, one of greater centrality and significance.

Aimee Dixon Anthony's chapter reinforces the intentions of this collection to disturb our somewhat rigid and ossified determinations of what constitutes New Wave cinema and, concomitantly, to challenge who gets to be a part of this story. Anthony demonstrates how, to a significant degree, the contributions of Black women filmmakers have not only been written out of the discourse of the New Wave but also how their absence is manifest across all of American film history. Anthony identifies the L.A. Rebellion's affinity with the emancipatory, decolonizing intentions of Third Cinema and demonstrates how throughout her career across short and feature films, L.A. Rebellion filmmaker Julie Dash has sought to emphasize the lives and experiences of women of color. In drawing a genealogical link between Dash and her predecessor, Zora Neale Hurston, who produced ethnographic films in the early days of cinema, Anthony shows how both made films that urge us to look again at our established histories to see the people who have been written out of them. Anthony urges us to continue in this endeavor to tell a story of the American New Wave and American cinema that is more inclusive.

Anthony's discussion of Dash, Hurston, the L.A. Rebellion, and their work through the 1980s and 1990s moves us into a consideration of the legacy of the American New Wave. In this section, we investigate how the spirit of independence and creativity that inspired many New Wave filmmakers has manifested itself in later periods in American filmmaking, as well as how the continued critical reverence for the films of the New Wave has driven specific filmmakers to draw upon the style and politics of the period in their own work (in these instances, to rather politically problematic ends).

Aimee Mollaghan engages with the style and politics of an example of New Wave-era filmmaking that, until recently, has been largely ignored in critical studies of the period. Mollaghan demonstrates how *Wanda* (Barbara Loden, 1970), far from romanticizing the open road as other films of the era do, chronicles a young woman who finds herself adrift, wandering across the American landscape. Utilizing landscape theory, consideration of realism, and a comparison with the documentarian impulse of Depression-era photographer Dorothea Lange, Mollaghan demonstrates how Wanda's drifting in the coal mining regions of Pennsylvania reflects on the industrial decline of the area during the late 1960s and early 1970s, and the hardship of rural life. She then moves to consider how Wanda's aimlessness is reflected in stories of women in more recent American independent filmmaking from Kelly Reichardt and Andrea Arnold. In so doing, Mollaghan draws a clear link between the politics of Loden's earlier film and the more recent work of Reichardt and Arnold, and how these films demonstrate the extent to which poor, young women are cut out of the financial and geographical discourses of mobility that constitute the dominant mythological construction of the American Dream.

Bringing us into the contemporary period, Karen Ritzenhoff and Hannah D'Orso examine comic book villain origin story *Joker* (Todd Phillips, 2019) and its allusions to the films of the New Wave era, particularly Scorsese's *Taxi Driver* and *The King of Comedy* (1982). They speculate about Phillips's intention in aligning his film so closely with Scorsese's work and argue that while his citations of these films may be superficial, they nonetheless emphasize the continued significance of the New Wave era in contemporary discourse regarding what constitutes aesthetically and politically significant filmmaking. Even those who criticized *Joker* in comparison with its New Wave forebears revealed their nostalgia for the earlier period, and the memory of a time when American cinema was politically charged and aesthetically vital (before the domination of blockbuster spectacle of the type *Joker* is nevertheless indebted as a comic book film). Ritzenhoff and D'Orso also consider *Joker*'s position in relation to Trumpian politics and the rising anxiety about white male supremacy in the United States, an aspect of *Taxi Driver*'s politics that also invites comparison.

The final chapter in this section, by Kim Wilkins, expands upon and develops some of the concerns of Ritzenhoff and D'Orso. In her examination of the rhetoric of independence during the Sundance and Miramax era, Wilkins demonstrates the significant extent to which this period of American cinema was framed around, and dependent upon, a mythological construction of the New Wave as the embodiment of the countercultural rebellion. However, as she reveals, this alignment of the Sundance–Miramax era with the New Wave results in deeply problematic elisions concerning gender and race. In her consideration of *Once Upon a Time ... in Hollywood* (Quentin Tarantino, 2019), Wilkins demonstrates how one of its standard-bearers evokes the New Wave era nostalgically as the era of maverick men who rescued Hollywood. Wilkins's analysis of some of the academic discourse around the New Wave, and its continued reinforcement of the story that Tarantino so lovingly retells about the period, implores us to be more reflective and critical about how we invoke the era when we want to discuss what constitutes aesthetically and politically significant filmmaking.

Conclusion

Our collection concludes with a substantive afterword from one of the most prominent scholars in the field. Peter Krämer offers a thorough exploration of the direction of travel for studies of the New Wave, examining more of the recent literature in the area, as well as suggesting directions for future research. He discusses the ongoing problems of defining a proper New Wave canon and an appropriate period for analysis, taking the debate in new directions. Taking into account the important work of recovery and reassessment of the politics of the New Wave that is ongoing, Krämer makes a compelling argument for continued attention to the industrial changes occurring in Hollywood at the time that the New Wave, or New Hollywood, flourished. What Krämer's continued work in this area demonstrates is how much there is still to be discovered and said about a period of American filmmaking that still holds such fascination for scholars and audiences alike.

Indeed, this collection is, as Krämer notes, one of many new books about the New Wave or New Hollywood that have emerged in the years since the fiftieth anniversary of *Bonnie and Clyde* and *The Graduate*, with more no doubt in the offing. What was clear from our conference in 2017 and the chapters in this collection is that the debate has shifted, in some cases quite markedly, away from the parameters by which it had been conventionally defined. The chapters here represent further contributions to our ongoing conversation about the position of the American New Wave in relation to film culture and engage in substantive debate about its constitution, meaning, and legacy.

The American New Wave was born in a period of political turmoil when the direction of the United States and its film industry was far from certain. This collection has been written and published in a period of comparable upheaval, though with its own contextual specificities. What will the American New Wave mean on its centenary in 2067? This collection, along with all the others recently published and in the pipeline, suggests there will still be fierce arguments about this subject over the next five decades, including one about the year in which that centenary should be commemorated.

Notes

1   Peter Krämer and Yannis Tzioumakis, "Introduction," in *The Hollywood Renaissance: Revisiting American Cinema's Most Celebrated Era*, ed. Peter Krämer and Yannis Tzioumakis (New York: Bloomsbury, 2018), xviii.
2   Jonathan Kirshner and Jon Lewis, "Introduction: The New Hollywood Revisited," in *When the Movies Mattered: The New Hollywood Revisited*, ed. Jonathan Kirshner and Jon Lewis (Ithaca, NY: Cornell University Press, 2019), 4–7.

3 J. Hoberman, "The Spirit of '76," in *When the Movies Mattered*, 163.

4 Krämer and Tzioumakis, "Introduction," xx.

5 Jeff Menne, *Post-Fordist Cinema: Hollywood Auteurs and the Corporate Counterculture* (New York: Columbia University Press, 2019), 24.

6 Peter Krämer, "Post-Classical Hollywood," in *The Oxford Guide to Film Studies*, ed. John Hill and Pamela Church Gibson (Oxford: Oxford University Press, 1998), 289–309.

7 For a thorough investigation of the New Wave auteur in the 1980s, see Chris Horn, *The Lost Decade: The Fortunes and Films of the "Hollywood Renaissance Auteur" in the 1980s* (PhD diss., University of Leicester, 2020), https://leicester.figshare.com/ articles/thesis/The_Lost_Decade_The_Fortunes_and_Films_of_the_Hollywood_ Renaissance_Auteur_in_the_1980s/12771071/1.

8 Krämer and Tzioumakis, "Introduction," xix.

9 Ibid.

10 Mel Gussow, "Movies Leaving 'Hollywood' Behind," *New York Times*, May 27, 1970, 36 in Maya Montañez Smukler, *Liberating Hollywood: Women Directors and the Feminist Reform of 1970s American Cinema* (New Brunswick, NJ: Rutgers University Press, 2019), 7.

11 Smukler, *Liberating Hollywood*, 9.

12 Ibid., 15.

13 Allyson Nadia Field, Jan-Christopher Horak, and Jacqueline Najuma-Stewart, "Introduction: Emancipating the Image: The L.A. Rebellion of Black Filmmakers," in *L.A. Rebellion: Creating a New Black Cinema*, ed. Field, Horak, and Stewart (Oakland: University of California Press, 2015), 3.

14 This was reflected upon by one of the contributors to this volume, Fjoralba Miraka, in her report on the conference held at Bangor University in July 2017. https://womensfilmandtelevisionhistory.wordpress.com/2018/01/15/ conference-report-women-in-the-american-new-wave-a-retrospective/.

2

The Great Shift in Hollywood Cinema: Men, Women, and Genre Revisionism of the American New Wave

Fjoralba Miraka

The revolution of 1960s and 1970s Hollywood led by the young generation of movie brats created a renaissance of American auteur cinema. This generation revised Classical Hollywood to reincarnate it in personal film narratives with a new stylistic and thematic approach. There is a general consensus[1] that genre films became a force in the 1970s mainly because of the relative security they offered in terms of box-office profit but also because this was the moment film was understood and appreciated as art by filmmakers who had for the first time studied it. Repetition and gradual transformation of key genres became inevitable as the young auteurs, driven by nostalgia for the classical films with which they grew up, as well as their desire for a personal signature in their own films in keeping with the European film waves of the time, created a canon of film texts that recycled and revived some of the most prominent Hollywood genres.

Genre revisionism in the 1970s entailed anything from parody and pastiche to demystification, transformation, allusion, and exploitation. As David Cook put it, "during the 1970s, genre was further destabilized by revision, parody, and hybridization, until by the 1980s an aesthetic of serious representation had become virtually impossible in genre-coded films."[2] The films of the era demonstrated familiar elements of past styles brought together with a fresh touch. The generic patterns available and exploited during the 1970s became vehicles for social commentary and for the widespread dissemination of ideological positions deeply embedded in the American psyche. Thus, the function of genres was to communicate in innovative yet recognizable structures, ideas, and ideals that persist and sustain the social fabric during turbulent times.

Taking as a starting point Linda Williams's assumption that melodrama is the all-encompassing expressive category of Hollywood cinema,[3] and also given the lack of consideration of this expressive category during this historical moment, my aim is twofold. First, my main concern is to recover and reassess what I perceive to be the great shift in the American cinema from the melodrama of the woman's film of the 1940s and 1950s—the era which was arguably the genre's pinnacle—to the "melodrama of beset manhood"[4] of the 1960s and 1970s, the widely defined Hollywood Renaissance period. Second, following up on the idea of the shift from the woman's film to the male melodrama, I proceed with the next obvious question of whatever happened to the women after their displacement from the melodramatic imagination. In order to answer the question, I look at the example of film noir and the ways in which women circulate in its American New Wave incarnations. My main argument will be that the simultaneous presence of the postmodern mood[5] in conjunction with the shift in gender roles from the 1960s onward has affected the melodramatic mode[6] tremendously and on multiple fronts. The shift is one that entails primarily the move from the woman's film such as the romantic melodrama, the family melodrama, and the maternal melodrama of the 1940s and 1950s to the films of the 1960s and 1970s that deal predominantly with the male psyche in the postmodern world.

The Melodramatic Mode

Melodrama as a category that designates an expressionistic and highly emotive mode of (re)presentation is among the most elaborately discussed aspects of cinema in the field of Film Studies as well as in other—predominantly literary and theatrical—contexts. More often than not, discussions of melodrama underline and center around what have conventionally and unanimously been confirmed as its basic tenets: its special relationship with the realist mode of presentation; its underlying and pervasive Manichean structure; the elaborate mode of excess, hyperbole, and exaggeration as an inextricable part of its visual rhetoric; and its highlighting of irony in its dramaturgy of the ordinary.

When we talk about the special position of women in melodrama we refer primarily to the fact that melodrama has been one of the few spaces open to accommodate female characters, to depictions pertinent to the realities of women and to issues that primarily concern women as a social group. The powerful dimension of melodrama as a space of resistance was the nexus of the feminist film criticism of the 1970s, and it is this dimension as well that makes it pertinent to discuss the implications of the shift from the woman's film to the male melodrama in the 1960s and 1970s. Discussing the woman's film and D. W. Griffith's role as father of this film form, Scott Simmon has concluded that from the moment of its origins in 1909, Griffith's *The Fascinating Mrs Fraser* constitutes a paradigmatic instance of the genre's much celebrated subversive potential, a genre that exposes the artificiality of the social conventions it portrays at the moment of their re-presentation.[7] His idea of the inherent resistances within the woman's film as the diachronic essential feature of the genre proves useful in understanding the woman's film as potentially subversive, if not "progressive," within the classical paradigm, which, for the feminist theorists of the 1970s (Mulvey for example), was an apparatus totally male-driven and male-oriented.

Mary Ann Doane and Jeanine Basinger moved across the same lines too. The former suggested that "there is an extremely strong temptation to find in these films a viable alternative to the unrelenting objectification and oppression of the figure of the woman in the mainstream Hollywood cinema."[8] By contrast, the latter identified and discussed this subversive potential of the genre, concluding that "the woman's film was successful because it worked out of a paradox. It both held women in social bondage and released them into a dream of potency and freedom."[9] It is true that by disclosing to female audiences examples of female behavior unacceptable and punishable by society because they were unnatural to her given social role, the woman's film indeed opened up new possibilities in its very portrayal of these "unnatural behaviors"; in effect, it gave voice and presence to a repressed reality and this is precisely the pivotal significance of melodrama.

Classical Hollywood has produced and exemplified certain woman-types deriving sometimes from the extensive collaborations of male directors with female stars. The Hawksian Woman, the Hitchcock Blonde, or Joseph von Sternberg's ideal woman in the image of Marlene Dietrich are some revealing examples. And they have all produced images, representations, and ideals of the female and the feminine that are transgressive while restrained in one way or another. It is pertinent then to ask, what happened to these woman types in the New Wave era, an age of distress, discomfort, and disillusionment, the era of Coppola, De Palma, and Scorsese? If melodrama is back, disguised in films such as *The Deer Hunter* (Michael Cimino, 1978), *Apocalypse Now* (Francis Ford Coppola, 1979), *Kramer vs Kramer* (Robert Benton, 1979), and *Obsession* (Brian De Palma, 1976), what is its subject matter, who are its characters, and what are its drives? If the Hawksian Woman and the Hitchcock Blonde are not here, then what is?

If melodrama is a genre/form that deals with portraying "stories about an emotional order ... threatened by an outside force,"[10] then it would seem to be the case that the histrionics of the melodramatic imagination were ever more pertinent and relevant in the films of the 1960s and 1970s: an era that in the United States encompassed an ongoing war that nobody understood, a political scandal with multiple and ongoing implications, a civil rights movement, the rise of minority groups, and the women's movement. One could discern the recurring commentary on each of these socially significant aspects of that time in films that derived from that very reality, almost as a direct corollary.[11] The most salient characteristic of those films is the prevalence of *males in distress* who struggle to cope with these realities and seem to be in constant search for a viable outlet for this distress and tension. How did we move from a hero in control (classical Hollywood) to a hero in distress (New Hollywood)?

The general tendency in film evidenced during this period is predicated on two strains: on the one hand, the classical American film hero is going through a transformative process that commenced with actors such as Montgomery Clift, Marlon Brando, James Dean, and James Stewart proffering alternative masculinities to the traditional macho type, and was completed in such new figures as Method actors Robert De Niro, Jack Nicholson, Dustin Hoffman, and Al Pacino. At the same time, gradually, the woman's film retreated during the 1960s and 1970s period of "New Melodrama" (to use Kehr's term again) and along with it Hollywood rid itself of some of the most interesting, intriguing, and rebellious women of the cinema.

For example, John Wayne's romantic masculine ideal, the matinee idol once worshipped for his ethos of character and handsome, flamboyant posture, has informed the films of many Renaissance directors. This idol has transformed now into the fragile heroes of the new melodrama as the aftermath of an American dream/ideal gone dire; and for every John Wayne character (Ethan Edwards, Tom Doniphon, Thomas Dunson) there is an emotionally confused Ted Kramer (Dustin Hoffman), a disillusioned Travis Bickle (Robert De Niro), a childish, irresponsible, and rebellious Jonathan, Robert, or R. P. McMurphy (Jack Nicholson), and an initially restless turned ruthless Michael Corleone (Al

Pacino). As Robert Burstein puts it, "the new actors attract attention by their intensity of feeling, rather than by physical attractiveness."[12]

The difference between the classical and the New Wave periods in terms of male characterization is indicative of the irrelevance of the masculine ideal of the proper melodrama of action that had for a long time informed the popular consensus about the myth of the quintessential male hero figure. That masculine ideal was in the 1970s unable to sustain that myth. Instead, it transforms and occupies a central place in the melodrama of passion in order to accommodate the particular need of mythologizing the hero into a concurrent figure representative of the everyday man of the 1960s and 1970s. The Romantic hero has transformed into a down-to-earth, next-door figure of the everyday life, a realistic character spreading from the image of the common man.

The postclassical melodrama is in effect not only the melodrama of *males in distress* but also the melodramas of their creators/artists trying to represent their perception and examination of the drama of the everyday life of their time. What seems to have happened in the 1960s and 1970s is a shift from the macho hero (quite often the director's alter ego) who dictated the action, the narratives, and the settings of the films to the emotional hero (also what Thomas Elsaesser called the unmotivated hero who struggles with his sense of self and his place in the society). At the same time, "the superfemale" and "superwoman"[13] of Davis, Crawford, Stanwyck, and Hepburn gave their place to dispensable female characters devoid of the class and glamor of their predecessors.

With the woman's film retreating into oblivion, the postclassical melodrama turned utterly masculine, capitalizing on that same "special" place once reserved for the "fair sex." The man's film has always been there in the war film (*All Quiet on the Western Front*, Lewis Milestone, 1930), the gangster film (*Little Caesar*, Mervyn LeRoy, 1931; *The Public Enemy*, William A. Wellman, 1931; *Scarface*, Howard Hawks and Richard Rosson, 1932), the action film (*Journey Into Fear*, Orson Welles and Norman Foster, 1942), film noir (*Double Indemnity*, Billy Wilder, 1944), and the western, the quintessential American film. In the 1960s and 1970s, the man's film extends into the category of film material once produced for and consumed by women, and the male hero is a central figure in both the melodrama of action and the melodrama of passion. It is important, thus, to explore the ways in which the melodrama of passion has accommodated the male psyche within a postmodern context, to see how the new aesthetics work in this new order while the woman is being pushed to the margins yet again.

To begin with, there seems to be a fundamental transformation in the relationship between melodrama and realism, two forms that have notoriously been perceived and analyzed as contradicting each other. If we accept the general assumption that classical melodrama conformed to a realist mode that drew from a predominantly middle-class reality and criticized it through a highly stylized mise-en-scène, postclassical melodrama turned to the everyday individual with a renewed sense of realism that not only rejects the illusionism of the "realist" mode of previous decades but also makes the audiences conscious of its artificiality. If *realist melodrama* is not too paradoxical a term, I would suggest that this could best define the nature of the mode of representation in the Renaissance films.

The realist melodrama, contrary to the classical melodrama, seems to sustain a congruence between content and form, that is, an agreement between the subject matter and the mise-en-scène. This brings new concerns in terms of the kind of relationship the two forms of realism and melodrama would formulate in postclassical Hollywood. And these concerns relate precisely to the kind of relationship that melodrama and women would move into. If the subversive potential of melodrama had up to that moment been predominantly predicated on its unique ability to promote a clash between content and form in order to reveal internal fissures, the realist melodrama has digressed from that mode, effacing all contradictions in favor of an attempt to achieve a realization of life as it is in actuality. The highly stylized mise-en-scène of classical melodrama has been replaced by other modes of excess, not only evident in the use of pastiche and allusion, for instance, but also evident in a *realism of extravaganza*, a documentary realism if you will—or a "down-to-earth realism"[14] in the words of Elsaesser—which draws on the real without putting any lenses on in order to examine and portray it in the most brutal, flat, and disturbing way.

Their realist visual rhetoric takes us back to questions of phenomenology as aesthetic movement and this phenomenological realism demonstrates as many possibilities as dangers. Phenomenological realism in the 1970s films is based on an aesthetics that operates through stylization, which is not employed in order to efface the tensions of reality. On the contrary, it is dedicated to representing reality as if through magnified lenses. In close proximity to the Italian neorealist films that made extensive use of phenomenological realism and whose "very essence of their forms is the tactile quality of the subject matter, their ponderable human mass,"[15] the Renaissance films employed an aesthetics of phenomenological realism that not only rejected the artificiality of classical realism but also set a new dimension of depicting the drama of real life—the drama of a graduate, the drama of a gangster, the drama of a detective, the drama of a soldier or a veteran, the drama of a psychopath.

This leaves us, then, with an unresolved issue. If the realist melodrama is not predicated on the tension between content and form but rather engages the former with the latter in a relation of reinforcement, then the melodramatic form loses its subversive potential as it was present in the classical paradigm. Thus, it becomes unusable for subversive purposes, which creates questions regarding the special position of women in melodrama and their relationship to its new form. Moreover, and in close relation to this, in its pretentious efforts to offer an unpolished mirroring of the real life, the realist melodrama runs the risk of validating the beliefs and idea(l)s of the artists and the society as a whole through recurring character-images. That is, the line between presenting and representing becomes too thin to discern, especially in such forms where the auteur is dedicated to depicting a reality with its places and people.

This becomes a problematic aspect for understanding, appreciating, and discussing the function of sex and gender in these films. For a whole generation of artists and audiences who rejected the conventions of representation of classical Hollywood in favor of more fresh and genuine representations, and who are then constantly presented with numerous images of women as prostitutes[16] versus men as heroes (even in distress), the realist melodrama does evolve into a significantly, if equally, oppressive system of representation in terms of gender identity and gender roles in its effacement of the multiple, variant, female characters of the past. Where the classical melodrama presented female audiences with alternative female identities in order to teach them the good and the bad models (and in doing so gave voice to what it sought to repress), the realist melodrama has generated a substantial wave of limited (arche)types that conform to a very basic, unthreatening, and even submissive model that is under constant attack and subject to physical, verbal, and textual violence (the best examples here are Martin Scorsese's films whose female characters are invariably abused physically, verbally, and textually—*Alice Doesn't Live Here Anymore, Mean Streets, Taxi Driver*).

Along with these changes in characterization, the mise-en-scène of the realist melodrama changed too. It has now moved from the closed inner space of home, which has traditionally been the space of the melodrama of passion of the women's film, to the public spaces that have traditionally been reserved for all other (male) genres. Male melodrama follows this conspicuous division of gender lines through a realization of film narratives concerned with male heroes and their presence mostly within the context of the contemporary world. Thus, the male melodrama of passion now occupies a central place in the urban spaces where the male protagonists are usually located: Scorsese's, Coppola's, and De Palma's leading characters are invariably located in big cities. Interestingly enough, the replacement of the central female figure of melodrama with the male figure of the realist melodrama has necessitated a dislocation and relocation of mise-en-scène, which allows the hero to retain his place in the public context and express emotions of distress, anger, and disappointment at his surroundings. It is hardly surprising that just when film became dedicated to portraying the open spaces, women and the woman's film were scarce.

Quite often the public spaces are inhabited by communities of men, whereas the woman (usually alone) occupies a conspicuously limited place (*Who's That Knocking at My Door, Mean Streets, All the President's Men, The Godfather I* and *II, The Deer Hunter*) or no place at all (*The French Connection, The Parallax View, Apocalypse Now, The Conversation*). The male bonding championed in most of these films works on multiple levels. It is a valid response and a strategy of standing up to the crisis of a postmodern context that throws into question all authorial positions—in which we also see an ongoing battle between a liberal ethos and conservative sensibilities. It is in various cases also a substitute for the domestic and romantic relations that engendered the subject matter of domestic melodrama but has now diminished. As Michael Ryan and Douglas Kellner have suggested, in the films of the 1970s one can see "the decline of romance."[17] They hold that in many films of the period "the real romance is between the men."[18] But what does this mean in terms of the function of the melodramatic imagination and the way it promotes the conservativism that overrides the films of such directors as Coppola, Cimino, De Palma, and Scorsese despite the general liberal ethos of the time? How did, in other words, melodrama transform from a potentially subversive mode into a suppressive one in the skilled hands of these directors?

The movie brats' films, in general, as well as most films of this whole generation of filmmakers, fall into the category of melodrama of psychology. The action and pathos of their dramas is placed and suffered respectively in the public domain in most cases and thus it follows a distinctly American way of thinking, which sets home and public spaces clearly apart and in stark contrast to each other. Their visual and moral rhetoric—a melodramatic rhetoric—claims highly political and politicized positionings and leanings (either consciously or unconsciously), which are made clear and emphasized through the pastiche of generic conventions that have traditionally been linked with the male psyche and identity.[19] This wave of "male genres" instantiates a validation of the male hero's propriety and responsibility to claim a strong and visible position in the public domain, which in its corruptibility and immorality constitutes a challenge to the ethos of the hero. The question, thus, remains: whatever happened to the women of the American New Wave?

Women in New Hollywood: The Case of Film Noir and the Femme Fatale

Conceptualized either as a genre or as a movement, or even a mood expressive of its historical specificity,[20] film noir in its highly visualized structure and emblematic character types has proven to be a source of much debate, and a space replete with social, cultural, and historical meaning. Much has been written on film noir,[21] in terms of "its historical resonances, its treatment of gender and its issues of style,"[22] as Helen Hanson has indicated in her *Hollywood Heroines*, and usually the icon of the femme fatale is an intricate part of it. She is usually the enigma-woman, the mystery that the male hero must solve, the sexual predator who preys on the male hero to use him for her own devious plans, the spider woman who is capable of any sort of behavior that goes against the stereotypical feminine type. In other words, the figure of the femme fatale can be understood as the single most dangerous figure in film history that poses an actual threat to the figure of the conventional male hero and everything he represents for American patriarchal society.

There have been film critics who have been engaged in deciphering the working of patriarchal order in film narratives and have commented on the repressive (or not) treatment of women in noir narratives and their visual style. There is debate over the idea that the configuration of the femme fatale is an empowering figure of female agency and subjectivity.[23] On the one hand, there is the position that suggests that the portrayal of women in film noir is an extremely negative one that works in tandem with patriarchal rules and ideologies in order to repress the female identity, in which case the femme fatale is not a liberating figure but a seductive trap to repress female agency. On the other hand, there is the counterargument that the femme fatale is an emblem of female agency, a portrait of empowerment and liberation from repressive patriarchal discourse.

There have been consistent attempts to finally stop vacillating between these two positions and settle it conclusively. However, the very fact that such a settlement has not yet taken place points to two issues. First, the pervasive and consistent workings of classical narratives—as part of the larger patriarchal order—to disguise their misogyny and their practices of degradation and subordination of female positions in highly stylized visualizations. Second, the fact that the femme fatale escapes a conclusive positive or negative definition suggests that she is a wandering figure with no definite identity. What has happened, thus, to this controversial female type in the 1970s film, what is her function, and how has it changed from the classical period?

The Graduate (1967)

Although *The Graduate* is not a film noir, I am considering it in this section for the significance of its central female character, Mrs. Robinson. Numerous studies of 1970s film culture consider this one of the key films that marked the beginning of a new era of filmmaking that would later be termed New Hollywood; however, very little consideration has been offered to the character of Mrs. Robinson as embodied by Anne Bancroft who had won an Oscar only five years earlier for *The Miracle Worker* (Arthur Penn, 1962). Although the unconventional narrative style is the most pronounced of the film's attributes, I am interested in delineating the position of Mrs. Robinson as a femme fatale: on the surface, she is a spider woman, a seductive sexual woman whose power naturally derives from this sexuality; she is amoral in an era of anxiety over middle-class sexual morals and she eventually seduces the confused male hero, leading him to a number of complicated situations. For this, the film treats her harshly in terms of both narrative and characterization.

If we were to dissect this character and analyze it in depth, we would find that she is in actuality a real rebel—like all femme fatales—who goes against convention to pursue what she desires, something that the graduate Benjamin (Dustin Hoffman) wishes he was able to do but is incapable of. She, thus, embodies the feminist of the 1970s who disregards social norms that confine her, and for that she is ridiculed throughout the film, is rendered absent from the narrative for a long time (a punishment that other women endure in the 1970s films such as Joanne (Meryl Streep) of *Kramer vs Kramer*), and eventually erased from it. It is as if the film was paying tribute to this classical icon but by incorporating it into a film narrative outside its context (the noir context) it lets it wither away, suggesting that the new film age is not willing to allow such anomalies to be reincarnated and to reemerge. As interesting a character as this is, however, the narrative structure is geared toward the male hero. The film progressively diminishes her allure and renders her a disturbed middle-aged woman with no control over her surroundings and the male hero. The film does not permit her any space for her background to be developed into a complete story and contains her within a one-dimensional image. The film employs a male point of view, that of Benjamin, and colors Mrs. Robinson according to youngster fantasies of being initiated into the world of sexuality by an older woman. The preoccupation with a graduate's anxiety over his future takes over the narrative and overshadows the very few hints we receive about Mrs. Robinson's own frustrations: a middle-class housewife suffering a problem that has no name in an unloving marriage. This is something that perfectly resonates not only with Betty Friedan's 1963 study of the position of women in America of the 1960s, *The Feminine Mystique*, but also with another femme fatale's story, that of Phyllis Dietrichson (Barbara Stanwyck) in *Double Indemnity*.

Klute (1971)

If in the character of Mrs. Robinson we find a parody of the femme fatale, in *Klute* we find a tamed version of her. We see how the dramatization of the conflict between good woman versus bad woman is played out in the roles of victim versus predator, embodied in the character of Bree (Jane Fonda). The usual threatening power of the femme fatale in this neo-noir is reduced and neutralized on two levels: narrative and character.

In terms of character, the femme fatale Bree embodies the (illusion) of the modern woman: she is the empowered woman who is assertive, independent, sexually active, and aware of her sex appeal—what better actor to portray such a character than Jane Fonda. She is conveniently placed in an urban environment, New York City, to enhance the idea of the modern woman having a social role in the public space—which is fittingly the space of film noir. She also plays the role of a prostitute; thus the plot already creates the scheme of the femme fatale as modern woman as prostitute, which consequently transforms the classic, mysterious, threatening woman into a modern common woman. It is as if what was left unspoken during the classical years (the femme fatale as a whore) is now fully reincarnated in the actual image of the woman as sex worker. On a symbolic level, the film also hints at the assumption that women in the public sphere are fallen women who need either punishment or reallocation in the private sphere. The move, thus, from the greater appeal of the enigma woman into the banal reality of a common prostitute renders the heroine a powerless, nonthreatening presence.

What enhances this transformation is also the positioning of the heroine as a victim of a (male) predator—a role which in the classical years of the genre belonged to her. Bree is being followed and threatened by Cable (Charles Cioffi), a man representative of the modern male social order that grows intolerant toward women's emancipation. His obsession with her is suggestive of the attitude of the American public during the 1970s toward the women's movement and everything it scrutinized and changed in relation to women's positions in the contemporary world of the time—this attitude became more open and direct during the backlash of the conservative 1980s. Cable is the personification of the wicked and perverse face of America, a rich businessman who stands on top of the world, he is everything immoral the American collective psyche represses and buries deep down. The heroine in the story is the one who threatens to bring this to the surface. The sex worker in the postclassical era is only a threat insofar as she encompasses the potential for the realization of the impure American self. She is a social ill and must be destroyed for the sake of moral salvation. The conflation, thus, of the predator/victim roles mitigates the threat that the femme fatale once posed for the male hero, especially as it is played out in the penultimate scene of Bree's confrontation with Cable during which she is framed as the conventional victim cornered by her predator.

Bree's repositioning from femme fatale to victim is further advanced by the narrative structure of the film. If the noir heroine posed an enigma for the male hero to solve, as discussed above, here she only plays a secondary role to the plot's enigma, which is the disappearance of a former client of hers, Mr Gruneman (Robert Milli), and the investigation of this case by John Klute (Donald Sutherland). To the latter she is not a sexually appealing model of woman—he resists her advances rather easily for a while. Rather, she is a fallen angel that needs to be restored in the house, as is implied by the end of the film. The working of the film is such that Bree starts as a competent modern woman and progressively is turned into a pawn of Klute's investigation into Gruneman's disappearance, then modeled as the disturbed lonely woman whose independence is only a superficial mask, and finally the female victim of a thriller who is saved by her hero at the very last minute and eventually (by implication) takes off with him, to become a "normal," respectable woman.

Chinatown (1974)

If Bree Daniels of *Klute* proclaimed the demise of the allure of the femme fatale over the male psyche by ending up a "tamed" woman, then Evelyn Mulwray (Faye Dunaway) of *Chinatown* has a similar fate in this 1970s neo-noir film. Glenn Man has suggested that "Polanski's film includes all the elements of the private eye *noir* genre: the hard-boiled but vulnerable detective, the femme fatale, antagonistic cops, henchmen and heavies, and a complex plot of murder and deceit, which the detective eventually exposes."[24] Indeed, in terms of visual and narrative style, the film works wonders in invoking the traditional film noir generic elements; in terms of characterization, however, it modernizes its hero by infusing in him all elements of 1970s cynicism, and depriving him of any romanticized idealism that was fundamental in classic noirs such as *The Maltese Falcon* (John Huston, 1941), *Murder My Sweet* (Edward Dmytryk, 1944), and *The Big Sleep* (Howard Hawks, 1946). He is implicated in the corruption he opposes and is eventually overrun by it.

With regard to the femme fatale of the film, Evelyn Mulwray, the question that arises is this: how far has this generic revisionism gone in modernizing the figure with aspects that speak to and of the 1970s paranoia and disillusionment? Evelyn is lascivious, mysterious, and eroticized for the voyeuristic gaze of the male hero and the audience; she is an enigma that Jake (Jack Nicholson) is struggling to resolve side by side with the second plot of the film, the dam plot, and she is dead by the end of the narrative, as expected in a noir text. However, before she is eradicated by the end of the film, she is finally resolved as an enigma and proven to be a victim of the same corrupt, malicious, patriarchal order that Jake cannot escape—she has been raped by her father Noah Cross (John Huston), impregnated by him, and tormented by the threat of him taking their daughter Katherine (Belinda Palmer) away from her, and finally killed for trying to escape him.

In a didactic fashion, Evelyn is too passive a femme fatale to stand in the world of the 1970s, and although her image, gestures, and style pay homage to the classic femme fatale, her treatment within the film discloses a deeply disturbing attitude toward what she represents. As if to ridicule the icon, she is stripped of her power little by little and gradually transformed in the eyes of Jake and the audience from a confident and self-reliant mystery woman into a victimized, fragile, scared, and, according to her father, "disturbed" woman. Contrary to the classical femme fatale who remains a mystery and holds some allure to the male hero and the audience even after her elimination, the neoclassical femme fatale is fundamentally broken into pieces.

Taxi Driver (1976)

In all three examples of femme fatale discussed above, we can discern the common pattern of initially rendering the heroine in the fashion of the classical femme fatale only to progressively take her power away either by means of narrative structuring or character ridicule, transforming her from a predator into a victim, and finally pushing her out of the narrative. Nowhere else is this taken to more extremes than in *Taxi Driver*. The film has acquired a reputation of mythic proportions, making Scorsese a mythic film figure. Its propensity to incorporate the classical westerner into a contemporary setting embodied in a modern antihero, its homage to screen violence, and its reflective nature toward the urban environment of New York make it probably the most explosive narrative of the decade. As a film noir, it relies on the narrative and stylistic aspects that make a film noir what it is: the dark urban environment, the lone hero in search of justice within a dirty, corrupt society, and the alienation of the modern man from his surroundings. But as a film noir *Taxi Driver* is missing a fundamental element: the femme fatale. The devious woman who is an intricate part of every film noir, and whose actions provide some justification and motivation for the hero's actions and decisions is conspicuously missing from this narrative. What we have instead is a child prostitute and an angel figure, Betsy (Cybill Shepherd), who according to Travis (Robert De Niro) is pure and above everyone else.

Usually in classical film noir and the neo-noir of the 1980s onward the angel figure is also part of the narrative. She is placed side by side with the femme fatale in order to create a stark juxtaposition with her and provide a healthy example of femininity compared to the unconventional example of the femme fatale. In *Taxi Driver*, Betsy is the angel in the house, as far as Travis is concerned, until he is disillusioned and rejects her for having rejected him first. At that point, she becomes a fallen woman, is "just like the others" as Travis puts it, and is punished both by the main character and the narrative. Travis grows indifferent to her by focusing all his energy into the character of the child prostitute, Iris (Jodie Foster). In the closing sequence Travis is completely indifferent to her, drops her off at her place, and we watch him drive away as he looks at her reflection fading away in the rearview mirror of his car. The camera is following her as she is left behind and little by little disappears eventually from the mirror and the screen, while Travis moves on wandering the streets of New York. The angel/devil has been eliminated.

In *Taxi Driver* we may have lost the femme fatale, but we have gained another character type. The film has substituted the empowering figure of the spider woman with the victimized figure of a child prostitute, Iris. If Scorsese's directorial preoccupations revolve around male anxiety, violence, alienation, and degradation in urban spaces, in the noir world of *Taxi Driver* he has transfused all those elements into this one character. Similar to Bree Daniels, Iris is a fallen angel that needs saving. By disposing of a threatening female presence that would only add to the hero's predicament and by offering instead a victimized child in which he can find a sense of purpose, *Taxi Driver* conclusively banishes the female presence from the public domain, offering no viable examples or alternatives for women. Betsy grows insignificant to Travis and the whole narrative; Iris becomes a focal point instead, insofar as she accommodates all his needs for self-definition and the narrative's need for closure by driving her *home*. In summary, both Betsy and Iris are two failed substitutes for the iconic figure of a film noir proper: the femme fatale.

Thus, speaking of genre revisionism in the 1970s, it becomes clear that starting from the end of the 1960s and moving into the 1970s, film noir has been reenvisioned with a twist to parody, tame, victimize, and eventually oust the single most empowering female figure not only of film noir but of all cinema in general: the femme fatale. The most celebrated noir narratives of the time demonstrate a clear hostile attitude toward this iconic figure to the point that her narrative function is reduced to that of a victim at best.

Conclusion

The great shift in Hollywood film that took place during the American New Wave is perhaps the single most significant challenge that the representation of women in the film industry (either in front of or behind the camera) ever faced. Stripping the woman's film from the big screen and replacing it with film narratives that speak of and to a male psyche brought significant changes in the ways women were represented during this specific moment in history, leaving them no room of their own, as well as no viable alternatives with which they can identify. The transformation of melodrama into a male pejorative led to the displacement of the woman from that single special place she had occupied during the classical period, leaving her vulnerable to diminishing, embarrassing, and offensive representations all made in the name of a selective genre revisionism.

Notes

1   Morris Dickstein, "Summing Up the Seventies: Issues," *American Film* (1979): 55–7; Stephen Schiff, Harlan Kennedy, Andrew Sarris, and Carrie Rickey, "Midsection: Dueling Genres," *Film Comment* 18, no. 2 (1982): 33–48; Robert Sklar, *Movie Made America: A Cultural History of American Movies* (New York: Vintage Books, 1994), 327–9.

2   David A. Cook, *Lost Illusions: American Cinema in the Shadow of Watergate and Vietnam 1970–1979* (California: University of California Press, 2000), 299.

3   Linda Williams, "Melodrama Revisited," in *Refiguring American Film Genres: History and Theory*, ed. Nick Browne (Berkeley: University of California Press, 1998).

4   I have borrowed this term from Nina Baym's illuminating article title "Melodramas of Beset Manhood: How Theories of American Fiction Exclude Women Authors," *American Quarterly* 32, no. 2 (1981): 123–39.

5   The term "postmodern mood" is widely understood as a mood that entailed questioning all prevalent ideals and ideas of a society around the 1960s.

6   As defined from its prototype examples of the French stage, the Italian opera, the English novel, and D. W. Griffith's proto-melodramas.

7   Scott Simmon, "'The Female of the Species' D. W. Griffith: Father of the Woman's Film," *Film Quarterly* 46, no. 2 (1992–3): 8–20.

8   Mary Ann Doane, *The Desire to Desire: The Woman's Film of the 1940s* (Bloomington: Indiana University Press, 1987).

9   Jeanine Basinger, *A Woman's View: How Hollywood Spoke to Women, 1930–1960* (London: Chatto and Windus, 1993), 6.

10 Dave Kehr, "The New Male Melodrama," *American Film* 8, no. 6 (1983): 43–7.

11 Some examples: *Kramer vs Kramer* is a direct assault against the women's movement and the new type of independent woman. *Taxi Driver* is a commentary on the postwar decline of New York and the psychological effects on a veteran who is struggling with the city's reality. *The Conversation* (Coppola, 1974) depicts a tormented surveillance expert who is dealing with demons of the past while working on a present case. *All the President's Men* (Pakula, 1976) is a commentary

on the Watergate scandal and *The Parallax View*, by the same director in 1974, deals with a presidential assassination and a corporate conspiracy.

12 Robert Brustein, "The New Hollywood: Myth and Anti-Myth," *Film Quarterly* 12, no. 3 (1959): 23–32.

13 Molly Haskell, *From Reverence to Rape: The Treatment of Women in the Movies* (New York: Holt, Rinehart and Winston, 1873), 160–1.

14 Thomas Elsaesser, "Tales of Sound and Fury: Observations on the Family Melodrama," in *Home Is Where the Heart Is: Studies in Melodrama and the Woman's Film* (London: BFI, 1987), 43–69.

15 Amede Ayfre, "Neo-Realism and Phenomenology," in *Cahiers du Cinema: The 1950s, Neo-Realism, Hollywood, New Wave* (Cambridge, MA: Harvard University Press, 1985), 182–91.

16 Scorsese's *Taxi Driver* and *Mean Streets*, Altman's *McCabe and Mrs Miller* (1971), Pakula's *Klute* (1971), De Palma's *Dressed to Kill* (1980) and *Blow Out* (1981), Schrader's Hardcore (1979), Brooks's *Looking for Mr Goodbar* (1977), and Russell's *Crimes of Passion* (1984).

17 Michael Ryan and Douglas Kellner, *Camera Politica: The Politics and Ideology of Contemporary Hollywood Film* (Bloomington: Indianapolis University Press, 1988), 150–1.

18 Ibid.

19 The film noir (*Taxi Driver*), the gangster film (*Mean Streets, The Godfather*), the conspiracy film (Pakula's trilogy of *The Parallax View, All the President's Men, Klute*), the buddy film (*Easy Rider*), the detective film (*The Conversation*), the thriller (*Sisters, Carrie, Obsession, Dressed to Kill*), and the war film (*Apocalypse Now, The Deer Hunter*), and even the western in its last breathing instances (*McCabe and Mrs Miller, The Wild Bunch, Straw Dogs*).

20 For an elaborate study of the genre, see Steve Neale's *Genre and Hollywood* (2000), Chapter 4, which brings together a wealth of sources discussing film noir's status as a genre, a movement, or a cycle.

21 A good starting point on the subject of the relationship of women and film noir is the 1998 edited collection *Women and Film Noir*, ed. E. Ann Kaplan, which captures a great deal of the debate within the feminist camp around the significance of the femme fatale for film noir.

22 Helen Hanson, *Hollywood Heroines: Women in Film Noir and the Female Gothic Film* (London: I.B. Tauris, 2007), 1.

23 Sylvia Harvey, Janey Place, Pam Cook, E. Ann Kaplan, Richard Dyer—all 1998.

24 Glen Mann, *Radical Visions: American Film Renaissance, 1967–1976* (Westport, CT: Greenwood Press, 1994), 139.

3

Formal Radicalism versus Radical Representation: Reassessing *The French Connection* (William Friedkin, 1971) and *Dirty Harry* (Don Siegel, 1971)

Cary Edwards

In the latter months of 1971, two of the most influential police thrillers of the New Hollywood era were released. William Friedkin's *The French Connection* was the first to be released, on October 9, and was met with critical acclaim and multiple Academy Award nominations (winning for Best Picture, Best Director, Best Actor, Best Adapted Screenplay, and Best Film Editing) alongside a box office pushing over $50 million.[1] The producers of *Dirty Harry* (Don Siegel), released on December 22, had to content themselves with a box office in the region of $35 million and a rash of critical opprobrium. Although both films engaged directly with contemporary issues of law and order and featured protagonists who not only broke policing rules but also displayed racist and violent behaviors, only the latter was regularly condemned by critics. This chapter seeks to understand the differing critical reactions and reassess how they comment and reflect on the New Hollywood period itself, and to reexamine how this initial critical reaction has limited our understanding of the latter film and its director.

Despite being of the same genre, a difference emerges from critical writings about the films. *The French Connection* is seen as an auteurist New Hollywood text, whereas *Dirty Harry* is labeled a fascistic reaction and throwback. However, the technical and thematic elements that define Siegel's work, particularly his embrace of moral ambiguity, suggest a different way of discussing the period beyond a binary of Old and New Hollywood, and the ideological views this implies. This discussion also concerns how the formal innovations evident in *The French Connection* were received positively in critical circles despite the problematic persona of the film's protagonist, Jimmy "Popeye" Doyle (Gene Hackman), whereas the self-reflexive representational and thematic elements of *Dirty Harry* were largely ignored as a consequence of its similarity to the form of Classical Hollywood. Furthermore, I explore how *Dirty Harry's* employment of form creates a viewing position that problematizes the spectator's alignment, creating complex moral problems. This is opposed to the cinema-verité techniques of *The French Connection* that allow the spectator to maintain a critical and moral distance from the action. *Dirty Harry* elides protagonist/cop "Dirty" Harry Callahan (Clint Eastwood) with antagonist/killer Scorpio (Andy Robinson) in such a way as to comment upon and complicate the film's moral position, pushing the spectator to identify that threat as internal to America. *The French Connection*, however, employs a binary between protagonist/cop, Doyle, and antagonist/drug smuggler, Charnier (Fernando Rey), externalizing America's crime problem. This then queries the ideological reading of *Dirty Harry* as a fascist/authoritarian film that was fixed by contemporary critics and asks questions of the divisions between Old and New Hollywood.

The French Connection and *Dirty Harry* as New Hollywood films

The narrative of the New Hollywood is one in which an auteur-led countercultural and youth-orientated cinema emerged from a broken Studio System. The Studio System created not only a standard cinematic language but also, through the Motion Picture Production Code, a moral and representational framework.[2] Mark Shiel describes the period of 1965 to 1970 as "an exceptionally intense period of change in American cinema, during which the old studio system … was finally swept away."[3] And, as Robin Wood explains, these shifts were not simply industrial in nature but ideological too, driven by "the major eruptions in American culture from the mid-60s and into the 70s."[4] This "breakdown of ideological confidence in American culture and values"[5] is often seen through the protagonists of the films whose countercultural nature attacked traditional morals.[6] Simultaneously, a self-conscious engagement with genre occurred[7] in which genre codes were knowingly employed. This produced, as Lawrence

Webb suggests, "two primary responses: a tendency towards self-reflexivity, genre deconstruction, and pastiche on the one hand, and the turn to docufiction and realist aesthetics on the other."[8]

Stylistically, this period shifted in ways that reflected the breakdown of the Hollywood industry. Exposure to international cinema introduced a new generation of filmmakers, audiences, and critics to alternatives to classical form. Perhaps most influential was the French New Wave, a cinema that "favoured location shooting," "source lighting," "auteur driven scenarios," and "naturalistic styles of acting."[9] This is not to say that the box office during the New Hollywood period was dominated by films featuring ideological or stylistic difference to Classical Hollywood. Such films as *Love Story* (Arthur Hiller, 1970) and *Airport* (George Seaton, 1971) displayed more conservative filmmaking techniques and attitudes to great success, establishing the technical and ideological opposition between films, and filmmakers, of the Old and New Hollywood.

How then to fit *The French Connection* and *Dirty Harry* into this formula? Traditionally, critics have been more comfortable with the former as a New Hollywood film than the latter. Partly, this is fixed by the production of each, with *The French Connection* fitting into the New Hollywood narrative more comfortably. By 1971, Friedkin was still a relative newcomer, despite several directorial credits in film and television. Prior to *The French Connection*, his films had enjoyed only minor financial and critical success and did little to herald the stylistic techniques he would come to use. He did, however, have a background in documentary, which, combined with a heavy French New Wave influence, came to define how *The French Connection* looks, placing it firmly into the New Hollywood movement. Friedkin employed an unplanned aesthetic to the film, imitating the French New Wave and Costa-Gavras's *Z* (1969), a link many of the contemporary critics noted and one that Friedkin has himself acknowledged.[10] Friedkin instructed his cinematographer Owen Roizman and camera operator Enrique "Ricky" Bravo to film freely, avoiding well-framed compositions. In Friedkin's own words "the camera could go anywhere."[11] This naturalism extended to the direction of actors such as Gene Hackman (Doyle) and Roy Scheider (Sonny Grosso) who were pushed to improvise lines and move freely on real New York locations. Some shots were even stolen and filmed without permission (most famously during the film's car chase) and "often the actors didn't know where the cameras would be."[12] Despite being based on a real crime, and Robin Moore's account of those events, it was a free adaptation; if an element of the true story was cinematic it was retained, if not something more dynamic was created. This includes the ending for the film that expresses a more negative scenario than originally occurred, in which most of Doyle's achievements are made redundant, producing a downbeat ending expressing much of the cynicism of the era.[13]

Dirty Harry, however, had much more conventional origins that bear the trace of the Old Hollywood. Siegel had worked in Hollywood since the 1940s, starting in Warner Brothers' montage department. Siegel and Eastwood had built an effective partnership—this was their fourth film together—and they worked on the various existing script drafts until they were happy (which included moving the location from New York to San Francisco).[14] Suggesting that the film was a product of the practices of Old Hollywood would be a mistake, however, as Siegel had long honed a production process that gave him a high degree of control over the filmmaking process. Partly this was out of necessity, driven by the low budgets he experienced during his B-movie days in the 1950s (most famously *Invasion of the Body Snatchers* (1956)), but it was also out of a desire to control final cut by shooting only what he needed. This script-led style was efficient and quick and he took a "non-interventional approach with his crew and actors."[15] This chimed well with Eastwood who had become disenchanted with mainstream practices that wasted time and money (his experiences shooting *Paint Your Wagon* (Joshua Logan, 1969) were key in this) and had taken an active role in managing his career through his Malpaso production company which coproduced *Dirty Harry*. A surface similarity to Old Hollywood style, through Siegel's formalized compositions, downplays his own signatures such as "the frequent use of hand-held camera to help promote a blurring of the image in the action sequences … high contrast lighting to heighten the effect of action movement, and … a style of backlighting … that loses figures in the foreground image."[16] In some ways, Siegel fits the auteur criteria of New Hollywood: he certainly demonstrates a consistent style across films, but his choice of genres, typically heavy on action, and the seeming familiarity of his style may have held such acclaim back.

Ironically, during the New Hollywood period, Siegel was gaining attention as an auteur, particularly in works by Alan Lovell[17] and Stuart M. Kaminsky.[18] His move away from B-movies toward greater budgets and box-office success, however, seems to have stalled his acclamation, as well as his association with Eastwood in which Siegel's work was to become subsumed. As Deborah Allison suggests, this has led to a divided view of Siegel's work, "at one extreme, a workmanlike director of taut action films, technically proficient but imparting little of his own individuality into each project; at the other, a right-wing misogynist whose films explicitly fan inflammatory social debates."[19] However, this ignores consistencies within Siegel's films that suggest his personal imprint. Lovell identifies several formal aspects throughout his work and a tendency toward moral ambiguity. Formally this includes not only an "uncluttered" visual style and simple narrative structure[20] refined throughout his career and reaching its peak in the late 1960s and early 1970s but also, as Allison summarizes, a "refusal to provide an unequivocal demarcation between heroic and villainous activity," suggesting "essential similarities between these characters."[21] This draws attention to the political and moral ambiguities that suffuse much of Siegel's work and allows, for example, a film such as *Invasion of the Body Snatchers* to be read as both pro- and anti-McCarthy.

Choosing to film in San Francisco gave access to a very different set of locations than the scenes of urban decay of *The French Connection*. Siegel chose to film alongside "monumental architectural landmarks from City Hall to Kezar Stadium, preferring wide open space" (filmed in 2.35:1 Panavision as opposed to the less expansive 1.85:1 ratio used in *The French Connection*).[22] These location choices have an important impact on both texts and how spectators relate to them. *The French Connection* was filmed in rundown streets and neighborhoods, whereas *Dirty Harry* takes place against a backdrop of municipal and public spaces—in the former crime is down a side street, in the latter it occurs in the public arena next to civic structures.[23] A consistent set of juxtapositions runs through the locations in *Dirty Harry* in which strip bars and playgrounds are seen to coexist, and through which both Callahan and Scorpio move freely. During this period New York was heavily associated with crime, whereas San Francisco had differing connotations as a city associated with the counterculture of the 1960s, and left-leaning institutions like the University of California, Berkeley, and also as one where the Mayor was willing to use tactical police squads to suppress student strikes. It had also experienced its own serial killer, the Zodiac killer, partly inspiring Scorpio who imitates the real-life killer's notes to the police.[24]

Despite their differing origins and production methods, both films display a key hallmark of the New Hollywood period: protagonists that "exist in the middle position between the 'official hero' and 'outlaw hero.' "[25] It is in this liminal space that Doyle and Callahan operate, simultaneously within and without the establishment. Critics, however, were more able to recognize this in *The French Connection* than in *Dirty Harry*.

Critical Reactions

Both films elicited negative responses due to the film's, and filmmaker's, assumed political positions; however, the notices for *Dirty Harry* were far more condemnatory. During this period, the impact of film critics had become more important as a more cine-literate audience emerged that directly engaged with a generation of critics who, in a similar way to how the new filmmakers displaced the old, had come to dictate what mattered about movies.[26] Film was being taken more seriously than ever before: "By the mid-1960s, treating movies as a lesser art or merely as an amusement had vanished for good,"[27] and the status of film critics had risen considerably.[28]

Critics like Pauline Kael, Andrew Sarris, and Vincent Canby in such publications as *The New Yorker, The Village Voice,* and *The New York Times* became key in shaping the discourse around films, suggesting dominant readings and fixing ideological takes. The initial critical reactions to both *The French Connection* and *Dirty Harry* continue to be echoed in more contemporary studies, limiting our own interpretations. Kael, no lover of Eastwood, described *Dirty Harry* as a "right wing fantasy" and "obviously just a genre movie, but this action genre has always had a fascist potential, and it has finally surfaced."[29] Kael's reaction to *The French Connection* was more circumspect, describing the film's "nightmare realism" of a world in which "there are no good guys" and accused the film and filmmakers of a "right-wing, left-wing, take-your-choice cynicism."[30] The emphasis on genre and fascism in Kael's review of *Dirty Harry* and realism for that of *The French Connection* is reiterated by much of the popular critical writing about both films. Garrett Epps's article for the *New York Times* titled "Does Popeye Doyle Teach Us How to Be Fascist?"[31] sums up much of this reaction. Comparing both films, Epps acknowledges that Doyle is a racist, and was read approvingly by some audiences for this, but the film "cannot be called fascist," as it offers no "unifying ideology." *Dirty Harry*, however, is "the simply told story of the Nietzschean superman and his sado-masochistic pleasures" in which Callahan is pitted against liberal authorities that prevent his enforcement of the law.[32] The impression is given that one film depicts the brutal realism of police enforcement and crime (in Sarris's words a "triumph of visual organization and engineering,"[33] which for Richard Schickel came "closer to the real thing [… more] than any other movie detective I've ever seen"[34]) without endorsing it, whereas the other exploits such issues to fascist conclusions. It is worth remembering that during the period leading up to the films' releases in the United States, crime had radically increased to become a dominant issue with Nixon running in 1968 on a law and order platform.[35] Crime, which had "doubled in the 1960s and tripled in the 1970s,"[36] much of it fueled by the growing drugs crisis, was ever present in headlines, as was the power of the police. Clearly larger sociopolitical concerns were at stake during this period and one wonders how far critical reactions were responding to these as much as the films themselves. What is clear is that the dominant reading of *Dirty Harry* that emerges precludes alternatives and denies the film's moral ambiguities.

Querying Textual Understandings

The narrative image[37] of the films, set through marketing and prior knowledge, helps set a spectator's subject position. I would contend that the spectator's understanding of a film is partly conditioned by the narrative image, especially with popular cinema, which is rarely consumed without some sort of forward knowledge, a set of expectations they take with them into theaters. For these two films, despite being in the same genre, the narrative images were remarkably different and suggest ways for us to consider how the spectator was positioned (although this does not fix all readings), and it complements the critical reactions to the films (which for many spectators form part of the narrative image).

20th Century Fox's pressbook for *The French Connection* fixes certain aspects of the film through its various posters. The main tagline, "In the great tradition of American thrillers," sets the film not only as a genre text but one particular to the United States. The main image places Doyle in the background shooting villain Nicoli (Marcel Bozzuffi) in the back, his arms outstretched in a pose reminiscent of crucifixion. A smaller image of Doyle himself sits by the title, in which he wears his trademark pork-pie hat. Other variants, all using the central image, promise that "The time is right for an out and out thriller like this" and that "Doyle is bad news—but a good cop." Various approving quotations from critics are included in some of the posters, but notably unemphasized are the director, star, or source material. In a section of the pressbook titled, "Exploitation," connections to the real-life story are made, as well as suggestions for promoting the film, including prevailing upon local press and law enforcement to engage with the film as "timely."[38] The main image itself possesses a grainy quality, which imitates newspaper photography, action frozen in time rather than posed in a studio.

At this point, Hackman, despite an Oscar nomination for *Bonnie & Clyde* (Arthur Penn, 1967), was yet to become a star and his identity is subsumed by Doyle in posters and the film's theatrical trailer. Opening with Doyle rousting a New York bar full of Black patrons, Doyle's persona is foregrounded both visually and, in a New York-accented voice-over, that intones, "Popeye Doyle, if he doesn't like you, he'll take you apart. And it's all perfectly legal because Doyle fights dirty and plays rough." Amid shots that showcase Friedkin's unplanned realist aesthetic, the images and voice-over emphasize the procedural aspects of the film, "The stakeout, the payoff, the chase, The French Connection." This firmly sets the film as one that spectators are positioned to see as realist.

The narrative image for *Dirty Harry* is markedly different, mostly because of the centrality of its star Clint Eastwood whose name appears above, and in the same size as, the title on promotional material. Two images of Eastwood dominate the posters—one in which he points his Magnum out toward the spectator, another that sees him in a full body pose pointing the gun to one side. This combination of Eastwood and gun builds on associations from previous films, especially Sergio Leone's *Man with No Name* trilogy, and went on to become the predominant image in marketing Eastwood's films throughout the decade.[39] The taglines for most of the film's various posters underline this image: "Detective Harry Callahan. He doesn't break murder cases. He smashes them" and "Detective Harry Callahan. You don't assign him to murder cases. You just turn him loose." An alternative poster offers, however, a different tagline and one that suggests a different emphasis to the film, "Dirty Harry and the homicidal maniac. Harry's the one with the badge." This alternative tagline suggests a narrative ambiguity and is repeated in voice-over as the theatrical trailer begins, which cuts between Scorpio and Callahan deliberately drawing a parallel. The trailer then moves into exploring what is "Dirty" about Callahan, suggesting "There are a lot of reasons they called him Dirty Harry. And he kept inventing new ones." As the trailer continues, it focuses on the film's action, as well as the conflict between Harry and his superiors, but it also takes time to include a scene in which Callahan explains his wife's death, implying a psychological depth to the character. Despite the clear elision between Eastwood and Callahan implied by the marketing, one article in the Warner Brothers pressbook suggests an attempt to create separation between actor and character, "Don't let Clint Eastwood's violent screen demeanor fool you. He's a pushover for kindness and consideration." Reading as a preemptory response to critical reactions, the article acknowledges how Eastwood's persona had grown out of Leone's films, but takes the time to reassure us that "Eastwood is truly an animal lover and abhors any kind of cruelty in the wild kingdom, as well as the domestic one." One can only speculate on the effect of this article, but it shows awareness of a growing critical opprobrium toward Eastwood and his films.

Before each film had begun, a differing sort of subject positioning had already occurred. For *The French Connection* it is one that suggests a high modality,[40] as if the film was a realist text or a style of "induced documentary." *Dirty Harry* was specifically advertised as a star vehicle, playing on Eastwood's persona, one which he had developed through Leone's Spaghetti westerns and in US productions such as *Coogan's Bluff* (Don Siegel, 1968) and *Hang 'Em High* (Ted Post, 1968). As Edward Buscombe notes, "The casting of Clint Eastwood, the last great totem pole of the Western, in the contemporary role appeared to authenticate the transference of the Western's traditional themes to the crime film."[41] During the 1960s, the western was in almost terminal decline as stars such as John Wayne aged and the genre became incapable of supporting its ideological framework in light of social change. Ideas such as manifest destiny had become deeply problematic, reflected in the changing representation of Native Americans, moving from a violent faceless other to victims of genocide in films such as *Soldier Blue* (Ralph Nelson, 1970). Eastwood, however, did not continue the genre as it had previously existed, playing a part in this demythologizing of the West. A part of the generic transformations of the era, Eastwood's westerns presented a nihilistic, selfish, cowboy hero at odds with traditional models. They were met with hostility by US critics, many of whom questioned their very legitimacy as westerns: "they *are* westerns, but unexpected ones, and to judge by their critical reception ... they are ones that are unwanted in some respects."[42] Christopher Frayling suggests one of the main critiques of the *Dollars* films, from US critics, was "for their destructive view of the West, for the detachment with which Leone treats brutality, and for their excessively rich visual style—an overdose of formalism."[43] The critical distance, experimentation, and self-reflexivity that the Spaghetti western often achieves served to re-present the genre in a new light, heightening the formal elements such as gunfights while simultaneously playing down, if not entirely eliminating, the traditional moral framework: "Traditional icons ... are all shown to be empty symbols of authority, rendered almost irrelevant by the brutality of the social context."[44] Released all at once in the United States, in 1967, Leone's films were influential on American westerns, but not accepted critically or understood for their reflexivity, a hostility that extended toward Eastwood himself. They also represented violence in a way not seen in the American western at that point, something that was often condemned despite the fact that "Leone's Westerns did not feature much spurting blood or squib work."[45] Violence and death were free from the traditional moral structures that had anchored the western. In Leone's films "violent death was quick, plentiful and was viewed dispassionately, stripped of the ritualizing codes."[46] That Leone's films were, in many ways, parodic and ironic was generally missed by critics at the time. Eastwood's persona is itself part of this generic transformation, an unrealistic superman version of the Western hero and an almost complete reversal of his appearance as Rowdy Yates on *Rawhide* (CBS Television Network Productions, 1959–65). Spectators approaching *Dirty Harry*, consciously a star vehicle, would have been aware of this persona. As Horsley notes, "A Clint Eastwood movie always features Clint Eastwood as Clint Eastwood."[47] This is, in turn, important for considering the subject position created by the film, of how Eastwood's persona affects the film's modality and whether this creates a critical distance between text and spectator.

Subject Positions in *The French Connection* and *Dirty Harry*

Key to reassessing each film is the question of subject positioning, which allows for a further discussion of how the films address their spectator, which then impacts on the availability of alternative ideological positions. *The French Connection* creates a distanced relationship between the spectator and text, a form of alignment[48] that avoids character subjectivity and therefore avoids the access to a character's state of mind required to build a strong allegiance. Along with a strong opposition between protagonist and antagonist this renders the problems depicted in the text (of crime and drug smuggling) as other and separate from the spectator. *Dirty Harry*, by contrast, deliberately parallels and blurs distinctions between protagonist and antagonist (as suggested by the film's tagline) through issues of recognition and parallel structures of alignment. Although a strong allegiance is created with Callahan (partly due to his character, but also Scorpio's appearance and behavior, and Eastwood's star persona) his moral legitimacy is constantly questioned, creating an ambiguity that resists simplistic ideological readings. Textual analysis of the opening sequences demonstrates how the films establish their subject positions, leading us to question how the spectator engages with each.

The French Connection's opening is intentionally discordant through the use of high-pitched non-diegetic sounds that accompany the titles, including a repeated dash that imitates a news telex service. In a prologue, the opening scene places the spectator in Marseilles. It lacks a direct relationship to the film's plot other than to show the spectator the antagonists Charnier and Nicoli. Primarily, the purpose of this sequence is to foreground not only violence, suggesting its immediacy, brutality, and casualness, but also its distance through the lack of recognition that occurs—the spectator is given little time or information to place the opening scene's characters into a schema before one is killed. The shooting of an undercover French police officer occurs after a sequence of mostly long and medium shots, filmed with a handheld camera. The officer is nameless, he follows Nicoli (whose identity is unknown at this point), and his death remains unconnected to the main plot. On one level, this opening serves to demonstrate the threat posed by Charnier's operation, but it also primes the spectator to expect sudden contextless violence without first establishing a secure character alignment, prevented by the lack of character information. The quick cuts between the undercover officer's face, Nicoli, and the gun give a sharp and sudden feel. The following moment in which Nicoli tears off and eats some of the officer's baguette not only underscores an ironic distance from the violence but also a casualness that fits the film's high level of verisimilitude. In a later scene, Doyle and others share expositional dialogue at the scene of a car accident—the bloodied bodies are shown in close-up despite their lack of place in the narrative. They not only help suggest the ever-presence of violence but also reinforce the distance from the action that the film has set up in the opening.

Issues of recognition and alignment are extended in the scenes that introduce Doyle and his partner Russo. Rather than being identified clearly, Doyle appears disguised as Santa Claus while Russo enters a bar to chase down a suspect. Literally hidden from the viewer by his fake beard and outsized suit, Doyle is placed in the rear of the frame. As the scene moves forward, a series of handheld shots observe Doyle and Russo as they go about their actions, although some subjective angles (such as point of view) are used generally, the camera remains distant, following the characters rather than taking or sharing their perspectives. During an interrogation in a back alley, the camera is placed behind objects or from angles that suggest a stolen image, such as from down a stairwell. This reinforces the high modality of the film, by employing the documentary aesthetic, and keeps the spectator at ground level with the action, while retaining distance from the characters. We watch Doyle and Russo, but we do not necessarily fully align with them—rather we are externally focalized. This is a complex system of identification that prioritizes objective shots and angles with some subjective elements throughout (most notably in the car chase). It allows for the spectator to watch Doyle but not to become involved or implicated in his actions, especially critical as these actions include a variety of racist insults and acts.

Another key element that affects our understanding of these processes is the opposition created between Doyle and Charnier. This conforms to a classic binary in which the values of the protagonist are opposed to those of the antagonist. Therefore, where Doyle is rough speaking and working class, Charnier is avuncular and wealthy. This is most clearly demonstrated in a sequence where Charnier sits with Nicoli for a three-course meal while Doyle watches on from outside in the cold (see Figure 3.1). Doyle's flaccid pizza and cold coffee are held in direct opposition to Charnier's gourmet dining. Given that Charnier is French and Doyle American, the locus of the criminal activity is placed outside of the United States, allowing the spectator to identify the problems in the film as external.

Figure 3.1 The clear separation between Doyle and Charnier (Doyle stands in the background) in *The French Connection* (Philip D'Antoni Productions, 1971).

Whereas the opening of *The French Connection* serves to distance the spectator from the action, the opening of *Dirty Harry* does the opposite. It places the spectator into a subjective position straight after a short prologue that features a memorial board for San Francisco police officers that reaches back to the 1800s (suggesting a textual link to the western). The subjective position is that of the antagonist Scorpio and it is a position returned to throughout the film and paralleled with that of Callahan. Initially, however, the spectator is placed as the victim, as the image of a rifle barrel juts toward them rendering them powerless. This then cuts to a point-of-view shot (see Figure 3.2), from down the rifle's scope, as the spectator shares Scorpio's gaze toward an unknowing female victim (rendered powerless partly by her ignorance and partly by her partially naked body). The non-diegetic sound juxtaposes this gaze, eliding violence and romance. It cuts to an overshoulder shot, from Scorpio's superior position and suggesting a subjective alignment.

The next cut returns us to the barrel, then to point of view. As the bullet is fired, we see a close-up of the trigger being pulled, then a cut to the victim who struggles and dies (seen from a similar angle to the point of view). The victim, young, slim, and blonde, suggests a scopophilic gaze that is then tied to violence—she has no identity other than as a body and a victim. Immediately the film has placed the spectator in a variety of positions offering alignment to the killer through the use of his point-of-view and reaction shots. This, however, is not necessarily an attractive alignment: we are clearly the antagonist and await Callahan's entry to the film as our main point of identification. But what the

Figure 3.2 Subjective alignment with Scorpio's scopophilic gaze in *Dirty Harry* (The Malpaso Company, 1971).

employment of these subjective shots suggests, when allied to similar shots from Callahan's point of view, is a similarity between protagonist and antagonist that draws the spectator's attention to their shared qualities. Two later sequences suggest a parallel through the use of similar subjective techniques: first when Callahan spies on "Hot" Mary (Lois Foraker) and then when Callahan and his partner Gonzales (Reni Santoni) watch for Scorpio on San Francisco's rooftops.

In the first instance, Callahan follows a suspect down an alley. Watching through a window he finds that the suspect is not Scorpio but a man returning home. With Callahan's face hidden, peering through the home's curtains, Callahan adopts a scopophilic gaze as Mary enters the frame. Long after Callahan realizes his mistake he lingers, to be discovered by some men who brand him a "Lousy Peeping-Tom" and attack him. The later scene focuses on Callahan's point of view (see Figure 3.3), his gaze down a pair of binoculars recalling the view down the scope from the opening scene, and he handles a rifle similar to Scorpio's. After following several people, Callahan's gaze comes to rest upon a window where he spies a young woman. Watching on, long after he needs to, Callahan sees her leave and then reappear naked with two guests. At first disgusted, Callahan watches on, saying to himself, "You owe it to yourself to live a little Harry." Both moments create parallels with Scorpio, drawing attention to their similarities, although Callahan's desire is framed as purely sexual, as opposed to Scorpio's desire to kill.

This is not to suggest that the spectator is encouraged to completely elide the characters—simply to recognize the similarities between the two. The recognition

Figure 3.3 Callahan's scopophilic gaze in *Dirty Harry* (The Malpaso Company, 1971).

of the differences between the two figures directs the spectator's alignment, and subsequent allegiance, to Callahan. Partly this is through the appearance of Scorpio, a character with somewhat androgynous features, such as a round face and long hair. Much initial criticism saw Scorpio as standing in for the counterculture movement, partly based on not only his hair but also his costume that includes a peace belt and neckerchief. These items of clothing, however, are introduced midway through the film once Scorpio has been released from custody. In the second scene to feature him, Scorpio is introduced via a close-up on his highly polished military boots. He handles a sniper rifle with confidence and professionalism, assembling it from its constituent parts and in a later scene uses a submachine gun capably. Rather than suggesting a clear opposition between Callahan (the establishment) and Scorpio (the counterculture), early scenes suggest an alternative reading of Scorpio, something intended and acknowledged by Siegel who suggested, "No verbal exposition is ever given, but to those who might have questioned his strange attire, it is possible that in his tilted fashion he could have returned from Vietnam bearing a crazed grudge."[49] His living quarters, in a groundskeeper's shack at Kezar Stadium, reinforce the suggestion that Scorpio is a returned veteran, left indigent. Scorpio is a mixture of signifiers, a composite of the Zodiac Killer and the campus shooter Charles Whitman who was as an "erstwhile altar-boy, former Eagle-Scout, ex-marine, and current student of architectural engineering" at the University of Texas, who "installed himself atop the library tower in the middle campus and began picking off victims—killing twelve and wounding another thirty one."[50] Scorpio targets Black people, young people, and homosexual men, all groups associated with the civil rights movement and counterculture; as Pierre Greenfield suggests, "Scorpio is the true redneck. 'My next victim will be a Catholic priest or a nigger,' is the last sentence of his ransom demand."[51]

Parallel to Scorpio is the representation of Callahan himself. As we have seen Eastwood's persona is key here (readily identifying him as the protagonist), but it is complicated in several ways. His status as a right-wing figure is often undermined; he too has long hair (his superior tells him to get it cut at one point). During a chase sequence, where Scorpio directs Callahan through San Francisco via public telephone, he is propositioned by a gay man in Mount Davidson. The man's approach to Callahan punctures Eastwood's masculine, heterosexual image—he is a reasonable target for homosexual advances. A reflective quality is repeatedly shown through the film. The famous speech, fetishizing the Magnum .44, is later parodied for its phallic connotations by

Scorpio, "My, that's a big one." Callahan's relationship to race is also more complex than many critics allowed, in part for one action sequence in which he interrupts a bank robbery in which the perpetrators are Black. The next scene, however, shows Callahan in a friendly relationship with a Black doctor and they discuss growing up in the same neighborhood, which is also the neighborhood where one of Scorpio's victims, a Black boy, is killed. In one of the more emotional scenes in the film we see the boy's mother's emotion and grief—the only time we see the impact of Scorpio's acts. This does not necessarily excuse or justify Callahan's other behaviors, such as his use of racist epithets, but it does complicate his figure and the reading of the film that sees it as simply anti-counterculture.

Eastwood's star persona, and therefore position in the diegesis, is further complicated by two other films released in 1971. Both *The Beguiled* and *Play Misty for Me* (the former directed by Siegel, the latter by Eastwood with a cameo by Siegel) share a deconstruction of Eastwood's persona. *The Beguiled* sees him as a Civil War soldier sheltering in a girl's school whose sexual dalliances with the staff and students end with first his leg being amputated and then his murder. Similarly, in *Play Misty for Me*, Eastwood is a hypermasculine disk jockey who has a one-night stand with a listener who then stalks and attempts to kill him. Both films interrogate and undermine the supposed machismo of Eastwood, emasculating his character.[52] During the bank heist in *Dirty Harry*, Callahan strides out, framed in front of a cinema playing *Play Misty for Me*—a severing of the diegesis that points to not only the film's artifice but also Eastwood's self-reflexive quality. Rather than displaying the fascist and authoritarian ideologies contemporary critics suggested, the film becomes a critique of such ideas by demonstrating the thin line between protagonist and antagonist and through its self-reflexive examination of Eastwood's star persona.

Conclusion

At the end of *The French Connection*, Doyle, having shot a colleague he mistook for Charnier, disappears off-screen chasing shadows. Text appears to inform us how much of the work in the film was undone and that Charnier escaped. This open ending, a characteristic of the New Hollywood, connotes an ambiguity familiar to fans of the French New Wave and chimes with the realist aesthetic employed in the film.[53] The openness continues the high modality of the film, eschewing any ideological closure—like life, and crime, it continues. The ending of *Dirty Harry*, although offering narrative closure as Scorpio has been eliminated, offers a different complication. During the advertising of the film the spectator's attention had been drawn to Callahan's legitimacy, connoted through his badge ("Dirty Harry and the homicidal maniac. Harry's the one with the badge"). Having killed Scorpio, Callahan throws away his badge, the symbol of society and his legitimacy, collapsing some of the distance between himself and Scorpio. Originally this was not to be the case. Indeed, the synopsis printed in the pressbook offers an alternate, "Harry turns and walks down the road, a solitary figure, his star in his pocket, the man they call *Dirty Harry*." A debate occurred in which director Siegel argued for Callahan to throw the badge away, Eastwood for him to keep it so as to imply a return to the police force and legitimacy. Eventually Siegel won out, and it gives the film a final subversive moment and helps assert Siegel's authorship of the film. Callahan ends outside of society, away from the legitimizing power of the state, leaving him much as Scorpio is at the start of the film.

Critical reactions fixed *Dirty Harry* as a right-wing text, a reaction to the liberal politics and innovative techniques of the New Hollywood. But by reassessing the film and acknowledging the parallels the film draws between antagonist and protagonist, forcing comparisons between the two, a more complex picture is drawn that undermines the initial readings and expresses a moral ambiguity indicative of the period. This reassessment pushes us to question our understanding of the New Hollywood period and the limitations of the auteur definition it assumes. In excluding *Dirty Harry*, and director Siegel, the dominant definitions of the New Hollywood period set a critical attitude that fixes some films, and filmmakers, as canonical and others as not, and also fixes ideological positions. Although *The French Connection* has been consistently placed as part of the New Hollywood canon, its box-office rival displays textual and ideological elements that sit just as happily within the period.

Notes

1 Box-office data is from www.boxofficemojo.com.
2 Stephen Prince, *Classical Film Violence: Designing and Regulating Brutality in Hollywood Cinema 1930–1968* (New Brunswick, NJ: Rutgers University Press, 2003), 197.

3   Mark Shiel, "American Cinema 1965–75," in *Contemporary American Cinema*, ed. Linda Ruth Williams and Michael Hammond (Maidenhead: Open University Press, 2006), 12.

4   Robin Wood, *Hollywood from Vietnam to Reagan and Beyond* (New York: Columbia University Press, 2003), 44.

5   Ibid., 23.

6   John G. Cawelti, *Mystery, Violence and Popular Culture* (Madison: University of Wisconsin Press, 2004), 206.

7   Paul Cobley, *The American Thriller: Generic Innovation and Social Change in the 1970s* (London: Palgrave, 2000).

8   Lawrence Webb, *The Cinema of Urban Crisis: Seventies Films and the Reinvention of the City* (Amsterdam: Amsterdam University Press, 2014), 111.

9   Jonathan Kirshner, *Hollywood's Last Golden Age: Politics, Society, and the Seventies Film in America* (Ithaca, NY: Cornell University Press, 2012), 28.

10 William Friedkin, *The Friedkin Connection* (New York: HarperCollins, 2013), 162.

11 Ibid., 163.

12 Ibid., 182.

13 Robin Moore's account, published in 1969, from which the film was freely adapted, includes the real-world fates of the criminals, with all major players being arrested and Eddie Egan and Sonny Grosso keeping their jobs—the ending of the film suggests most of the criminals were released and that Egan and Grosso were transferred out of narcotics. See his *The French Connection* (London: Bloomsbury, 2005).

14 The script had circulated around Hollywood, in various forms, and had been offered to stars including Frank Sinatra and John Wayne before Eastwood accepted.

15 Paul Smith, *Clint Eastwood: A Cultural Production* (Minneapolis: University of Minnesota Press, 1993), 71.

16 Ibid., 72.

17 Alan Lovell, *Don Siegel: American Cinema* (London: BFI, 1975).

18 Stuart M. Kaminsky, *Don Siegel: Director* (New York: Curtis Books, 1974).

19 Deborah Allison, "Siegel, Don." *Senses of Cinema*, July 2004, http://www.sensesofcinema.com/2004/great-directos.siegel, accessed November 20, 2019,.

20 Lovell, *Don Siegel*, 27.

21 Allison, *Senses of Cinema*.

22 Webb, *The Cinema of Urban Crisis*, 140.

23 The finale, however, takes place outside the city. Yvonne Tasker suggests Callahan's violence is legitimized by the urban environment. The finale makes it "asocial." See her *The Hollywood Action and Adventure Film* (Chichester: Wiley-Blackwell, 2015), 114.

24 Joe Street, *Dirty Harry's America: Clint Eastwood, Harry Callahan and the Conservative Backlash* (Gainesville: University Press of Florida, 2016), 63.

25 Christian Keathley, "Trapped in the Affection Image: Hollywood's Post Traumatic Cycle (1970–1976)," in *The Last Great American Picture Show: New Hollywood Cinema in the 1970s*, ed. Thomas Elsaesser (Amsterdam: Amsterdam University Press, 2004), 303.

26 Raymond J. Haberski Jr., *"It's Only a Movie": Films and Critics in American Culture* (Lexington: University Press of Kentucky, 2001), 178.

27 Ibid., 173.

28 Ibid., 2.

29 Pauline Kael, *Deeper into Movies* (London: Marion Boyars, 2000), 385–8.

30 Ibid., 313–18.

31 Garrett Epps, "Does Popeye Doyle Teach Us How to Be Fascist?," *New York Times*, May 21 (1972), Section D, 15.

32 Ibid.

33 Andrew Sarris, "Films in Focus," *The Village Voice*, October 21, 1971, 77.

34 Richard Schickel, "A Real Look at a Tough Cop," *Time*, November 19, 1971, 13.

35 Kirshner, *Hollywood's Last Golden Age*, 21.

36 Paul Johnson, *A History of the American People* (London: Phoenix, 1997), 987.

37 John Ellis defines this as "An idea of a film ... widely circulated and promoted ... the cinema industry's anticipatory reply to the question 'What is this film like?'" See his *Visible Fictions* (London: Routledge, 1992), 30.

38 Suggestions include "prevailing on their local press to do a special feature, interviews or even editorial on the work of the narcotics squad people in your area" and "invite local civic leaders, police officials, attorneys, social workers and press to your opening nite [sic] to do a private screening to gain their endorsements."

39 David Frangioni and Tom Schatz, *Clint Eastwood Icon: The Ultimate Film Art Collection* (London: Titan Books, 2009), 66.

40 According to Bob Hodge and David Tripp, "modality 'concerns the reality attributed to a message." The concept of a modality (a term borrowed from linguistics) is used to describe how the audience attributes different levels of reality to different texts. The higher the modality the more "real" a film is understood to be. See their *Children and Television* (Cambridge, MA: Polity Press, 1986), 104.

41 Ed Buscombe, *The BFI Companion to the Western* (London: BFI, 1998), 53.

42 Smith, *Clint Eastwood*, 19.

43 Christopher Frayling, *Spaghetti Westerns: Cowboys and Europeans from Karl May to Sergio Leone* (London: I.B. Taurus, 1998), 180.

44 Ibid., 187.

45   Stephen Prince, *Savage Cinema: Sam Peckinpah and the Rise of Ultraviolence* (Austin: Texas University Press, 1998), 18.

46   Ibid.

47   Jake Horsley, *The Blood Poets: A Cinema of Savagery* (Lanham, MD: Scarecrow Press, 1999), 89.

48   Analysis of subject positions refers to Murray Smith's "structure of sympathy," the concepts of recognition, alignment, and allegiance that help us understand how spectators relate to a text:

>   In this system, spectators construct characters (a process I refer to as *recognition*). Spectators are also provided with visual and aural information more or less congruent with that available to characters, and so are placed in a certain structure of *alignment* with characters. In addition, spectators evaluate characters on the basis of the values they embody, and hence form more-or-less sympathetic or more-or-less antipathic *allegiances* with them.

See his *Engaging Characters: Fiction, Emotion and the Cinema* (Oxford: Oxford University Press, 1995), 74.

49   Don Siegel, *A Siegel Film: An Autobiography* (London: Faber and Faber, 1993), 370.

50   J. Hoberman, *The Dream Life: Movies, Media and the Mythology of the Sixties* (New York: New Press, 2003), 152.

51   Pierre Greenfield, "Dirty Dogs, Dirty Devils & Dirty Harry," *Velvet Light Trap* 16, no. 34 (1976): 36.

52   This self-reflexivity would become more recognized in Eastwood's later films such as *Tightrope* (Richard Tuggle, 1984), *Unforgiven* (Clint Eastwood, 1992), and *Gran Torino* (Clint Eastwood, 2008).

53   True to form, Hollywood gave us a closed ending in *The French Connection II* (John Frankenheimer, 1975) when Doyle finds and kills Charnier. The tagline, "This is the climax!," suggests an audience dissatisfaction with the first film's ending.

4

A Wave of Their Own: How Jewish Filmmakers Invented the New Hollywood

Vincent Brook

Introduction

The Jewish New Wave in American cinema is old news. That an extraordinary number of Jewish actors (Woody Allen, Alan Arkin, Richard Benjamin, Albert Brooks, Mel Brooks, Richard Dreyfus, Elliott Gould, Charles Grodin, Dustin Hoffman, Madeline Kahn, Carol Kane, Zero Mostel, Carl Reiner, George Segal, Barbra Streisand, and Gene Wilder, among others) burst on the scene from the mid-1960s through the 1970s, unprecedentedly proclaiming rather than hiding their Jewishness—on- and off-screen—has been extensively covered. This treatment, however, has been generated largely within Jewish Studies, thereby ghettoizing the Jewish New Wave within the larger New Hollywood narrative (mid-1960s through the 1970s) to which it crucially contributed. Less explicably, and more egregiously, a second marginalization has occurred within both the larger narrative and Jewish Studies: namely, the near-complete neglect of the outsize and overarching significance of Jewish *directors* to the onset and development of the New Hollywood.[1]

Outsize and overarching, indeed. For though the New Hollywood would be incalculably diminished without the bountiful contribution of the above Jewish actors, it is unthinkable without the seminal, iconic, and numerically disproportionate films directed by the likes of Arthur Penn (*Mickey One, Bonnie and Clyde, Alice's Restaurant, Little Big Man, Night Moves*), Mike Nichols (*The Graduate, Carnal Knowledge, Catch 22*), Sidney Lumet (*The Pawnbroker, Dog Day Afternoon, Serpico, Network*), Stanley Kubrick (*Lolita, Dr. Strangelove, 2001, A Clockwork Orange, The Shining*), Woody Allen (*Take the Money and Run, Bananas, Sleeper, Love and Death, Annie Hall, Manhattan*), Mel Brooks

(*Blazing Saddles, Young Frankenstein, The Producers*), Paul Mazursky (*Bob & Carol & Ted & Alice, Alex in Wonderland, Blume in Love, Next Stop Greenwich Village, An Unmarried Woman, Willie and Phil*), Roman Polanski (*Rosemary's Baby, Chinatown*), Bob Rafelson (*Five Easy Pieces, The King of Marvin Gardens*), Peter Bogdanovich (*The Last Picture Show, Paper Moon*), Alan J. Pakula (*The Sterile Cuckoo, Klute, The Parallax View, All the President's Men*), William Friedkin (*The French Connection, The Exorcist, The Sorcerer*), Sydney Pollack (*They Shoot Horses, Don't They?; The Way We Were*), John Schlesinger (*Midnight Cowboy*), Herbert Ross (*The Owl and the Pussycat; Play It Again, Sam; Funny Lady*), Elaine May (*A New Leaf, The Honeymoon Kid, Mikey and Nicky*), Haskell Wexler (*Medium Cool*), Ralph Bakshi (*Fritz the Cat, Heavy Traffic, Coonskin, Wizards, The Lord of the Rings*), Richard Lester (*Petulia*), Frank Perry (*Diary of a Mad Housewife, Play It as It Lays*), Jeffrey Schatzberg (*Panic in Needle Park, Scarecrow*), and Steven Spielberg (*Sugarland Express*), among many others.[2]

Whatever its cause, this gaping elision is overripe for revision, not least given the privileged place in film history of the New Hollywood period—to which, of course, numerous non-Jewish directors also contributed. Diane Jacobs in *Hollywood Renaissance* (1977), one of the first surveys of the epoch, singled out the more prominent of these—Robert Altman, John Cassavetes, Francis Coppola, and Martin Scorsese (Paul Mazursky was the lone Jew to make her short list)—to which I would add, at the very least—Hal Ashby, Brian De Palma, Bob Fosse, George Roy Hill, Sam Peckinpah, and Richard Rush.[3] My argument remains, however, that the influence of Jewish filmmakers, especially on the New Hollywood's formative period, was demonstrably greater than that of non-Jews, with only Italian Americans (directors Coppola, Scorsese, and De Palma and actors Robert De Niro, Al Pacino, and Joe Pesci) offering even the slightest ethnically tinged competition. Moreover, though the Jewish aspect of my reconsidered narrative needn't rely solely on explicitly Jewish characters or themes in Jew Wave films, I do propose, and hope to show, that a determining role was played, to a greater or lesser degree, by the directors' Jewishness, broadly conceived.

Although references to Jewish religious practice or belief are rare among the Jew Wave films (except as fodder for satire), faith in Judaism, unlike with other religions, has not been, in the modern era, a prerequisite for Jewish identification. My analysis focuses rather on a more recent, historically grounded, ideologically informed relation to Jewishness. Enabled by the sociocultural and religious freedoms of the French Revolution-inspired *haskalah* (Jewish Enlightenment) from the late 1700s onward, this form of identification, while drawing on the ethical strand in the Talmudic tradition, gains its greatest strength from Jews' heritage of persecution and marginalization, and expresses itself in an "insider/ outsider" perspective aimed at perfecting the world and improving the lot of the least among us.[4] From this newly empowered, yet still empathetic, and largely secular Jewishness, first in Europe and later in America, emerged a distinctively Jewish orientation toward progressive social change and cultural innovation. In addition, as it did for American Jewish activists and artists in general, a micro-geographic and demographic component affected the Jew Wave directors specifically. As the title of Nathan Abrams's recent monograph, *Stanley Kubrick: New York Jewish Intellectual*, highlights, a shared Jew York City upbringing and outlook among several of the prominent Jew Wave directors helped to engender and reinforce the liberal political and avant-garde artistic aspects of their work.[5]

The Canon Game: Arthur Penn

Of the forty-plus Jew Wave directors who propelled and helped sustain the New Hollywood, five stand out for their ur-influence, trendsetting films, and distinctive oeuvre: Arthur Penn, Mike Nichols, Sidney Lumet, Stanley Kubrick, and Woody Allen. Penn earns pride of place for his New Hollywood precursor (*Mickey One*), several prominent sustainers (*Alice's Restaurant*, *Little Big Man*, *Night Moves*, *The Missouri Breaks*, and *Four Friends*), and above all for his having helmed the film touted by critics and historians as the avatar of the American New Wave, *Bonnie and Clyde*.[6]

Alone among the Big Five for his Philadelphia rather than New York City upbringing, Penn more than compensated intellectually and artistically: first, by attending the avant-garde-oriented Black Mountain College in North Carolina; second, by cutting his directing teeth on the New York stage and in early television, then centered in New York, whose ranks were rife with Jewish writers and directors who would later contribute to the New Hollywood.

After "graduating" to the movies and having several films butchered by the Hollywood studios, Penn's *Mickey One* was his first stab at a more personal, "European-American" film.[7] True to its pre-New Hollywood genesis, the film's Kafkaesque scenario about a troubled stand-up comic and its surrealistic

French New Wave style proved too much for critics and the public to take at the time. Star Warren Beatty, however, was impressed enough to hire Penn for *Bonnie and Clyde*, which Beatty both starred in and produced. A period-piece send-up of the famed Depression Era bank robbers, in which the eponymous leads (played by Beatty and Faye Dunaway) are portrayed not as ruthless criminals but as sexy, underdog antiheroes, not only clicked but resonated strongly with a counterculture mounting a collective attack on traditional American values and US foreign policy. The film's radical content, jarring shifts in tone, and brutal gunning down of the doomed couple, depicted as a tragic slow-motion ballet, were attuned to the 1960s in other ways. A Production Code in limbo since 1966 enabled the aestheticized ultra-violence, and Penn's finger on the pulse of the period added historical specificity to the New Wave influence. "This was the time of Marshall McLuhan," he explained (referring to the social critic who coined the concept "the medium is the message"). "The idea was to use the medium as a narrative device" and to reference recent events, such as the image at the end of Clyde's head "blown away by a bullet" evoking the Kennedy assassination.[8]

Penn's next film, *Alice's Restaurant*, dispensed with allegory. Like the other New Hollywood icon of 1967, *The Graduate*, it took the counterculture head-on and straight from the horse's mouth. An adaptation of Arlo Guthrie's folk song "Alice's Restaurant Massacree" and starring Guthrie as himself, the film is based on real events, including Guthrie's visits to his dying (then already deceased) folk-singing legend father, Woody Guthrie (played by Joseph Boley). The era's youthful rebelliousness is captured in all its rambunctious glory, while the film's comedic element, as in *Bonnie and Clyde*, belies a "noir backbeat of betrayed romanticism," and its "madcap autobiography [is] driven by the military draft and the Vietnam War."[9] Though opposed to the war, Penn was not uncritical of the counterculture's grounding in white privilege. "The characters in *Alice's Restaurant* are middle-class whites," he explained. "They aren't poor or hungry or working class. They are not in the same boat as African Americans. But they're not militants either ... From this point of view, this film depicts a very specific social class. It's a bourgeois film."[10] It's also a Jewish film in more than the outsider theme and progressive politics characteristic of most of Penn's work, as both the real-life Guthrie, who was bar mitzvahed, and the titular Alice Brock were born to Jewish mothers (the latter's mother having financed the famous restaurant).[11]

Emboldened by the budding New Hollywood movement and increasing studio encouragement that *Bonnie and Clyde* helped propel, Penn's next film, *Little Big Man* (1970), was his boldest to date—in style and content. It also upped the Jewish ante in starring Jew Wave icon Dustin Hoffman as fictional Little Big Horn survivor Jack Crabb. Once again resorting to allegory but more pointedly satirically than in his previous films, Penn uses Crabb's alleged raising by the Cheyenne and serving as Custer's scout to conjure both identity politics and Vietnam War opposition. And more reflexively than *Bonnie and Clyde*'s upending of gangster genre conventions, *Little Big Man* reverses the good-guy/bad-guy binary of the cavalry-and-Indian western in its semi-fictional yet full-throated revisioning of Anglo-American/Native American history. As a further sign that the Jew Wave both reflected and helped reproduce the social upheaval of the period, where *Bonnie and Clyde* clearly resonated with the Marxist-oriented (and heavily Jewish constituted) Weather Underground's politically motivated bank robberies of the late 1960s and 1970s, *Little Big Man* heralded and perhaps helped inspire the American Indian Movement's 1973 standoff with the FBI at Wounded Knee.

If Penn's first three Jew Wave films also exhibited noir attributes—ambivalent protagonists, crime themes, dark views of society—his *Night Moves* fit fully into the film noir revival (or neo-noir, as it came to be known, itself a product of the New Hollywood). Set in the contemporary period and adopting noir's telltale shadowy lighting and expressionist mise-en-scène, *Night Moves* sealed the deal by appropriating a classical noir trope for contemporary purposes: "a private detective [played by Gene Hackman] who ends up circling the abyss, a no-exit comment on the post-1968, post-Watergate times."[12]

Penn's other noteworthy films of the 1970s, *The Missouri Breaks* and *Four Friends*, returned to familiar territory: the former to the anti-western, the latter to the coming-of-age counterculture tale. More resolutely noir than *Little Big Man*, *The Missouri Breaks* failed critically and commercially upon its release, but subsequent assessments, such as that of *The New York Times*'s Xan Brooks, place it firmly in Penn's allegorical and socially hyperconscious Jew Wave mold: "Derided [initially] as an addled, self-indulgent folly, [in 2003] its quieter passages resonate more satisfyingly, while its lunatic take on a decadent, dying frontier seems oddly appropriate [and how much more so post-2016!]."[13] *Four Friends*' most distinctive Jew Wave aspect is the ethnicity of the main member of the titular quartet, Yugoslavian Jew Danilo Prozor (Craig Wasson), who, as with

Arlo Guthrie's *Alice's Restaurant* character, is autobiographically related to the film's screenwriter, Steve Tesich.

Mike Nichols

The autobiographical Jewish connection to Mike Nichols's New Hollywood oeuvre begins not with his films' characters but with Nichols himself. Born Mikhail Igor Peschkowsky to a Russian-German family in Berlin in 1931, Nichols described his fate as "insanely, unfairly, ridiculously lucky. All Jews went to the camps, but we not only didn't go to the camps, we were allowed to leave the country."[14] Escaping the Holocaust but not the anti-Semitism of his childhood upbringing in New York City, Nichols recalled how Jew-hatred, along with his German accent and permanent loss of all his hair from a whooping cough vaccine, affected his character and filmmaking in two ways: turning him into "as far outside as an outsider can get," but also linking him, via his "Russian Jewish parentage ... to a great generation of Central European émigrés ... that stretches from Ernst Lubitsch through Billy Wilder."[15]

Nichols's Jewish pedigree was further overdetermined by his stand-up comic's profession, as Elaine May's partner in the hit Nichols and May comedy team of the 1950s and early 1960s. Yet the depth and breadth of his extratextual Jewishness could not prevent the Jewishness in his films, as with most of the Jew Wave directors, from almost wholesale neglect by critics and historians. This de-Judaizing pattern prevails even in discussion of the second of the breakthrough New Hollywood films, *The Graduate*. One of the more astute analysts of Nichols's work, J. W. Whitehead, in his discussion of this "visual watershed" and "milestone in cinema history," broaches its Jewish aspect only in coded terms.[16] Whitehead describes protagonist Benjamin Braddock (Dustin Hoffman, in his breakout role) generically as having "ethnic features" and refers (Jewish insinuatingly) to both Benjamin and his father (the Jewish William Daniels) as "small men" of "diminutive size."[17] Another Jewish stereotype, Papa Braddock's miserliness, Whitehead doesn't mention at all, nor is the striking Jewish/Gentile contrast between Benjamin and Carl Smith (Brian Avery), his tall, blond, uber-WASP romantic rival, worthy of comment.

Whitehead's Jew/WASP elision is especially curious in regard to *The Graduate* because, as Jewish Studies scholars had long pointed out, Nichols and Hoffman had drawn attention to this very subject. Nichols had originally slated blond, blue-eyed hunk Robert Redford for the lead, given Benjamin's Aryan-esque description in Charles Webb's novella. He went with Hoffman instead because Hoffman was the opposite of the "walking surfboard" character in the book, "a dark, Jewish, anomalous presence, which is how I experience myself."[18] Hoffman, meanwhile, recalls having protested to Nichols: " 'I'm not right for the part, sir. This is a Gentile. This is a WASP. This is Robert Redford.' And Mike said, 'Maybe he's Jewish inside.' "[19]

Nichols's Jewishness, inside and out, informs the bulk of his Jew Wave (and later) work. His adeptness (per Whitehead) at critiquing hegemonic structures, cultural dysfunction, and late-capitalist objectification, commodification, and conformity, in his Jew Wave films especially (*The Graduate, Carnal Knowledge, Catch 22, The Day of the Dolphin*), is directly traceable to his self-admitted outsider complex and similarly Jewish-inflected empathy for the marginalized and oppressed. It also explains his leaning toward source material and/or screenplays written by fellow socially minded Jews. During the Jew Wave period this included Buck Henry (*The Graduate; The Day of the Dolphin*), Joseph Heller (*Catch 22*), and Jules Feiffer (*Carnal Knowledge*) and continued with Nora Ephron (*Silkwood*, 1983; *Heartburn*, 1986), Neil Simon (*Biloxi Blues*, 1988), Carrie Fisher (*Postcards from the Edge*, 1990), Elaine May (*The Birdcage*, 1996; *Primary Colors*, 1998), Garry Shandling (*What Planet Are You From?*, 2000), and Tony Kushner (*Angels in America*, 2004).

Whitehead partially atones for his Jewish blind spot toward Nichols's work in acknowledging at book's end that Woody Allen—"smart, funny, New York, Jewish," with a career trajectory from stand-up to theater to film directing— may be Nichols's "closest analog."[20] Yet another smart, not so funny, Jew Wave director, who also moved from theater (and TV) to film, Sidney Lumet, offers perhaps the most suitable match with Nichols.[21]

Sidney Lumet

Brian Neve's study of the "social tradition" in American film focuses on six politically oriented directors from the classical Hollywood period (1930s–1950s): Orson Welles, Elia Kazan, Abraham Polonsky, Robert Rossen, Joseph Losey, and Jules Dassin, of which only Welles and Kazan were not Jewish.[22] Jewish émigrés fleeing Hitler played a similarly predominant role in classical film noir (1940s–1950s), as I have detailed elsewhere and Alain Silver affirmed in his selection of the "ten best" noirs: "I did have one rule: a single movie per director, otherwise [Jewish émigrés] Siodmak, Lang, Wilder, and Ophuls might have overwhelmed the field and made it an all-émigré list."[23]

In the postclassical period (1960s on), Jewish neo-noir and politically oriented directors have continued to "overwhelm the field"—and Sidney Lumet has figured prominently in both groups.[24] Indeed, with the exception of Nichols and three other Jewish directors—Stanley Kramer, Fred Zinnemann, and Martin Ritt—no American filmmaker has been more closely aligned than Lumet with a cinema dominated by "a deep and abiding commitment to social justice."[25] As for films featuring Jewish characters and themes, only Woody Allen can hold a torch to Lumet. Encouraged by the ethnic pride movement of the 1960s and fueled further by identity politics, Lumet's explicitly Jewish films include the proto-Jew Wave *The Pawnbroker*; the Jew Wave-period *Bye Bye Braverman* (1968) and *Just Tell Me What You Want* (1979); and post-Jew Wave *Daniel* (1983), *Garbo Talks* (1984), *Running on Empty* (1988), and *A Stranger Among Us* (1992).

Few directors, Jewish or Gentile, have matched Lumet's relentless probing of the modern city's, specifically New York City's, problematic core. The investigation went beyond his addressing police corruption, as in *Serpico* (1973), or antiestablishment sentiment and transgender issues, as in *Dog Day Afternoon* (1975). It extended boldly into areas of race and ethnicity, as David Desser and Lester Friedman observe: "The presence of a multiracial, multiethnic mise en scene is unmistakable, and not merely tokenistic [in Lumet's films], [drawing] precisely on the conflicts that rage within a multicultural society."[26]

Lumet's emphasis on (Jewish) angst is another distinctive feature of his films, but again, given their political bent, is directed outward, at topical social issues. Lumet, "the street Jew," as he called himself, though by no means eschewing psychological or philosophical dimensions, invariably places issues of personal guilt and responsibility in the context of social engagement in the public sphere.[27] Lumet's documentary-style aesthetic, similarly, is more neorealist in inspiration than *nouvelle vague*, whose devices he also engages but gears them more toward a heightening of the connection to social reality.

Lumet's liberalism also diverges from Nichols's in its insider rather than outsider genealogy. As he explained in a 1989 interview: "I guess when you're a Depression baby, someone with a typical Lower East Side poor Jewish upbringing, you automatically get involved with social issues."[28] Both of Lumet's parents were Polish émigrés who became Yiddish theater actors in New York. Lumet himself debuted on the Yiddish stage in 1928 at age four, became immersed in secular Jewish activism in the 1930s, and by the late 1940s was taking on lead roles in Jewish-themed, politically oriented plays.[29] After a stint directing for early television, he made his film-directing debut in 1957 with the TV drama-adapted, Oscar-nominated *Twelve Angry Men*, whose issues of guilt, justice, and individual responsibility would dominate his subsequent work.

The Pawnbroker proved Lumet's cinematic breakthrough, from a Jewish and Jew Wave perspective. Although a few Hollywood films had dealt with the Nazi death camps—Zinnemann's *The Search* (1948), Edward Dmytryk's *The Juggler* (1953), George Stevens's *The Diary of Anne Frank* (1959), and Kramer's *Judgment at Nuremberg* (1960)—*The Pawnbroker* was the first "to confront the permanent scars of the Holocaust" on those who survived the camps.[30] It also foreshadowed, and immeasurably influenced, the New Hollywood—stylistically and in terms of personnel. The impetus for the film's radical, New Wave-style flash-cutting technique came from Jewish editor Ralph Rosenblum, whose extensive work on key New Hollywood films, along with that of the Jewish Dede Allen, all but clinches the case for renaming this period the Jew Wave.

Besides his crucial contribution to *The Pawnbroker*, Rosenblum went on to become Woody Allen's editor throughout his Jew Wave period, from *Take the Money and Run* through *Interiors* (1978), while Dede Allen, along with editing Penn's path-breaking *Bonnie and Clyde* and a string of his other Jew Wave films from *Alice's Restaurant* and *Little Big Man* to *Night Moves* and *The Missouri Breaks*, also cut Lumet's *Serpico* and *Dog Day Afternoon*. Rosenblum and Dede Allen, Paul Monaco summarizes, "imitated devices from several French films …, but [they] also extended them. . . . More importantly, [their] innovations shifted editing away from its traditional reliance on telling a story to the creation of a new and penetrating subjectivity in the feature film."[31] Warren Buckland went further. In a paper delivered at the American New Wave conference in 2017, Buckland added only Nichols's non-Jewish editor Sam O'Steen to Rosenblum and Dede Allen as "The Film Editors who invented the New Hollywood."[32]

Arguably, Lumet's greatest, and certainly most prescient, contribution to the Jew Wave was *Network* (1976), a brutal satire written by the Jewish Paddy Chayefsky and edited by the Jewish Alan Heim. *Network*'s indictment of television's uber-capitalist obeisance to the bottom line and ruthless co-opting of leftist ideals, while reflecting the disillusionment of the mid-1970s, also seemed farcically over the top—at the time. By the 2000s, however, with a rabid right-wing news analyst (Glenn Beck) patterning himself after *Network*'s lunatic leftist anchor Howard Beale (played by Peter Finch) and a Reality TV star turned commander in chief (guess who) channeling Beale's "We're mad as hell and we're not going to take this anymore!" refrain, *Network*'s hyperbolized dystopia had come to pass, and not only on TV.[33]

Stanley Kubrick

Among prominent Jew Wave directors, Kubrick was furthest ahead of the curve. The poster boy, per Nathan Abrams, for New York Jewish intellectual directors, only Production Code proscriptions kept his trademark tragicomic irony from bursting into full bloom as early as his 1962 adaptation of Vladimir Nabokov's controversial novel *Lolita*, Kubrick's "first film as a mature, independent director."[34] Forced to resort to innuendo in addressing the novel's notorious pedophilia theme, Kubrick's version still managed to capture the book's satirical tone and wry critique of American culture, both of which he would henceforth make his own. Besides the inferred, self-critical Jewishness of decadent playwright Clare Quilty (played with salacious glee by Jewish actor Peter Sellers), an underlying "Jewish-inflected humor" infuses the film, Abrams argues, which Kubrick uses "to make serious points about post-Holocaust Jewish masculinity."[35]

In *Dr. Strangelove: How I Learned to Stop Worrying and Love the Bomb*, Kubrick's farcical companion piece to Lumet's serious take on nuclear war, *Fail Safe* (also 1964), the wraps came off in content and style. In the film's madcap approach, Abrams sees a nod to an "alternative" Jewish cultural bent, as opposed to the "high moral seriousness" of the Jew York intellectuals, with examples of the former ranging from Paul Krassner's *Realist* and Harvey Kurtzman's *Mad* magazines to satirical cartoonist Jules Feiffer, cabaret singer-songwriter Tom Lehrer, and the radical Jewish stand-ups.[36] Capping *Dr. Strangelove*'s French New Wave-indebted cross-cutting of documentary and comical modes is a pointed (literally) post-Holocaust allusion—in the Nazi salute of the eponymous (Gentile) Werner von Braun/(Jewish) John von Neumann-like scientist, whose "interfaith marriage" (including Strangelove's portrayal by Peter Sellers) upholds Kubrick's non-denominational sense of mankind's propensity for evil.[37] Uniquely Kubrickian, and New Hollywood-esque, is the irreverent musical "mismatch" of a Second World War pop-era love song (Vera Lynn's "We Will Meet Again") with the final images of nuclear Armageddon.

2001: A Space Odyssey would take musical incongruity to new heights, literally, in melding Strauss's Blue Danube Waltz to a spaceship's dance around the blue planet on its way to the moon. Even more revolutionary, literally and figuratively, was the formal/thematic match cut from the bone hurtled skyward in slow motion by a prehistoric ape (after wielding it to kill a rival ape for control of a watering hole) to the like-shaped spaceship circling Earth hundreds of millennia hence. The visual and chronological sleight-of-hand was (and remains) thrilling aesthetically and intellectually, in its devastatingly irrefutable message: that at the heart of human evolution and technological progress lies lethal weaponry and intraspecies warfare. The rest, as the Talmudic says, is commentary—among which is Abrams's attribution of a Jewish "religious turn" to the film's admittedly ambiguous ending. Although the death and embryonic rebirth of the astronaut protagonist David Bowman (Keir Dullea) can be read Christologically, even stronger mystical elements, Abrams avers, are tied to the Kabbalah—specifically, the *ein-sof* (Hebrew for "without end" or "the infinite") "used to describe the supreme entity or the Godhead."[38]

Kubrick's next two films, *A Clockwork Orange* and *Barry Lyndon*, were based on British novels (by Anthony Burgess and William Makepeace Thackeray, respectively), but Kubrick's New Hollywood auteurism (and New York Jewish intellectualism) prevailed. Abrams, while acknowledging Kubrick's fraught relationship with his Jewish identity (compounded by his marriage to the niece of notorious Nazi film director Veit Harlan), again regards the director's concern with issues of masculinity, ethical responsibility, and the nature of evil as existing in dialogue with the New York Jewish (and here British) literary milieu. In *A Clockwork Orange*'s dystopian, near-future tale of ultra-violence run amok, the intellectual point is made musically once again—most boldly, and controversially, in the classical ("The Thieving Magpie") and popular ("Singin' in the Rain") accompaniments to gang rape.

As for *Barry Lyndon*, much like Hitchcock's high-key lighting and insouciant air counterpoising his films' macabre themes, Kubrick's sumptuously beautiful adaptation of the Thackeray novel—hailed for its candle-lit, symmetrically composed, slow reverse-zooms—belies its savagely ironic take on a ruthlessly ambitious Irish scamp (partly an avatar for Kubrick himself), whose qualities of character (and lack thereof) both enable his rise and propel his fall in a corrupt and repressive society.[39]

In *The Shining*, Kubrick, though still living and working in England, cast his jaundiced eye back on his native United States. The dysfunctional nuclear

American family at the center of the allegory bears the brunt of the ire-ony, but associations with Native American genocide undergird the overall critique. The Overlook Hotel (based on the historic Stanley Hotel) in Estes Park, Colorado, the microcosmic setting for the film, not only is located near the nation's Continental Divide but, most resonant with the supernatural horror story Kubrick concocted from a Stephen King novel, was constructed atop ancient American Indian burial grounds. America's collective criminal past comes back with a vengeance during the brief period the Torrance family (played by Jack Nicholson, Shelley Duvall, and young Danny Lloyd) serve as sole-dwelling, off-season caretakers (along with Scatman Crothers's African American cook) of the cavernous hotel.

The Shining—its title a reference, as the cook explains, to a special psychic gift possessed by the young boy—has become a cult classic and inspired, not copycat crimes but a plethora of theories about the film's alleged esoteric meanings and a documentary, *Room 237* (2012), devoted to examining them. Abrams again weighs in from the intellectual angle, this time pointing to Kubrick's reading of Central European Jews (Freud and disciples, Brunos Bettelheim and Schulz, and Simon O. Lesser) as underpinning the film's fraught father–son relationship.[40] Other, more subjective theories posited in *Room 237* range from the reasonable (First Peoples' revenge) to the ridiculous (Kubrick's penance for helping the government fabricate the moon landings, as imagined in 1977's fictional *Capricorn One*). Somewhere in between, from a Jew Wave perspective, is academic Geoffrey Cocks's notion of *The Shining*'s conscious allusion to the Holocaust, for which his book *The Wolf at the Door: Stanley Kubrick, History, and the Holocaust* (2004) offers intriguing evidence.

Beginning with Kubrick's longtime desire to make a Holocaust film, more forthrightly than *Dr. Strangelove* but still in an "oblique" manner, Cocks points to several corroborative elements in *The Shining*.[41] Among these is (Kabbalah-inspired?) numerology, specifically the prevalence of 42—Room 237's three numerals multiplied equaling 42, Danny's tee shirt bearing that number, and his mother Wendy's taking 42 swings of the baseball bat at deranged husband Jack—a number which since the early 1970s "was seen as an ominous metonym for the Final Solution, which was launched at the Wannsee Conference in 1942."[42] Jack's typewriter (on which he can't manage to compose any "poetry after the Holocaust"), Cocks additionally explains, is an Adler Eagle typewriter—"a German machine, pictured almost to make it a character, a clear representation of the bureaucratic killing machine."[43] Most compellingly, given Kubrick's emphasis on metaphoric music, are the repeated uses of "The Night Music" section from Bartók's *Music for Strings, Percussion and Celesta* and Penderecki's *The Awakening of Jacob*. The piece by the "fiercely anti-Nazi Hungarian Bartok … suggests trepidation about Nazism," while the Shoah connection to Penderecki is more direct. A Christian Pole in whose oeuvre "Jewish motifs recur," Penderecki said that "all his music is freighted with the horror [of the Holocaust]."[44] *The Awakening of Jacob*, the title itself a reference to the Hebrew patriarch, plays over the film's most iconic scene, in which blood gushes from the elevators. The image alone, Cocks opined in an interview, is "as good a visual metonym for the horror of the 20th century as has ever been filmed," while the music "is also known as the 'Auschwitz Oratorio' for the time when it was played at the former camp at a ceremony in the 1960s."[45]

Woody Allen

As director, writer, and star of most of all his Jew Wave films since *Take the Money and Run* (1969), Allen is a triple threat—quadruple if you include his chief editor and New Hollywood co"inventor," Ralph Rosenblum. Allen's films also, largely through the neurotic New York Jewish persona he created, are the most distinctly Jewish of any of the Jew Wave directors. Other Jew Wave actors (e.g., Richard Benjamin, Richard Dreyfus, Elliott Gould, Charles Grodin, Dustin Hoffman, and George Segal) contributed to the emergence of a new American breed of romantic leading man, one decidedly more vulnerable, alienated, sensitive, and emotionally involved than the more conventionally masculine, predictably non-Jewish matinee idols of the classical Hollywood period such as Clark Gable, John Wayne, Cary Grant, or Humphrey Bogart. Allen's modern schlemiel characters, additionally, didn't merely disclose their Jewishness; they reveled in it. Most crucially, and most divergent from the stock type of Yiddish lore from which his American version derived, Allen's "schlemielitude" didn't signify a loss of sexual potency or erotic charge.[46]

Allen's earliest efforts through *Love and Death* (1975) tended to rely on a farcical parody formula akin to that for which Mel Brooks would become the standard bearer. How much the stylistic and thematic leap in his Oscar-winning *Annie Hall* (1977) can be attributed to his stint as an actor-only in fellow Jew Waver Martin Ritt's blacklist satire *The Front* (1976), the divergence from Allen's pre-*Front* work is pronounced. Besides proclaiming Allen's coming-of-age as a filmmaker, *Annie Hall* marked the coming together of his on- and off-screen selves and a loosening of the social and sexual constraints of the classic schlemiel. Both *The Front* and Allen's earlier written and starring *Play It Again, Sam* (1972, directed by Herbert Ross) had shifted the schlemiel's center of gravity (and levity) from the shtetl to New York City and turned the caricature of Yiddish folklore into a recognizable human being. *Annie Hall* capped the transformation by making the connection between the Neurotic New York Jew and Woody Allen explicit. Henceforth, at least in the films in which he appears as prime or coprotagonist, the "fictionalized versions of Allen's own manufactured identity as Woody Allen" became an essential ingredient of his conjurer's art.[47]

Allen's Jew Wave-influenced aesthetic continued from *Annie Hall* through the three films that followed: *Interiors* (1978), *Manhattan* (1979), and *Stardust Memories* (1980). His uniquely Jewish take on the European art cinemas, most specifically Bergman and Fellini, centered on self-reflexive flourishes and existential angst distilled through (Jewish) humor, not only on the redemptive power but also on the problematic of art (particularly cinema) and relationships (largely of the shiksa variety), and on the Jewish insider/outsider complex.

Jew Wave form and content converge most compellingly—and originally—in Allen's exploration of the relation between documentary and fiction. While present in his work as early as the quasi-mockumentary *Take the Money and Run*, the reality/illusion dialectic peaked, among his Jew Wave films, in *Stardust Memories*.[48] On one level a comedic homage to Fellini's solipsistic *8½* (1963), about a director's creative conflict in the making of the very film we're watching, *Stardust Memories* extends the autobiographical conjunction of Allen's life and corpus to the breaking point. The dilemma that acclaimed director Sandy Bates confronts during a festival retrospective of his work in Atlantic City mirrors to a tee that which Allen experienced at the time: between continuing to make Jewish-infused comedies like the critical and box-office hits *Annie Hall* and *Manhattan* (as his surrogate fans at the faux festival urge him to do), or venturing further into the Bergmanesque dramas to which he aspires but may not be suited (as *Interiors*' roundly panned flop seemed to indicate).

An added Jewish element in *Stardust Memories* is that both fans and critics at the retrospective's microcosmic setting are almost all Jews and played by Jewish actors. As Patricia Erens observed, "The rolling credits probably contain the longest list of Jewish names in film history, apart from the Yiddish cinema of the 1930s."[49] The ethno-religious tribute is countered, and partial revenge achieved, by the send-up, some would say trashing, of fans and critics alike, leading to accusations—not the first or last—of Jewish self-hatred on Allen's part. Allen paraphrased Kafka in various rebuttals to the charge, such as his Allen-esque character in *Deconstructing Harry* (1997) asserting, "I may hate myself, but not because I'm Jewish." Desser and Friedman came to his rescue with *Stardust Memories*, specifically, pointing out that besides the film's grounding in Fellini-esque grotesquerie, "Allen's clearest target is himself. His most vicious barbs are directed inward."[50]

Another common criticism of Allen's work has been its derivative aspects, as Sam Girgus summarizes: "All of the presumably fresh elements and concepts that are said to comprise his work are largely derivative, 'Xeroxed' borrowings."[51] The criticism, however, unwittingly has an anti-Semitic ring. It was "the Jew's mimicry of a world which he could never truly enter," Sander Gilman capsulizes the received anti-Semitic wisdom, "which produced works which were felt to be creative but, in fact, were mere copies of the products of *truly* creative individuals."[52] Clearly, however, quite the opposite has been the case. Jews' insider/outsider status, rather than a handicap, has proven an "epistemological advantage," per Isaac Deutscher, borne of living "at the margins between cultures" and spurring some of the boldest thought of the modern age.[53] This extended from Marx, Freud, and Einstein in the social and physical sciences to Schoenberg's atonal music, Kafka's angst-driven literature, and a Heine-inspired, American-tinged humor combining the comic and the cosmic—the "ironic deflation," the "lofty perspective laid low by the common desire," the "encounter of learning and business in the same culture," the "self-conscious byplay of *Kunst* and candy store"—which Allen made his trademark.[54]

Best of the Rest

Mel Brooks and Paul Mazursky follow closest behind the "big five" Jew Wave directors, both for the New Hollywood distinctiveness of their work and its Jewish element. Brooks's métier was parody, but of a particular, and particularly vulgar, Jewish variety steeped in the insider/outsider complex. Parody, Jeremy Dauber explains in his historical study of Jewish humor, derives from intimate, affectionate "familiarity with a culture one feels oneself to be outside." Vulgarity, to be clever rather than merely vulgar, "involves an intimate understanding of [what is] ridiculous" about a society and is therefore "ripe for being deflated ... under the right times, conditions, and places ... and by the right people."[55]

The 1960s/1970s were the right time and the United States the right place for at least some of Brooks's vulgar parody, including the generic spoofs *Blazing Saddles* (1974), *Young Frankenstein* (1974), *Silent Movie* (1976), and *High Anxiety* (1977). *The Producers* (1967) was ahead of its time, but it would return from the repressed in a 2001 Broadway musical and 2005 film remake. Another Jewish aspect of Brooks's Jew Wave period, especially, was his ensemble of largely Jewish actors, which besides himself (on occasion) included Gene Wilder, Zero Mostel, Madeline Kahn, Marty Feldman, Harvey Corman, and Sid Caesar.

Like Brooks, Mazursky wrote most of all of his directed films, performed in several of them (though generally in bit parts), and prominently featured Jewish actors in central roles: Elliott Gould and Dyan Cannon in *Bob & Carol & Ted & Alice* (1969); George Segal, Susan Anspach, and Shelley Winters in *Blume in Love* (1973); and Lenny Baker and Shelley Winters in *Next Stop Greenwich Village* (1976). Like Allen, Mazursky is unabashed about his European art cinema indebtedness, as in *Alex in Wonderland*, his homage to *8½*, and *Willie & Phil* (1980), his remake of Truffaut's *nouvelle vague* classic, *Jules et Jim* (1962).

An autobiographical element explicitly infuses *Next Stop, Greenwich Village*, a coming-of-age tale of a Brooklyn-bred, theater-oriented Jew who takes a chance on Hollywood. The film also shares with Allen, Brooks, and Lumet a common Jew Wave motif of exploring, "with equal portions of censure and compassion ... the new values that usurp the role of traditional religious precepts."[56]

Conclusion

Another distinguishing feature of the major Jew Wave directors, besides their predilection for Jewish actors, characters, subtexts, and themes, lies in their career routes to theatrical filmmaking. The prototypical springboard to the big screen for non-Jewish New Hollywood directors, notably Coppola, Milius, De Palma, Rush, and Scorsese, were the still fledgling film schools: most prominently USC (Milius), UCLA (Coppola and Rush), and NYU (De Palma and Scorsese). And while Altman and Cassavetes, in starting their careers in the young medium of television, were exceptions, not so for seminal Jew Wavers. Besides Penn and Lumet, Ritt and Frankenheimer directed some of the prestigious anthology dramas of TV's so-called "golden age" of the 1950s. Allen and Brooks famously got their start (along with Carl Reiner and the Jewish Larry Gelbart, Neil and Danny Simon, and Mel Tolkin) on the legendary writing staff of Sid Caeser's

Your Show of Shows (1950–4). Before crafting screenplays, Mazursky wrote for *The Danny Kaye Show* (1963–7) and penned the pilot episode of the *Monkees* (1966–8). Nichols and May's cinematic paths, while circumventing television, overlapped with Allen's in starting with stand-up in their highly successful (on stage and LP) comedy team. And Nichols's segue into stage-directing nurtured his move into filmmaking via the screen adaptation of Edward Albee's Tony-winning *Who's Afraid of Virginia Woolf* (play 1962, film 1966).

This brief overview of Jew Wave backstories must remain, due to space limitations, as cursory as the discussion of the larger movement's directors and films. A more expansive venue would have required more than honorable mention of other significant Jewish contributors to the New Hollywood such as Bogdanovich's *The Last Picture Show* (1971), Polanski's *Rosemary's Baby* (1968) and *Chinatown* (1974), Schatzberg's *Panic in Needle Park* (1971), Schlesinger's *Midnight Cowboy* (1969), and Wexler's *Medium Cool* (1968). Additional standouts among films with explicitly Jewish characters and themes include Ted Kotcheff's *The Apprenticeship of Duddy Kravitz* (1974), May's *The Honeymoon Kid* (1972), and Micklin Silver's *Hester Street* (1975). Lower-budget efforts, which Charles Taylor has thankfully reclaimed in his book *Opening Wednesday at a Theater or Drive-In Near You: The Shadow Cinema of the American '70s* (2017), include Larry Cohen's blaxploitation-ish *Hell Up in Harlem* (1972) and *Black Caesar* (1973), Monte Hellman's road film-ish *Two-Lane Blacktop* (1971), and Russ Meyer's softporn-ish *Vixen!* (1968) and *Beyond the Valley of the Dolls* (1969).[57] Ralph Bakshi's ultra-racy animated features (1972's *Fritz the Cat* was X-rated) belong in a Jewish class all of their own.

Far from the last word on the Jew Wave, this rewriting of New Hollywood historiography serves rather as incentive for additional rethinking of a key period in American cinema. It also commands acknowledgment, at the very least, that without Jewish filmmakers—actors, writers, editors, producers, and especially directors—the New Hollywood would have been delayed in its formation and deprived of much of the originality its—now arguably dated—sobriquet suggests.

Notes

1   David Desser and Lester D. Friedman's *American-Jewish Filmmakers: Traditions and Trends* (Urbana: University of Illinois Press, 1993) does discuss several Jewish

directors from a Jewish perspective, but not specifically in relation to the New Hollywood.

2 For a more extensive list, see my like-titled article in *Journal of Jewish Film and New Media* (Fall 2020).

3 Diane Jacobs, *Hollywood Renaissance* (New York: A.S. Barnes, 1977).

4 See among others, David Biale, Michael Galchinsky, and Susannah Heschel, eds., *Insider/Outsider: Jews and Multiculturalism* (Berkeley: University of California Press, 1998).

5 Nathan Abrams, *Stanley Kubrick: New York Jewish Intellectual* (New Brunswick, NJ: Rutgers University Press, 2018).

6 David A. Cook, "Auteur Cinema and the 'Film Generation' in 1970s Hollywood," in *American Cinema*, ed. Jon Lewis (Durham, NC: Duke University Press, 1998), 11–37, 12.

7 Peter Biskind, *Easy Riders, Raging Bulls: How the Sex-Drugs-And-Rock 'n' Roll Generation Saved Hollywood* (New York: Simon & Schuster, 1998), 28.

8 Quoted in Biskind, *Easy Rider*, 35. McLuhan introduced the "medium is the message" concept in *Understanding Media: The Extensions of Man* (New York: Penguin, 1964).

9 James Grady, "Thanksgiving at Alice's Restaurant: The Guthries' American Dream Lives On," *Politics Daily*, November 25, 2009.

10 Arthur Penn, *Arthur Penn: Interviews* (Jackson: University Press of Mississippi, 2008).

11 Bernard Starr, "Surprising Connections: 'Alice's Restaurant,' Judaism, and Donald Trump," *Huffpost*, December 19, 2017, https://www.huffingtonpost.com/entry/surprising-connections-alices-restaurant-judaism_us_5a22c9b7e4b04dacbc9bd79a.

12 Manohla Dargis, "Arthur Penn, a Director Attuned to His Country," *New York Times*, October 8, 2010, http://www.nytimes.com/2010/10/10/movies/10dargis.html.

13 Xan Brooks, "The Missouri Breaks," *The New York Times*, May 22, 2003, https://www.theguardian.com/culture/2003/may/23/artsfeatures2.

14 Quoted in J. W. Whitehead, *Mike Nichols and the Cinema of Transformation* (Jefferson, NC: McFarland, 2014), 13.

15 Ibid., 14.

16 Ibid., 36, 38.

17 Ibid., 38, 41.

18 Gavin Smith, "Of Metaphors and Purpose: Mike Nichols Interview," *Film Comment*, May 1999 (quoted in Joshua Louis Moss, *Why Harry Met Sally: Subversive Jewishness, Anglo-Christian Power, and the Rhetoric of Modern Love* [Austin: Texas University Press, 2017], 104).

19 Sam Kashner, "Here's to You, Mr. Nichols: The Making of 'The Graduate,'" *Vanity Fair*, March 2008: 6.

20 Whitehead, *Mike Nichols*, 301.

21 See Vincent Brook's "review of J.W. Whitehead's *Mike Nichols and the Cinema of Transformation*," *Jewish Film and New Media* (Spring, 2018).

22 Brian Neve, *Film and Politics in America: A Social Tradition* (New York: Routledge, 1992).

23 Vincent Brook, *Driven to Darkness: Jewish Émigré Directors and the Rise of Film Noir* (Piscataway, NJ: Rutgers University Press, 2009); Alain Silver, "Introduction," in *Film Noir Reader 4: The Crucial Films and Themes*, ed. Alain Silver and James Ursini (New York: Limelight, 2004), 3.

24 David Bordwell, Janet Staiger, and Kristin Thompson, *Classical Hollywood Cinema: Film Style and Mode of Production to 1960* (New York: Columbia University Press, 1985).

25 Desser and Friedman, *American-Jewish Filmmakers*, 161.

26 Ibid.

27 Quoted in Don Shewey, "Sidney Lumet: The Reluctant Auteur," *American Film* 8 (December 1982): 33–4 (cited in Frank R. Cunningham, *Sidney Lumet: Film and Literary Vision*, 2nd ed. [Lexington: University Press of Kentucky, 2001], 15).

28 Quoted in David Margolick, "Again, Sidney Lumet Ponders Justice," *New York Times*, December 31, 1989: H9 (cited in Cunningham, *Sidney Lumet*, 1).

29 Desser and Friedman, *American-Jewish Filmmakers*, 164.

30 Ibid., 203.

31 Paul Monaco and Charles Harpoe, eds., *The Sixties, 1960–1969* (Berkeley: University of California Press, 2003), 92–4.

32 Warren Buckland, "The Film Editors who invented the New Hollywood," paper presented at "The American New Wave: A Retrospective" conference; Warren Buckland, "The Film Editors Who Invented the Hollywood Renaissance: Ralph Rosenblum, Sam O'Steen and Dede Allen's *Bonnie and Clyde* (1967)," in *The Hollywood Renaissance: Revisiting American Cinema's Most Celebrated Era*, ed. Peter Krämer and Yannis Tzioumakis (New York: Bloomsbury, 2018), 19–34.

33 Alan Jay Levinovitz, "It's Not Relative," *Chronicle Review* (March 10, 2017): B4–5; B4.

34 Abrams, *Stanley Kubrick*, 93.

35 Ibid.

36 Ibid., 97–8.

37 Ibid., 126.

38 Ibid., 118, 128.

39 Email from Nathan Abrams to the author, April 9, 2018.

40   Abrams, *Stanley Kubrick*, 193.

41   Geoffrey Cocks, *The Wolf at the Door: Stanley Kubrick, History, and the Holocaust* (London: Peter Lang, 2004); Marc Tracy, "Kubrick's Holocaust Film: The Subtext of 'The Shining,'" *Tablet*, January 30, 2012. http://www.tabletmag.com/scroll/89719/ kubrick%E2%80%99s-holocaust-film.

42   Tracy, "Kubrick's Holocaust." Abrams (in *Stanley Kubrick*), 127.

43   Tracy, "Kubrick's Holocaust"; the "no poetry after the Holocaust" quote is from Theodore Adorno's article "Cultural Criticism and Society," trans. Samuel and Shierry Weber, in *Prisms* (1951), 34.

44   Tracy, "Kubrick's Holocaust"; Filip Leach, "Notes on Pederecki," *Culture.Pl*, November 11, 2013. http://culture.pl/en/article/notes-on-penderecki.

45   Tracy, "Kubrick's Holocaust."

46   See Ruth R. Wisse, *The Schlemiel as Modern Hero* (Chicago: University of Chicago Press, 1971).

47   Sam B. Girgus, *The Films of Woody Allen*, 2nd ed. (Cambridge: Cambridge University Press, 2002), 1.

48   The pinnacle of Allen's docu-fictional bent is *Zelig* (1983), also one of the first feature-length mockumentaries.

49   Patricia Erens, *The Jew In American Cinema* (Bloomington: Indiana University Press, 1984), 371.

50   Desser and Friedman, *American-Jewish Filmmakers*, 57.

51   Girgus, *The Films of Woody Allen*, 109.

52   Sander Gilman, *The Jew's Body* (New York: Routledge, 1991), 129, 134.

53   Isaac Deutscher, "The Non-Jewish Jew," in *The Non-Jewish Jew and Other Essays* (Oxford: Oxford University Press, [1958] 1968), 30; Thorstein Veblen, "The Intellectual Preeminence of Jews in Modern Europe," *Political Science Quarterly* 34 (March 1919), reprinted in *The Writings of Thorstein Veblen*, ed. Leon Ardzrooni (New York: M. Kelley Bookseller, 1964), 223.

54   Mark Schechner, "Dear Mr. Einstein: Jewish Comedy and the Contradictions of Culture," in *Jewish Wry: Essays on Jewish Humor*, ed. Sarah Blacher Cohen (Detroit: Wayne State University Press, 1987), 141–57; 147, 151, 153.

55   Jeremy Dauber, *Jewish Comedy: A Serious History* (London: W. W. Norton, 2017), 130.

56   Ibid., 224, 233.

57   Charles Taylor, *Opening Wednesday at a Theater or Drive-In Near You: The Shadow Cinema of the '70s* (New York: Bloomsbury, 2017).

5

New Hollywood's "Zany Godards": A "Shirley" Serious Assessment of Zucker-Abrahams-Zucker

Emilio Audissino

Despite its significant role and position, studies have tended to overlook the field of comedy in New Hollywood and the American New Wave. A key component of such movies as Woody Allen's *Everything You Always Wanted to Know about Sex* (1972), Mel Brooks's *Young Frankenstein* (1974) and *Blazing Saddles* (1974), and Carl Reiner's *Dead Men Don't Wear Plaid* (1982) was homage through affectionate spoof and parody derived from cinephilia, a central characteristic of the American New Wave. It was also one of its strongest links with the eponymous French *nouvelle vague* (new wave), whose filmmaking was fueled by an almost inescapable cinephile elan and "a deep affection for American genre film."[1] At the same time, American New Wave films were characterized by "a deconstruction of traditional genres"[2] and an "intensification of Hollywood's traditional practices."[3] Homage, cinephilia, deconstruction, and intensification constitute keywords for the American New Wave, but they were also the foundational elements of the comedy cinema of Zucker, Abrahams, and Zucker (ZAZ).

Despite having been influential models and box-office hit-makers—their directorial debut, *Airplane!* (1980), cost $3.5 million and grossed more than $83 million in the domestic market alone (boxofficemojo.com)—and despite the fact that their cinephile and revisionist poetics places them legitimately within the American New Wave, as we will presently see, ZAZ have received little to no proper academic scrutiny. While other comedic directors, especially

Allen and Brooks, have been the subject of various academic studies,[4] ZAZ's cinema has been ignored. When one finds mentions of the ZAZ trio, it is mostly in the form of cursory and brief references in general histories of Hollywood cinema—if they are mentioned at all—or in books on film comedy, and when they are mentioned, their essence is typically misinterpreted or their specificity is downplayed.[5]

Their classification within the parody/spoof genre is possibly one of the main reasons for the underconsideration of ZAZ as auteurs. They are just seen as parody comedians, like many others in Hollywood's history, including Bob Hope, Bing Crosby, Dean Martin, and Jerry Lewis. Furthermore, the ZAZ trio did not "evolve" into "serious" authorship as Allen did in his post-*Annie Hall* Bergman/Fellini-influenced filmography. Neither did they have a career as lengthy and graced with accolades as Brooks, who is one of the rare EGOT (Emmy, Grammy, Oscar, Tony) winners, which makes it difficult to ignore his work.[6] Another reason may be that the parodic core of ZAZ's cinema is considered to be too derivative and the silly behavior of their characters too lowbrow for serious academic consideration.

Furthermore, there is the added difficulty of individuating the defining features of ZAZ's "authorial" mark, the specific character that distinguishes their approach to comedy from that of others who operate in similar parody-based territories. Benny Hill too made parodies of low-budget crime films such as "The Police Raid in Waterloo Station" (*The Benny Hill Show*, April 25, 1979). Mel Brooks built his reputation as a parodist, for example, taking aim at Hitchcock in *High Anxiety* (1977). Instances of parody can be also found in Woody Allen—the mockumentary *Take the Money and Run* (1969)—and in Monty Python, including their Sam Peckinpah spoof in the episode "Salad Days" of *Monty Python's Flying Circus* (November 30, 1972). When ZAZ are conflated with these parody authors, the result is a normalization of their comedy. As I will demonstrate below, theirs are parodies with a stronger deconstructionist impetus and style.

ZAZ have been as influential on comedy cinema as the celebrated "serious" authors of the American New Wave have been on cinematic drama. Their "irreverent attitude" and the "seriousness about being funny" resonate with an ethos that is fully germane to the American New Wave: a revisionist/deconstructionist impulse combined with a knowledgeable and competently serious approach to film. In this chapter, I attempt to fill this gap. By providing some preliminary and tentative definitions of ZAZ's brand of comedy, I argue that a way to individuate their position within the American New Wave is to compare ZAZ's role within the movement to that of Jean-Luc Godard, "the most idolized of the New Wave directors,"[7] and "a certified *enfant terrible* with a taste for the innovative … and the offbeat."[8] While I do not claim that ZAZ's cinema had the same weight or canonical importance as Godard's, if we want to find a level of irreverence and deconstruction in the American New Wave comparable to that of Godard in the French New Wave, it is to ZAZ we must look.

Background

The Wisconsin-born trio started out in 1971, in Madison. With Dick Chudnow, they were the founding members of the "Kentucky Fried Theater," a blend of vaudeville nonsense and college-lampoon irreverence that combined "video satires of TV commercials and a stage show"[9] and, in contrast to the trend of the Nixon era, favored "media jokes" over political satire.[10] A reviewer for the *Badger Herald* recalls: "Of course they were very funny … but what I was the most impressed with is how serious they were about being funny."[11] Kentucky Fried Theater, in the words of Tino Balio, "embodied that irreverent attitude that mocked all things traditional of the popular culture of the 1950s and early 1960s. It's a style that still reverberates and influences comedy today."[12]

ZAZ moved to Los Angeles in 1972, where they "rented a warehouse, put in 140 seats and did the show for another five years."[13] They also made a few TV appearances, for example, in *The Midnight Special* (1972–81). After the release of *The Kentucky Fried Movie* (directed by John Landis), in 1977, they focused on cinema, collectively taking the director's chair in their subsequent works *Airplane!*, *Top Secret!* (1984), *The Naked Gun* trilogy (1988, 1991, 1994, with the third installment directed by Peter Segal), and the six-episode TV series *Police Squad* (1982, for which they directed the Pilot Episode and executive-produced the others).[14] ZAZ's films had a considerable influence on Hollywood comedy thereafter; for example, the Farrelly Bros., Seth MacFarlane, the Wayans Bros., and Matt Groening are all indebted to ZAZ to some degree.

To attain a thorough definition of ZAZ's comedy style, many aspects should be addressed; here, it seems appropriate at least to mention some of them to inspire future investigations. The influence of French cinematic surrealism is essential, not only as to the dark and macabre humor that is found in both—consider the "United Appeal for the Dead" segment of *The Kentucky Fried Movie*, with the disturbing presence of a kid's corpse—but also as to the absurd universes that both construct: for example, the pigeon monument in *Top Secret!*, which will be mentioned below, looks as if taken from a surrealist film. Other influences to be taken into account are vaudeville and the Theater of Absurd, particularly Ionesco's comedy-tinted works—considering that ZAZ started as a theater group. Another is silent-cinema comedy and animated shorts, based on sight gags, a type of "comedy that derives from exploiting the magical properties of cinema, a comedy of metaphysical release that celebrates the possibility of substituting the laws of physics with the laws of the imagination."[15] The impossible physical laws of cartoons are recurrently replicated in ZAZ's narrative worlds; for example, the soldier in *Top Secret!* that falls off the wall and, on the impact of the ground, shatters as if made of ceramic.

Jewish humor and its penchant for incongruity, lateral thinking, logical dissection, and disruption of conventions is another major influence.[16] So is the cinephile culture of the baby-boomer—the "film generation"[17]—and "varsity" lampoon. Like the members of Monty Python, ZAZ were college-educated and started as a university comedy team. The satirical humor typical of the *Harvard Lampoon* magazine—for example, the *Lord of the Rings* parody *Bored of the Rings* by Henry N. Beard and Douglas C. Kenney (1969)—probably had a substantial formative influence. Another influential publication, in which Jewish humor and lampoon converge, is the *Mad* magazine, which is directly acknowledged by Jerry Zucker and Jim Abrahams as "our biggest and earliest influence ... [e]specially ... a section called 'Scenes We'd Like to See.'"[18] Here, though, in order to gauge their place within the American New Wave/New Hollywood, I will focus on the comparison with Godard.

Godard, Cinephilia, and Intertextuality

In the nouvelle vague, cinephilia and intertextual references to cinema can be found in other filmmakers who hailed, like Godard, from the ranks of film criticism such as Eric Rohmer and François Truffaut, to name two. Yet, in Godard, "we find intertextuality aplenty—citations, allusions, borrowings— as well as ... 'hypertextuality,' the derivation of one text from another by transformation (satire, parody) or imitation (pastiche, remake)."[19] Godard's is a cinema about cinema, showing a strong investment in the deconstruction of the cinematic conventions, often taking the move from a critical appropriation of the traditional genres: the noir (*Made in U.S.A*, 1966), the sci-fi (*Alphaville*, 1965), the gangster film (*Bande à part*, 1964), the melodrama (*Une femme mariée*, 1964), or the musical (*Une femme est une femme*, 1961). As Jean-Michel Frodon states, "Godard will become even more so the sole director to make clear in his own films a commentary on cinema, on staging, on the stakes of the relation between images, the real, the articulation of the sound track and the image track, etc."[20] In other nouvelle vague authors, intertextuality rarely takes the form of a foregrounded deconstruction but works in more integrated and unostentatious realizations. In Godard, classical storytelling is often halted or fragmented to make room for moments of metatextual or metalinguistic showcase: a character watching a film (*Vivre sa vie* (1962) or *Une femme mariée*), or an entire film being about filmmaking (*Le Mépris*, 1963). A conspicuous characteristic of Godard's—not present to such extent in the other French auteurs—is that technical choices are often not motivated and hence seemingly gratuitous, drawing attention to the artifice of film itself. For David Bordwell, "Godard ... raises as does no other director the possibility of a sheerly capricious or arbitrary use of technique."[21] If, as David Sterritt suggests, "classical filmmakers are like puppeteers who want us to forget their string pulling and accept the actions of their marionettes as natural events," with Godard it is as if he were

> waving to us from behind the stage, reminding us of [his] presence and inviting us to enjoy [his] string pulling as an essential and meaningful part of the spectacle. The result is a brand of cinema more self-aware and proudly artificial than classical stylists find acceptable.[22]

If the French New Wave was a revolutionary way of considering cinema and making film, then Godard was the revolution's most "radical" leader.[23] If the films of the other French auteurs, though innovative, were "perceived to exist essentially within certain broad traditions," Godard's *À bout de souffle* (1960) "was clearly revolutionary."[24]

Godard represented the epitome of the auteur/filmmaker and thus his daring style and self-reflective narration were soon imitated worldwide, including by Hollywood's new generation. Some founding films of the American New Wave come to mind: the documentary look, provocative themes, handheld camera, and location shooting of *Easy Rider* (Dennis Hopper, 1969); the use of telephoto lenses and flattened images in *The Parallax View* (Alan J. Pakula, 1974); and the jump cuts in *The Graduate* (Mike Nichols, 1967) and *Bonnie and Clyde* (Arthur Penn, 1967). This latter film also opens with detail-shots and extreme close-ups reminiscent of *Une femme mariée*, and its script was initially pitched to Godard himself.[25]

Godard's techniques, though, were imported in a diluted form. The auteurs of the American New Wave were moved by a revisionist desire, but they were nevertheless conscious of their working for an industry, within a solid tradition, and with one eye on the box office. The attitude of the French New Wave— irreverence, intertextuality, deconstruction, prevalence of metalinguistic and metatextual showcase over storytelling, and "arbitrary use of technique"—that was adopted in more domesticated forms by the auteurs of the American New Wave can be often found at almost Godardian levels in ZAZ.

"Zany Godards" of the New Hollywood?

The parallel with Godard is instrumental in detecting ZAZ's peculiarity, and hence their authorial signature, within the American New Wave. Both ZAZ and Godard make the move from a kind of cinephilia that mixes affection for and irreverent desecration of the Hollywood tradition, manifested through a keen interest for metalanguage. More importantly, both ZAZ and Godard take these characteristics to unique idiosyncratic extremes that set their works apart from those of others.

When ZAZ's comedy is discussed, the specificity of their authorial mark is often missed. Kristin Thompson and David Bordwell, for example, state: "[they] savaged the disaster film in *Airplane!* (1980). Such zany treatment of genre conventions had already been employed in silent slapstick and in the comedies of Bob Hope and Bing Crosby and Dean Martin and Jerry Lewis. Mocking Hollywood was itself a Hollywood tradition."[26] A first essential element that is overlooked here, and which precisely distinguishes ZAZ from the likes of Bob Hope and Jerry Lewis, is the absence of comedians. David Zucker stresses this difference, when talking about "zany treatment of genre conventions": "It had been done before …. Mel Brooks did it with *Blazing Saddles*. What was different was that we didn't use comedians."[27] The past examples cited by Thompson and Bordwell *all* involve comedians parodying serious genres, and this is also the case with Brooks, Allen, among others. These are instances of "comedian comedy."[28] In comedian-comedies, according to Steve Neale and Frank Krutnik, the comedian and his 'deviant' behaviour are set in playful conflict with the conventions .... In each of these films, it is as if the comedian—the disruptive element in the smooth functioning of the genre—is dropped into the fictional world by accident and, like a child, proceeds to toy with the rules.[29]

Most scholars conflate ZAZ's films with comedian-comedy parodies, which ZAZ's are not. For comic effects, ZAZ use *non-comedians* that act and react with obtuse impassibility, "almost as if the characters in the movie didn't realise they were in a comedy."[30] Their trademark actor, Leslie Nielsen, might be perceived now as a comedian because of the exposure he received as the star of many of their films, but before ZAZ he used to be a straight actor. The choice was subversive at the time. As ZAZ recall,

We were proposing a big broad comedy without comedians—a completely new concept. Nobody understood the idea of serious actors playing it straight, but for us that was everything. ... The studio wanted Bill Murray or Chevy Chase, the reigning comic actors at the time. We loved them but they weren't right. Lines like "I am serious—and don't call me Shirley" would have been 50% less effective.[31]

ZAZ's revisionist act of assigning comedy to drama actors is one of the primary ways to turn "audience expectations around."[32] Theirs, essentially, is the opposite of the "comedian-comedy" mechanism: we do not encounter a comedian that, put in serious situations, overturns them with ridiculous antics, but instead we have a serious actor placed in ludicrous situations that have no impact at all on her/his wooden composure. The casting of an actor famous for serious roles, like Peter Graves from *Mission: Impossible* (1966–73), placed in the absurdly ludicrous situations of *Airplane!* and yet instructed to act even more seriously than her/ his usual standards is a central ingredient of ZAZ's humor. ZAZ's approach does not consist in a direct upsetting of the generic expectations—as when in *High Anxiety* (1977) Brooks turns the menace of a bird-flock attack from the conventional beak-stabbing into an excremental bombing—but a subtler comic contrast between Graves's gravitas and the ridiculous events that surround him. Moreover, in comedies, conventional devices are typically used to foreground the comicality of the gags and jokes, and to cue the audience's laughter. These devices are featured in most comedian-comedies, and they range from the "Pavlovian" laugh track (in television comedy), comic reaction shots (eye rolls or farcically exaggerated surprise or outrage), commentary asides, breaches of the fourth wall with direct interpellation, and so on. In the tracking-shot incident in *High Anxiety*, when the camera crashes through the window pane—thus breaking the fourth wall and baring the cinematic apparatus—the characters react by startling and observing the mishap with comic embarrassment, a reaction whose function is to emphasize the comicality of the gag.

ZAZ's comedy style is essentially "serious" in tone, dispensing from the above-mentioned devices conventionally implemented to emphasize the comic. "You could have cast funny people and done it with everybody winking, goofing off and silly. ... But the whole point was (the) serious style," explains Jerry Zucker.[33] ZAZ expanded on the concept: "we took the story seriously. We did all these ridiculous jokes, but always come back to grave danger. It makes the jokes more unexpected. On some moronic level, [watching *Airplane!*] people do care whether the plane lands and whether Ted and Elaine get together."[34]

More than parodies in the most common sense—the one that has been in use since Aristophanes (comedians comically desecrating tragedies)—ZAZ's work is parodic in the less-common usage of the word: imitation/paraphrasis, as used in musicology.[35] Parody here is meant as a rework of previously existing texts within a different context or for a different use—for example, the borrowing of secular music in the creation of Masses in Baroque music. Linda Hutcheon has provided nuances to the concept:

> Nothing in *parodia* ... necessitates the inclusion of the concept of ridicule. ... Parody ... in its ironic "trans-contextualisation" and inversion is repetition with difference. A critical distance is implied between the background text being parodied and the new incorporating work, a distance usually signaled by irony. But this irony can be playful as well as belittling: it can be critically constructive as well as destructive. The pleasure of parody's irony comes not from humor in particular but from the degree of engagement of the reader in the intertextual "bouncing" between complicity and distance.[36]

ZAZ's works belong to this *lato sensu* notion of parody, which can be humorous, but is, above all, an imitation, reuse, inversion, trans-contextualization, all laced with irony, whose etymology is from the Greek word for "to dissemble," to put on an appearance of. ZAZ's films put on an appearance of seriousness, they pretend to be drama films despite the patently ridiculous events, and *that* is the principal source of their comic effect.

Their films can be called "comic remakes." The serious tone is heightened and stiffened, the conventions intensified, the absurdities pile up to such an extent that everything turns comic—what I call "nonsensical accumulation."[37]

In *The Kentucky Fried Movie*, for example, the longest segment of this parody of a television schedule is titled "A Fistful of Yen" and takes aim at *Enter the Dragon* (Robert Clouse, 1973), intensifying all the aural and visual clichés of kung fu films until they reach a breaking point and slip into the ridiculous. *Airplane!* is often discussed as a spoof of the air travel disaster movie genre and of *Airport* (George Seaton, 1970), but it is more precisely an exaggerated paraphrasis of *Zero Hour!* (Hall Bartlett, 1957), a B-movie about a potential plane crash that was imitated so verbatim that Paramount had to pay a licensing fee for using so much dialogue and narrative material from the original (see Figure 5.1).[38] David Zucker elaborates on the process:

> [*Zero Hour!*] actually had exactly the same plot. The doctor on the plane even says, "Stewardess, I want you to know exactly what our chances are, to find someone back there who can not only fly this plane but didn't have fish for dinner." That line survived in the movie. … We found that characters always said, "You can't be serious" and another character replied, "I am serious," we simply added, "Don't call me Shirley." Half the movie was written for us by hundreds of hack writers, dozens of years back.[39]

ZAZ's TV show *Police Squad!* was the comical remake of *M Squad* (1957–60), featuring a verbatim reshooting of its title sequence (through comical intensification and nonsensical accumulation) and borrowing bits of dialogue from the original. *Top Secret!* blends the Elvis Presley musicals with the espionage B-movies and remakes passages of *The Dirty Dozen* (Robert Aldrich, 1967).

As can be seen, the two key characteristics of the American New Wave, self-reflexive "deconstruction of traditional genres" and "intensification of Hollywood's traditional practices," are not only present in ZAZ's cinema but are central to it, realized in the form of comic remakes and nonsensical accumulation, respectively. Exactly like other auteurs within New Hollywood, ZAZ revisit the Hollywood tradition through the informed and critical eye of the "film generation," which makes them legitimate members of the movement. They distinguish themselves from other comedy authors of the American New Wave by adopting a peculiarly, "authorially" idiosyncratic approach to comedy. They reject the old-school comedian-comedy approach. Further, their comic inspiration comes not so much from "standard" comic situations—on the one side of the spectrum, the slapstick quality of someone slipping on a banana peel; on the other side, the more sophisticated real-life observational humor in the tradition of the "Catskill Mountains Comedy"[40]—as from the self-conceited

Figure 5.1 Dramatic perspiration in *Zero Hour!* (Paramount Pictures, 1957) and its intensification in *Airplane!* (Paramount Pictures, 1980).

seriousness, formulaic routines, and dramatic stiffness of the run-of-the-mill productions of Old Hollywood, America's "cinéma de papa." Their irreverence toward the "cinéma de papa" plays to a degree that echoes Godard's own irreverence, and they bring deconstructionism and intensification to Godardian extremes as well.

In both Godard and ZAZ, the self-reflective deconstruction of cinematic conventions and the provocative upsetting of the viewer's expectations extend to the point of deliberately seeking a style that looks "wrong" or "sloppy" or "amateurish" to the eye accustomed to the classical style. We have already discussed how Godard manifests his authorial presence by deconstructing the technique, by bringing to the foreground the apparatus that generally tells the story unobtrusively, most famously through his trademark jump cuts. In *Une femme est une femme* and in *Bande à part* the soundtrack presents abrupt cuts and clearly audible jolts and gaps, as if faulty or the result of an ill-executed editing. In *À bout de souffle* the killing of the policeman—the plot twist that determines the following events—is presented as a quick action rendered in a confusing cutting that makes the comprehension of the event difficult, to the point that *Positif* claimed that Godard "had salvaged the unwatchable *Breathless* by convincing the public that badly made movies were now in style."[41] In a similar fashion, ZAZ recreate technical faults or clumsy filmmaking to draw the attention to the artificial nature of Hollywood's films and create a comic effect through an absurd intensification.

A very common slippery ground in filmmaking is continuity, that is, the sustained appearance of a consistent and uninterrupted space/time continuum in the filmic presentation. Continuity mistakes are often detectable, for example, in the level of liquid in a drinking glass: full in one shot; then half-full in the reverse shot; then almost empty in the subsequent master-shot. In Episode Five of *Police Squad!*, Lieutenant Drebin engages in a fistfight with some mobsters, and he is the one who pulls most of the punches, looking perfectly tidy and in control in the master-shot. At the end of the fight, he leans down to pick up a gun; we cut to a close-up of him as he rises: his hair is suddenly rumpled, his face bruised, with his nose bleeding and one black eye. We cut to the damsel in distress he has just rescued as she sighs in relief; then we cut back to Drebin, and now he is again perfectly tidy: no blood, no wrinkles, no bruises.[42]

Another staple of Hollywood's routines that invites derision is the use of back-projection to shoot camera-car dialogue, stage-coach rides, or faux exterior shots. Instead of filming on location or in a moving vehicle, actors play with a screen behind them onto which are projected landscapes of various natures, or a moving background previously filmed from the rear of a car. Easier and less costly than the real thing, back-projection produced almost invariably an artificial look of flattened perspective and a discrepancy of grain and contrast between the actors and the background. The phony look of back-projection scenes has always carried the risk of spoiling dramatic circumstances with an unintentional ludicrous hue, such as when Arborgast (Martin Balsam) falls down the staircase in *Psycho* (Alfred Hitchcock, 1960). Back-projection is given a comic twist in *Airplane!*: during a serious camera-car dialogue, the back-projection goes awry, first offering a patently unnatural and laughable fast motion, then configuring an impossible trajectory for the car before showing a cyclist being run over (unbeknownst to the driver), and finally a totally incongruous black-and-white backdrop from an old western, with "Indians" chasing the car. At the end of the film, another cliché of the Hollywood happy ending is comically intensified by saccharine musical accompaniment. As the "boy" finally gets the "girl" and the romance subplot comes to a denouement when they kiss, Elmer Bernstein's orchestra and choir score the moment with blissful soaring modulations, but the choir is forced to soar so high in pitch that we hear the strained voices trying to extend out of their natural register[43]—an author- and apparatus-revealing handling of the soundtrack reminiscent of Godard's aforementioned baring of the device.

A stylized type of acting is also an ingredient of the faux-sloppy look that is shared by ZAZ and Godard. Acting style is not following the naturalistic conventions of Hollywood or of the "cinéma de papa" but willingly seeks an artificial look. In ZAZ films, acting is deliberately "wooden" and anti-naturalistic. For them, *Airplane!* is basically "a satire on a style of acting .... Robert Stack [raised to fame by 1950s Hollywood melodramas] who played Captain Rex Kramer, used to say: 'I get it—we're the joke!' "[44] In Godard, acting is similarly distant from Hollywood's naturalism, subjected to an intensification on both extremes, from Jack Palance's histrionic satire of the bossy American type in *Le mépris* and Belmondo's contrived mimicking of Bogart in *À bout de souffle*, to Jean Seberg's unjustified aloofness in the same film. As the action of Godard's characters typically lacks the logical motivation and realistic well-roundness of the classical Hollywood—in *À bout de souffle* "it is unclear why Patricia even bothers with Michel, and she becomes a satirical representative of the American college woman abroad"[45]—so, in ZAZ, characters are oblivious pawns in comic games, almost cardboard types.

The deconstruction of the classical centrality and pertinence assigned to dialogue is yet another ingredient of ZAZ's comedies shared with Godard. Dialogue, in Godard and ZAZ, is often deprived of its classical functions: namely, exposition (to pass pieces of information), characterization (reveal something about the character), and action (express subtextual actions).[46] In Godard, dialogue presents frequent non-sequiturs, digressive tendencies, and emphasized literalness, and it often turns into a sort of voice-over commentary. In *Vivre sa vie*, Anna Karina is introduced during a long dialogue scene in which she is framed from behind, frustratingly impeding us to see her face; the classical synchronized dialogue is thus deconstructed by disconnecting her voice from her moving lips. Godard's is a "collage style" in which images can be used as illustrations for the sound, or vice versa sound as a commentary to the images.[47] ZAZ's signature "audiovisual disjunction"[48] similarly deconstructs the classical audiovisual unity—dialogue tells one story (typically a contrivedly serious, deliberately dull, and often pointless one) in the foreground; visuals show another in the background (a bizarre comic event). In *Top Secret!*, a maudlin dialogue scene in a park is coupled with a surrealistic reverse-world gag in the background: a giant monument of a pigeon is surrounded by flying men who land on and then soil it (see Figure 5.2).

Godard's and ZAZ's unconventional authorial intervention and "capricious use of the technique" also spill over those areas of the film that are generally considered merely functional framing elements, peritexts: the opening titles and end credits. Filmmakers might intervene on these in terms of graphic design and general appearance to foretell key themes and moods. In the French New Wave the borders between the film text and its end credits peritext were further eroded, famously with the final freeze-frame of Truffaut's *Les Quatre Cents Coups* (1959): the text's image stretches into the peritext, a

Figure 5.2 ZAZ's audiovisual disjunction in *Top Secret!* (Kingsmere Properties, 1984).

trespassing that was also imported in the American New Wave, for example, in the freeze-frame finale of *Butch Cassidy and the Sundance Kid* (George Roy Hill, 1969). What the French New Wave did, Godard brought to "capricious" excesses: in *Une femme est une femme* Godard's authorial presence spills into the peritext forcibly, as we hear the backstage sound from the set, "Lights," "Camera," "Action"; in *Le Mépris* the opening titles are not in written form but read in voice-over.[49] Similarly, what the American New Wave did with the peritexts, ZAZ brought to "ridiculous" excesses. In *Police Squad!*, we have the announcer reading a wrong title in the opening, and the freeze-frame at the end of the episodes is profilmic: it is not the final frame that is frozen to be held as a backdrop for the end credits, but it is the actors who stand still, showing comical signs of fatigue in prolonging this uncomfortable pantomimic task, and also having to ignore accidents and actions that go on despite the freeze-frame regime. ZAZ scatter these "peritextual jokes" also within the end credits lines, thus "imposing" a Godardian "capricious" authorial presence even on a part of the film that typically is merely perfunctory—giving credit to the film's cast and crew.[50] At the end of ZAZ's films, those who sit through them will find, among the regular credits, intruders like "Author of *A Tale of Two Cities*: Charles Dickens" (in *Airplane!*) or other more extended instances (see Figure 5.3).

Second Unit Director	ROBERT K. WEISS
Set Decorator	MICKEY S. MICHAELS
Set Designer	JAMES TOCCI
Camera Operators	ALLEN D. EASTON JOE THIBO
Assistant to David Zucker	LESLIE MAIER
Sound Mixer	RICHARD BRYCE GOODMAN
Mr. Goodman's Hearing Aid	BEVERLY HILLS EAR BOUTIQUE
First Assistant Film Editor	KEVIN NOLTING
Assistant Film Editor	VINCENT LAINO
Supervising Sound Editors	GEORGE WATTERS II F. HUDSON MILLER
Music Editor	JEFF CARSON
Production Coordinator	RITA GRANT MILLER

Figure 5.3 Peritextual jokes in the end credits of *The Naked Gun 2 ½: The Smell of Fear* (Paramount Pictures, 1991).

Comedy of Stylistic Excess

Classical narration favors an approach in which the narrative progression is the dominant element, and every device is at the service of narrative clarity and cause-effect logic. Devices are primarily used with a *compositional motivation* (an element is used to build the causal, temporal, or spatial system of the narrative) and a *realistic motivation* (an element is used because its presence is plausible according to our experience of the real world). Style is "transparent" or "invisible," it must not attract attention to itself but be at the unobtrusive service of storytelling. Both ZAZ's and Godard's is a cinema designed to draw the attention to the technique and whose style is not invisible. In Godard and ZAZ the principal motivations are *transtextual* (an element is in the film because it references other films or some generic or cinematic convention) and *artistic* (an element has no other motivation than an aesthetic or authorial-mark one).[51] This latter claim may sound unspecific for ZAZ, because it is not unusual for comedy in general to feature moments—"outré scenes"[52]—where artistic motivation overtakes compositional motivation.[53] Yet, as in the previous cases of conflation of ZAZ with other parody auteurs working on comedian-comedies, in this case too an overlook of the degree and handling of the artistic motivation can lead to a fallacious normalization of ZAZ.

In traditional comedies, the artistically motivated gags, jokes, and "outré scenes" are foregrounded and cued by those already-mentioned devices aimed at stressing the comic nature of the event—reaction shots, pantomimic gesturing, laugh track, and so on. Brooks and others might mock Hollywood and its conventions, but they make sure that such mockeries are well under the spotlight and fully noticeable—as in Allen's harpist-in-the-closet gag in *Bananas* (1971) or Brooks's window-crashing camera in *High Anxiety*. In ZAZ the artistically motivated devices seem to be layered more to configure a peculiarly absurd universe corresponding to their authorial vision (nonsensical accumulation) rather than to elicit an immediate laughing reaction, to the point that in many cases there seems to be an overabundance, almost a waste of comic ideas. Sometimes the overall design seems to defy the rules of efficient compositional motivation, enacting a gratuitous squandering of elements consisting of multiple off-center sight gags or dispersed humorous details. This happens in the wordplay on "key" displayed in the background of the locksmith's shop in *Police Squad!* (Figure 5.4).

Figure 5.4 A ridiculously ample choice of "keys," *Police Squad!*, Episode Five (ABC, 1982).

Another instance that signaled a defense of one's own authorial vision and a contest of the traditional devices was ZAZ's firm opposition to the use of a laugh track—a *de rigueur* helping hand in traditional sitcoms—to help signal the gags in *Police Squad!*, despite the network's pressure.[54]

What distinguishes ZAZ from other comedic auteurs, and makes them akin to Godard within the landscape of the American New Wave, is a "style-centered" approach that employs a "parametric narration" that "allow[s] the play of stylistic devices a significant degree of independence from narrative functioning and motivation."[55] As Godard within the nouvelle vague context presents a strong penchant for parametric narration—"style disrupts rather than clarifies Godard's story"[56]—so do ZAZ within the context of the American New Wave. The transtextual motivation ("hypertextuality") and artistic motivation ("a sheerly capricious or arbitrary use of technique") gain greater importance in both, and in both they take the move from a "serious" parodic intent, in the Hutcheonian notion of the term, as noted by David Bordwell:

> *Alphaville* and *Made in U.S.A* satirize the hard-boiled detective tale, *Une femme est une femme* parodies the musical. ... Similarly, Godard will mock the art cinema as well, with Bergman forming a frequent target (the film-within-a-film of *Masculin féminin*, Corinne's erotic monologue in *Weekend*).[57]

As ZAZ's humor is strongly incongruity-based and the product of playing on the viewer's conventional expectations, Godard's critical cinema seeks a systematic overturn of the viewer's expectations through stylistic choices incongruous with the classical style. In parametric narration, "the replete approach is constantly foregrounding stylistic events in that each discrete stylistic event will tend to instantiate a deviant procedure. … More is put in than we can assimilate, even on repeated viewings. Like decorative art, parametric cinema exploits the very limits of the viewer's capacity."[58] Besides the already-discussed scattered humorous details, in ZAZ this "replete approach" takes the form of audiovisual disjunction, that is, the already-considered instances of sight gags or absurd actions in the background masked by overserious and deliberately badly written dialogue in the foreground.

A striking instance of this capriciousness, gratuity, and squandering that makes ZAZ akin to the parametric, style-centered cinema of Godard is in *Top Secret!*. At the beginning of the second act we encounter an overelaborate gag that required complex technical virtuosity and production effort that are not really paid off by a commensurate direct comic result. The two protagonists must visit a Swedish antiquarian bookshop to retrieve a message left there by the resistance leaders. The whole scene is spoken in a mysteriously sounding language—mock Swedish the viewer might initially assume. The scene becomes increasingly weird, with the actors' movement looking mechanical and jerky, until we eventually realize, thanks to actions that contradict the physical laws, that the entire scene is shot and acted in reverse (from end to beginning) and then reverse-printed, thus creating the strange language (English spoken backward) and the odd movements. Moreover, this convoluted sequence also has extra sight gags hidden within: one of the antique books in this austere shop, elegantly bound in leather, bears the title, "Lesbian Bars of North Carolina." I would call the use of such an elaborate staging and camerawork to obtain so little comic effect an instance of "Excess," as used by Kristin Thompson (after Roland Barthes): "Analytically there is something absurd about it."[59]

Excess "implies a gap or lag in motivation," is "counternarrative" and "counterunity,"[60] and can be one of the extreme manifestations of the "replete approach" of parametric narration. Analyzing "Excess" at work in comedic territories, Kristin Thompson thus describes Tati's *Play Time* (1967): "we cannot fully distinguish the comic from the non-comic. Everything begins to look strange and funny."[61] This description could also be applied to ZAZ's Swedish bookshop. In comedy, "Excess" may take the form of an overload that risks pushing the final result in the category of the "Silly," defined as "something so ridiculous or ludicrous it isn't even funny,"[62] as in Godard "Excess" is at risk of impeding comprehension. Traditional comedians and comedy authors would stay clear from the potentially unprofitable terrain of the "Silly" and favor a more direct, economical, compositionally motivated approach that can guarantee laughter as a more predictable and immediate response.

The playfulness, revisionism, and irreverence realized through a deconstruction and intensification of the conventions at the core of ZAZ's poetics are what make them legitimate auteurs within the American New Wave. It is ZAZ's idiosyncratic style (audiovisual disjunction and nonsensical accumulation) and their commitment to pursue it beyond more standard and immediately effective comic strategies that qualifies them for the assignation of the New Wave title of "auteurs." Arguably, they are those who stayed truer to Godard's radical lesson in parodic irreverence and subversion. Nichols, Scorsese, Coppola, Penn, and others might have adopted the Godardian jump cuts, tele-photo lenses, and handheld camera. Yet, in the end, these were insertions of Godard's superficial "quirks" into a narration that essentially remained compositionally motivated and storytelling-centered. As Robert Kolker has pointed out, "as delighted as they were … by the formal possibilities of their medium, as conscious as they were of the genres they emulated or attacked, most only stepped slightly in front of the conventional stylistics of classical American film."[63] If we want to find an equivalent of Godard's serious parody, style-centered approach, and parametric narration in the American New Wave/New Hollywood, it can be "Shirley" found in ZAZ's cinema.

Notes

1   Jonathan Kirshner and Jon Lewis, "Introduction. The New Hollywood Revisited," in *When the Movies Mattered: The New Hollywood Revisited*, ed. Jonathan Kirshner and Jon Lewis (Ithaca, NY: Cornell University Press, 2019), 2. On cinephilia, see Marijke de Valck and Malte Hagener, eds., *Cinephilia. Movies, Love and Memory* (Amsterdam: Amsterdam University Press, 2005).

2   Geoff King, *New Hollywood Cinema. An Introduction* (London: I.B. Tauris, 2002), 128.

3   Kristin Thompson, *Storytelling in the New Hollywood. Understanding Classical Narrative Technique* (Cambridge, MA: Harvard University Press, 1999), 3.

4   See, for example, Nick Smurthwaite and Paul Gelder, *Mel Brooks and the Spoof Movie* (Belleville, MI: Proteus, 1983); Peter J. Bailey and Sam B. Girgus, eds., *A Companion to Woody Allen* (Chichester: Wiley-Blackwell, 2013).

5   There is no trace at all of ZAZ in King, *New Hollywood Cinema*; Barry
    Langford, *Post-Classical Hollywood. Film Industry, Style and Ideology since 1945*
    (Edinburgh: Edinburgh University Press, 2010); Kirshner and Lewis, eds. *When
    the Movies Mattered*; Stephen Prince, ed. *American Cinema of the 1980s. Themes
    and Variations* (New Brunswick, NJ: Rutgers University Press, 2007); Linda Ruth
    Williams and Michael Hammond, eds., *Contemporary American Cinema* (London/
    New York: Open University/McGraw Hill, 2006). In Andrew Horton and Joanna
    E. Rapf, eds. *A Companion to Film Comedy* (Chichester: Wiley Blackwell, 2016),
    other than a single (and misspelled) passing mention in Charles Morrow's chapter
    to the "Zucker/Abrams [*sic*] team" (264) - there is nothing else on the trio. ZAZ's
    works are often mentioned not as an object of study per se but as examples of one
    specific comic mechanism, thus reducing their peculiarity or emphasizing, for the
    sake of argumentation, aspects that are only of secondary relevance, for example,
    parody based upon incongruity (Brett Mills, *The Sitcom* (Edinburgh: Edinburgh
    University Press, 2009), 83) or toilet/bodily humor (Nick Marx and Matt
    Sienkiewicz, eds., *The Comedy Studies Reader* (Austin, TX, University of Texas Press,
    2018), 18).

6   On Brooks's longevity, see Alex Symons, *Mel Brooks in the Cultural Industries:
    Survival and Prolonged Adaptation* (Edinburgh: Edinburgh University Press, 2012).

7   David Sterritt, *The Films of Jean-Luc Godard: Seeing the Invisible* (Cambridge:
    Cambridge University Press 1999), 1.

8   Ibid., 61.

9   Duane Dudek, "25 Years and still Laughing. 'Airplane!' Maintains Its Cruising
    Altitude with a Non-stop Zany Attitude." *Milwaukee Journal Sentinel*, June 11,
    2005, online, https://web.archive.org/web/20080430053901/http://www.jsonline.
    com/story/index.aspx?id=332493, accessed January 30, 2020.

10 ZAZ in Jon Brooks, "Chat with the Creators of *Airplane!*" (video), *YouTube*,
    February 1, 2011, https://youtu.be/ikP_xKoZyUM, accessed January 30, 2020.

11 George Hesselberg, quoted in Rich Markey, "Finger Lickin' Funny." *On Wisconsin*,
    Wisconsin Alumni Association, Spring 2007, online, https://web.archive.org/
    web/20140703025902/http://www.uwalumni.com/home/alumniandfriends/
    onwisconsin/archives/spring2007/funny.aspx, accessed January 30, 2020.

12 Ibid.

13 Dudek, "25 Years and still Laughing."

14 I concentrate in particular on ZAZ's 1977–84 period, the one closer to the birth of
    the New Hollywood, thus leaving aside the *Naked Gun* trilogy, in which some of
    the early characteristics of ZAZ were normalized; for example, the increased use of
    comic reaction shots. *Ruthless People* (1986) has also been omitted because it was
    directed but not written by ZAZ.

15   Noël Carroll, "Notes on the Sight Gag," in *Theorizing the Moving Image* (Cambridge:
     Cambridge University Press, 1996), 146.

16   ZAZ's humor has antecedents in the Marx Brothers, *Hellzapoppin'* (H. C. Potter,
     1941), and has affinities with Allen, Brooks, and Carl Reiner. On Jewish humor see
     Jeremy Dauber, *Jewish Comedy: A Serious History* (New York: Norton, 2018). On
     humor in American cinema, see Guido Fink, *Non solo Woody Allen: la tradizione
     ebraica nel cinema americano* (Venice: Marsilio, 2001).

17   Robert Sklar, *Movie-Made America: A Cultural History of American Movies*, 2nd ed.
     (New York: Vintage, 1994), 302.

18   Quoted in Dudek, "25 Years and still Laughing." On film parodies in the *Mad*
     magazine, see Grady Hendrix, "Cahiers du Cinémad," *Film Comment* 49, no.
     2 (March 2013): 43–7; on *Mad*'s intersections with Jewish culture, see Nathan
     Abrams, "A Secular Talmud: The Jewish Sensibility of Mad Magazine," *Studies in
     American Humor* 3, no. 30 (2014): 111–22.

19   David Bordwell, *Narration in the Fiction Film* (Madison: University of Wisconsin
     Press), 312.

20   Jean-Michel Frodon, "From Pen to Camera: Another Critic," in *A Companion
     to Jean-Luc Godard*, ed. Tom Conley and T. Jefferson Kline (Chichester: Wiley-
     Blackwell, 2014), 12.

21   Bordwell, *Narration in the Fiction Film*, 312.

22   Sterritt, *The Films of Jean-Luc Godard*, 18.

23   Richard Neupert, *A History of the French New Wave Cinema*, 2nd ed. (Madison:
     University of Wisconsin Press, 2007), xvi.

24   Ibid., 231.

25   Jonathan Rosenbaum, "New Hollywood and the Sixties Melting Pot," in *The Last
     Great American Picture Show: New Hollywood Cinema in the 1970s*, ed. Thomas
     Elsaesser, Alexander Horwath, and Noel King (Amsterdam: Amsterdam University
     Press, 2004), 141.

26   Kristin Thompson and David Bordwell, *Film History: An Introduction* (New York:
     McGraw Hill, 2010), 489.

27   Quoted in Ian Nathan, "You Can't Be Serious," *Empire* (November 1996): 127.

28   Steve Seidman, *Comedian Comedy: A Tradition in Hollywood Film* (Ann Arbor, MI:
     UMI Research Press, 1981).

29   Steve Neale and Frank Krutnik, *Popular Film and Television Comedy* (London:
     Routledge, 1990), 105.

30   David Zucker quoted in Nathan, "You Can't Be Serious," 127. The exception to this
     is Stephen Stucker in *Airplane!*, a comedian whose Don DeLuise-like flamboyancy
     is in strident contrast with the general deadpan countenance.

31   Simon Bland, "How We Made: *Airplane!*," *The Guardian*, May 25, 2020, https://www.theguardian.com/film/2020/may/25/how-we-made-airplane-the-movie, accessed May 29, 2020.

32   Leonard Maltin quoted in Dudek, "25 Years and still Laughing."

33   Ibid.

34   Bland, "How We Made: *Airplane!*."

35   Robert Falck, "Parody and Contrafactum: A Terminological Clarification," *Musical Quarterly* 65, no. 1 (January 1979): 1–21.

36   Linda Hutcheon, *A Theory of Parody: The Teachings of Twentieth-Century Art Forms* (London: Routledge, 1985), 32.

37   Emilio Audissino, "*Police Squad!*. The Zucker-Abrahams-Zucker Style VS the Substance of Early 1980s Television," in Sarah Cardwell, Lucy Donaldson, and Jonathan Bignell, eds., *Moments in Television. Substance/Style* (Manchester: Manchester University Press, forthcoming).

38   *Late Night with David Letterma*n (video), March 15, 1982, https://youtu.be/TPwNVG14OIM, accessed January 30, 2020.

39   Quoted in Nathan, "You Can't Be Serious," 127.

40   David Marc, *Comic Visions: Television Comedy and American Culture*, 2nd ed. (Malden, MA: Blackwell, 1997), 31–2.

41   Neupert, *A History of the French New Wave Cinema*, 34.

42   This continuity-based gag is reprised in *A Naked Gun 2 ½: The Smell of Fear*.

43   On the music for *Airplane!*, see Tim Summers, "'Shirley, Bernstein Can't Be Serious?': *Airplane!* and Compositional Personas," *Journal of Film Music* 6, no. 1 (2013): 75–86.

44   Bland, "How We Made: *Airplane!*."

45   Neupert, *A History of the French New Wave Cinema*, 214.

46   Robert McKee, *Dialogue: The Art of Verbal Action for the Page, Stage, and Screen*. (New York: Twelve, 2016). The demotion of dialogue is an element that also connects ZAZ to Jacques Tati. For more on ZAZ/Tati similarities, see Audissino, "*Police Squad!*."

47   Bordwell, *Narration in the Fiction Film*, 317.

48   Audissino, "*Police Squad!*"

49   This had already been done by Orson Welles for the end credits of *The Magnificent Ambersons* (1942).

50   ZAZ's interventions on the peritexts also include the typeface of "The End" title card in *Airplane!* and *Top Secret!*—which reprises the old Warner Bros. look—as well as the signature use of the exclamation point in their titles (*Airplane!*, *Police Squad!*, *Top Secret!*), which is itself an intensifier used to parody the sensationalist dramatic tone of many B-films.

51 A discussion of the four types of motivation is in Kristin Thompson, *Breaking the Glass Armor: Neoformalist Film Analysis* (Princeton, NJ: Princeton University Press, 1988), 16–20.

52 David Bordwell, Janet Staiger, and Kristin Thompson, *The Classical Hollywood Cinema: Film Style & Mode of Production to 1960* (New York: Columbia University Press, 1985), 22.

53 Neale and Krutnik, *Popular Film and Television Comedy,* 31–2.

54 See Audissino, *"Police Squad!"*

55 Thompson, *Breaking the Glass Armor,* 247.

56 Neupert, *A History of the French New Wave Cinema,* 215–16.

57 Bordwell, *Narration in the Fiction Film,* 315.

58 Ibid., 285, 306.

59 Kristin Thompson, *Eisenstein's Ivan the Terrible: A Neoformalist Analysis* (Princeton, NJ: Princeton University Press, 1981), 287.

60 Ibid., 293.

61 Thompson, *Breaking the Glass Armor,* 259.

62 Neale and Krutnik, *Popular Film and Television Comedy,* 67.

63 Robert Kolker, *A Cinema of Loneliness,* 4th ed. (Oxford: Oxford University Press, 2011), 10.

6

Design as Authorship: Polly Platt's New Hollywood Aesthetic

Aaron Hunter

Polly Platt's production design bears a recognizable authorial stamp. She began her Hollywood career on the first four films directed by Peter Bogdanovich. She continued to develop and deploy her personal approach to narrative and design on films by directors including Michael Ritchie, Robert Altman, Carl Reiner, and James L. Brooks, before transitioning to producing in the 1980s. Platt's approach to design would prove a formative influence during and after the New Hollywood era. Her strict attention to details of period and location, and her drive to craft an aesthetic grounded in a new realism would help usher in an era of authenticity in Hollywood design. In addition to her visual contributions to 1970s Hollywood cinema, her understanding of design as a key component of narrative and character development added nuance and depth to the films she worked on.

However, while Platt's contributions to crafting these films' distinctive visual palettes are undeniable, it is the directors of the films who have been recognized as auteurs. Like many creative women of the New Hollywood era, Platt's authorial role in filmmaking has been marginalized. This marginalization perpetuates the single-author, auteurist paradigm that dominates New Hollywood scholarship. It also helps maintain the notion that New Hollywood was fundamentally a cinema of creative men. This chapter employs archival research and formal analysis of Platt's 1970s films to argue not only that her authorial contributions can be discerned, but that those contributions were essential to the development of a "vision" in the films. As with other interventions in this collection, my intention is not simply to reassess Platt's work or even her style, as it were. Rather it is to centralize, or at the least demarginalize, a figure whose creativity and labor played a significant role in developing vital aspects of New Hollywood style, a role that has been overlooked due to the historical framing of the era as one dominated by the figure of the male auteur.

New Hollywood Auteurism

The architecture of New Hollywood history and scholarship is built upon a foundation of auteurism. The strain of auteurism that emerged in the 1970s, and the films and filmmakers it elevates, is so thoroughly welded to critical and scholarly conceptions of the era as to be virtually inseparable. While much research has enumerated and interrogated the various factors that allowed the New Hollywood era to flourish, however briefly,[1] most of that research, varied and intricate as it may be, ends up promulgating an era of "directors' cinema." There has been, since its inception, some resistance to this framing. Pauline Kael famously disputed Andrew Sarris's formulation of an auteur theory (despite much of her criticism being director-centered in nature); Richard Corliss made eloquent claims for a screenwriter-centered criticism; Graham Petrie argued that auteurism distorts film history; and feminist and production studies scholars have long argued that auteurism is an incomplete model for understanding film production. Despite such efforts to construct a more nuanced critical and scholarly apparatus for understanding New Hollywood filmmaking—with such efforts strengthening in recent years—the auteur paradigm continues to dominate the functional organizing of New Hollywood scholarly and popular engagement.

At the heart of this construction lies a paradox that is difficult to resolve. The concept of the auteur changed significantly between its articulation in the pages of *Cahiers du Cinema* and its popular flourishing in 1970s Hollywood. Truffaut and his colleagues had devised a strategy for discerning auteurism by means of analyzing mise-en-scène and detecting a consistent visual style despite the rigid constraints of the studio system. The *Cahiers* auteur did not so much impose his vision upon a film, as smuggle it into the film via patterns of shot selection, framing, or camera movement and details of location, set, and prop. Sarris developed this idea significantly by insisting that visual consistency was only one of the necessary components of auteurism: the work of a true auteur must also exhibit a consistency of theme. While Sarris's early work looked back at the directors of the Classical-era studio system, his conjoining of visual style and thematic development undergirded the primacy of the director's singular vision that has continued to dominate understanding of the auteur filmmaker. This expansion of the concept significantly influenced the popularized notion of auteurism that emerged in 1970s Hollywood. Unlike the formulation of the *Cahiers* writers, for post-Sarris auteurists, a director's vision is imposed upon the film.

Many factors led to the preeminent position that directors were allowed to assume in 1970s Hollywood, including studio upheaval, generational shifts, changes in distribution and exhibition strategies, technological advances, and the influence of popular art cinemas from outside the United States. Auteurism bound these various influencing factors into a simple concept and allowed it to flourish. Early in the era, New Hollywood directors made films that were financial and critical hits, endowing those directors with reputational capital that they could convert into future projects that were also (for a time) successful, endowing them with more reputational capital, and so on. As products of this system, the films became seen as products, almost solely, of their directors.

The paradox then is one of rhetoric versus practice. Rhetorically, assigning everything of value in a film to its director serves many functions. It assists in the categorizing, marketing, and canonization of films. For example, the term "a Scorsese film" at once describes a type of film—gritty, urban, criminal (despite Scorsese's frequent forays into other genres)—but also a product for film consumers ("I like Scorsese films, I'll purchase a ticket to see this one, too") and a status (a film by one of global cinema's "greats"). It also makes attribution of quality much easier. Speaking practically, on the other hand, a film crew consists of numerous practitioners who contribute to the visual style and themes of the film utterance. Film scholars and critics know this and, on occasion, acknowledge the contributions of cinematographers or, less frequently, production designers. This is particularly true when the cinematography or design calls attention to itself, such as with stunning golden hour shots or the exuberant design of musicals and science fiction. Yet, once the acknowledgment is made, discussions generally return to the director. Thus, even though the concept and nuances of auteurism have changed and developed over time, the result still involves attributing a film's mise-en-scéne and its potential meanings to the director.

The New Hollywood film industry was brimming with innovative, imaginative cinematographers who worked closely with directors to create a new look for American cinema. Gordon Willis, John Alonzo, Owen Roizman, Haskell Wexler, Laszló Kovács, Vilmos Zsigmond, and others are recognized for their skill, artistry, and individual contributions.[2] However, their authorship, partial or otherwise, is rarely recognized. Nobody would refer to *The Godfather* (Paramount, 1972) as "a Gordon Willis film" or *Chinatown* (Paramount, 1974) as "a film by John Alonzo."[3] Furthermore, while it is often cinematographers who first embrace emerging camera, lens, and lighting technologies—for example, the Panaflex or the Steadicam—it is generally directors who receive credit for deploying them. In practice, these increasing developments required more responsibility on the part of the crew. As Charles Tashiro explains, "the cinematographer and designer increased in production importance, but rarely in critical recognition or discussion."[4] Thus, even as advancements in technology and the demands of location shooting required more highly developed skill sets on the part of cinematographers, as well as an accompanying creative imagination for using them, directors continue to reap the rewards of those creative developments.

Production designers tend to be less well known even than cinematographers. While New Hollywood films are often described in terms of their visual presentation—gritty, realistic, with an often documentary-like approach to detail—the designers who created the worlds through which the characters and cameras move have been subject to little evaluation. Few of them are known and none of them are discussed extensively in any critical fashion. Yet, the design strategies of Richard Sylbert, Dean Tavoularis, and Polly Platt, among others, were crucial to creating the look that New Hollywood films are known for. This lack of recognition is due in part to the nature of the films and their design. In aiming for a "realistic" visual style, the design of 1970s films rarely calls attention to itself, even, arguably, in the era's many period pieces. This unnoticeable quality, however, is due to the efforts of designers to create a lived-in reality (often in hand with meticulous location scouting). Herein, again, lies the paradox: through all its iterations, auteurism relies on an analysis of mise-en-scéne—all that is visible within the frame—but the work of the filmmakers who design, build, light, and shoot those elements of a film— who literally determine the frame and its contents—remain unacknowledged for their work.

The career of production designer Polly Platt exemplifies the tension between these rhetorical and practical formulations. Her career is often framed in the context of her relationship with Peter Bogdanovich and the films they made together. Platt designed the first four films Bogdanovich directed: *Targets* (Paramount, 1968); *The Last Picture Show* (BBS/Columbia, 1971); *What's Up, Doc?* (Warner Bros., 1972); *Paper Moon* (Paramount, 1973). Earlier, she worked alongside him on his first forays into directing for Roger Corman, helping him rewrite the script and direct the second unit on *The Wild Angels* (AIP, 1966) and designing the additional footage he directed for *Valley of the Prehistoric Women* (The Filmgroup/AIP, 1968). In histories of the era, Platt's role is often framed in one of two ways. Sometimes she is cast as a professional muse to Bogdanovich. Alternatively, because in addition to production design, she also usually oversaw location scouting and costume design and contributed to script decisions, she is sometimes framed as an unofficial "codirector" of the films. For example, regarding *The Last Picture Show*, Peter Biskind quotes star Ben Johnson as "whispering that [Platt] directed the film as much as [Bogdanovich] did."[5]

However, neither of these formulations properly grapples with the lasting contributions Platt made to Hollywood cinema, and both center Bogdanovich as much they do Platt. First, casting Platt as Bogdanovich's muse, or even his inspirational collaborator, replicates many of the chauvinistic tropes about female partners that riddle Hollywood history. If Platt functioned only as Bogdanovich's muse, then her usefulness in Hollywood can be read as having expired after the couple's creative separation. Histories of the era often treat her this way, ignoring her further three decades of work. For example, Platt figures prominently in the first third of *Easy Riders, Raging Bulls*, and Biskind often credits her with much of the creative motivation for the first four films—like for seeing the possibility of *The Last Picture Show* having a European flair. However, once she and Bogdanovich separate, she virtually disappears from the book, with occasional mention as one of the wives abandoned by their director husbands (see also Toby Rafelson and Marcia Lucas).[6] On the other hand, depicting Platt as an unofficial codirector replicates the auteurist rhetoric that only as a director could her contributions have mattered. Thus, even when she is recognized it is rarely for her talent and contributions as a designer. Those contributions, however, are too varied and too vital to be reduced to such tropes. As a production designer beginning in 1967, Platt played a significant role in crafting Hollywood's new visual directions.

New Hollywood Production Design

New Hollywood films often walk a fine line between realism and expressionism, deftly blending elements of both in their mix of conventional and nonconventional styles of filming, editing, design, and sound. Geoff King describes this as "seemingly contradictory"[7] and describes how this playfulness came about as directors in the early 1970s were given greater creative freedom due to studio upheaval. This continuum between the expressive and realistic might better be understood as a dialogue rather than a contradiction. Filmmakers of the era, equally influenced by the studio films of Classical Hollywood of their youth and the more experimental films of various European New Waves, felt comfortable blending expressive and realistic narrative and stylistic modes in ways that most previous Hollywood filmmakers had not (or had not been allowed to). The result in these instances is often a film that seems grounded in the real world, in which the implications and ramifications of events and character actions take on a more expressive, personal quality.

Take, for example, *Bonnie and Clyde* (Warner Bros., 1967), often noted as the film that set New Hollywood in motion. The opening scene announces the film's subtle departure from classical conventions in an effort to convey Bonnie's dissatisfaction with life. Bonnie (Faye Dunaway) paces her cramped bedroom alone, frustrated and naked. In addition to the groundbreaking, if mild, nudity, the sequence employs jump cuts with awkward, shaky camera movements to convey a sense of uneasy boredom. These stylistic flourishes call attention to themselves in ways that circumvent traditional Hollywood practices of "invisible" style. The production design, on the other hand, grounds the sequence in a drab realism that indicates the film's Depression-era setting and the simple, plain life that Bonnie desperately wishes to flee. The visible ceiling, the degraded quality of the mirror, the dusty photographs hanging askew on the wall, the shaky brass bedstead through which Bonnie peers like prison bars all create an intensely realistic space. This realism remains "invisible," but it is the appearance of reality that allows the more expressionistic camera work and editing to convey Bonnie's interiority so efficiently.

Robert Kolker describes how the scene's elements "give the viewer a sense of immediate, if confused, attachment to the character."[8] Yet, in describing the color, the close-ups, the editing, Kolker never mentions production designer Tavoularis, cinematographer Burnett Guffey, or editor Dede Allen; everything about the sequence that works (or does not work) is credited to director Arthur Penn. Clearly, though, the talents of all three (and more)[9] are vital to the sequence. Guffey has discussed the attempt to create an unglamorous realism on the film: "Nothing was to be beautiful. Everything was to be, you might say, *harsh*—and that's the way it was through the whole picture" (emphasis in original).[10] This harshness was facilitated by the film's location shooting and production design. Tavoularis wanted to do something new in the film, "to rebel against the *Pillow Talk*, Hollywood movie look … I had looked at rooms in places like Waxahachie, and I knew what a modest house looked like—I wanted those old ceilings with wallpaper on them to be visible."[11] To capture Penn's desired realism in the spaces that Tavoularis designed, Guffey was forced to rethink forty years of experience and resort to using fewer and smaller lights, with smaller cameras and rigs.[12] The result combined all three men's efforts to capture the stark reality of Bonne and Clyde's Depression-era existence.[13]

While the design on *Bonnie and Clyde* was not completely new—Tavoularis admitted to being inspired by Sidney Lumet[14]—it made a noticeable contribution to what would rapidly become the standard approach to film design in New Hollywood. A major factor was that the drive for realism, in both contemporary films and period pieces, was coupled with a desire to shoot on location. Lawrence Webb explains how "the move away from studio production, under way since World War II, was now accelerating at a new pace" and describes the increased desire to shoot on location as an effort to replicate "authenticity, realism, immediacy, contemporaneity, social awareness, imperfection."[15] Production designers working on location had three broad options for shooting interiors: repurposing and accentuating existing structures and interiors; completely renovating interiors (e.g., tearing out walls and building new ones or redesigning building facades); and building new sets from scratch. This sometimes meant building freestanding structures and on other occasions hiring local soundstages or warehouses.

Because of this intimate relationship between locations and sets, in the early years of New Hollywood production, designers regularly oversaw location scouting. Tavoularis says, "You used to always location scout yourself, and it was fun. Although it's a time consuming thing—hundreds of hours really."[16] Like Tavoularis, Richard Sylbert (*Chinatown, Shampoo*), Michael Haller (*Harold and Maude, Bound for Glory*), Polly Platt (*The Last Picture Show, Paper Moon*), and many other production designers of the early 1970s played significant roles in determining the shooting locations of their films. In not only constructing and dressing sets but also deciding where those sets are located, how they look inside and out, and working closely with the cinematographer to light them, New Hollywood production designers significantly crafted the mise-en-scéne of their films. Furthermore, they made conscious decisions about these designs based on how they might affect narrative and character. Tavoularis fashioning visible ceilings was as much about refining Bonnie's character as it was striving for period authenticity. In designing sets and locations for *Chinatown*, Richard Sylbert describes how "every building that Gittes visits will be above his eye level, because it's harder to go uphill than down."[17] Thus, in crafting their films' visual milieu, designers were intentionally contributing to elements of their thematic authorship as well.

Polly Platt's contributions were perhaps even more significant. With her background in theater design, she had already developed a sharp eye for how specific design, props, and costumes accentuate and refine a scene's narrative content. In her early twenties, she had sewn piecework in a factory and later worked retyping well-known Hollywood scripts for Larry Edmund's Bookshop on Hollywood Boulevard.[18] At the former, she says, "I learned how to sew fast," while the latter "taught me a lot about screenwriting." Both would become fundamental components of Platt's design. In the first instance, although regularly uncredited, Platt designed costumes—including sewing several costumes herself—on almost every film she designed. She also made significant script contributions, although she rarely received a writer's credit.[19] And like other more celebrated contemporaries, Platt's time working as a production assistant, writer, and even editor for Roger Corman taught her how to navigate a film set from a variety of positions and how to do so efficiently, cheaply, and with an eye for how the finished film would come together. Thus, by the time Platt began her career in Hollywood films, her actual roles included production design, costume design, location scouting, and script contributions. This combination of talents meant she played a tremendous role in determining those films' mise-en-scéne. For the remainder of this chapter, I will discuss how specific contributions that Platt made to the films she designed in the 1970s represent aspects of the films' authorship. While I will focus in part on the four films she designed with Bogdanovich, I will pay particular attention to two of the films she is less well known for: *The Thief Who Came to Dinner* (Bud Yorkin Productions, 1973) and *The Bad News Bears* (Paramount, 1976).

Polly Platt's New Hollywood Design

Platt is probably best known for her early career work with Bogdanovich, to whom she was married from 1962 to 1971.[20] Her later career in production design, on films as varied as *A Star Is Born* (Warner Bros., 1976), *Terms of Endearment* (Paramount, 1983), and *The Witches of Eastwick* (Warner Bros., 1987), is rarely mentioned and certainly not the subject of any scholarly or critical research. Alternatively, fans of *The Simpsons* may know her for having introduced producer James L. Brooks to cartoonist Matt Groening in 1985. Her career, however, extends backward and forward from both of those periods, including a highly creative interval in between, after her creative relationship with Bogdanovich ended.

Platt's interest in production design began during childhood. Her father, John, a colonel in the US Army, had several posts in Europe, including as a presiding judge in the Dachau trials, so Platt spent much of her childhood in postwar Germany (and later France).[21] As much as she had been conditioned to hate Germans during the war, she recalls being saddened by the poverty and destruction the war had wrought. "I longed for supernatural powers to rebuild the towns and feed and clothe the starving people … I think my later accomplishments as a production designer in movies came out of an overwhelming desire to see these buildings rebuilt."[22] During a stint back in the states between trips to Europe, she was taken to see a summer stock production of Shaw's *Arms and the Man* (1894), and she wandered "back stage" (behind a barn) during the intermission, where she saw lighting technicians at work while the cast changed costumes. "I knew right then that this was what I wanted to do. I wanted to be part of the theater and design the sets and costumes."[23] After returning from Europe for good, she joined her school's theater group, "building scenery and painting it and being the prop girl."[24] In college at Skidmore and then Carnegie Tech (which would become Carnegie-Mellon), she studied art and drama and took jobs doing set design for summer stock productions. She recalls reading plays and sketching ideas for them, trying to interpret how the plays might look with different color and design styles.[25] At Carnegie Tech, she was told that, as a woman, she was not strong enough for production design but could do costume. "I didn't care. I was happy to learn costumes design. I would get what I needed from Summer Stock work. I took a drafting class in the Architecture department so I could read and draw blueprints."[26] The sexism is notable and, sadly, typical not only of the era but of the sexism that Platt would face throughout her career. As important, though, is how it demonstrates Platt's ability and willingness to make difficult situations work to her benefit: both the costume design and architectural studies she undertook in lieu of production design would become components of the all-encompassing design strategy that she would employ in Hollywood.

She did not graduate. Instead, having married a young playwright named Philip Klein, she drove out west to California with her new husband in the hopes of establishing residency and reenrolling at UCLA. It was here that she worked as a seamstress and learned how to sew quickly and accurately. Later, they moved to Tucson to join friends from Carnegie Tech who were starting a repertory theater there, with Platt responsible for costumes and sets. Sadly, Klein died in an automobile accident on his twenty-first birthday, and Platt decided to leave the theater company and move back east. After some time drifting between her parents' home in Massachusetts and Tucson, Platt decided to try making it in theater in New York City. It was there, in the spring of 1961, that she met Bogdanovich.

The relevance of these biographical details is that when Platt met Bogdanovich, she already had several years' training and experience designing, building, and painting sets and crafting costumes. She had studied architecture and, through her formal and informal study of drama, was well-versed in the narrative and character conventions of playwriting. She would hone these skills over the next several years, first in New York theater and then, after she and Bogdanovich moved to Los Angeles, on several Corman productions—including their first full film together, *Targets*. Thus, when evaluating and analyzing Platt's career as a production designer, with Bogdanovich and later, it is necessary to remember that in her films, she was the driving creative force behind set design, costume design, and location scouting.[27] In the following section, I will briefly trace how she deployed those skills on the films she made with Bogdanovich before moving on to consider her work on some of the other New Hollywood films she made.

Early Career

Platt's first four films were shot at least partially on location; some included studio sets as well. Set design entailed either constructing entire sets on a studio lot or repurposing existing structures. In terms of building sets, *Targets* is highly instructive of how Platt's attention to details of color and architecture added nuance to the emotional tone of a given scene. *Targets* was a low-budget

Corman production, and the crew had to make use of one stage for most of the film's interiors, including a studio screening room, Beverly Hills restaurant the Polo Lounge, mass shooter Bobby's (Tim O'Kelly) bungalow home, and the Beverly Hills Hotel suite of retiring actor Byron Orlok (Boris Karloff). For the latter two, each set was designed to convey elements of the main characters' emotions, as well as the feel of the space itself. *Targets* comprises two different stories—one about a mass shooter and the other about a horror film star—and the stories only come together in the film's climactic scene: Bobby's shooting spree leads him to the drive-in cinema where Orlok's final film is premiering. The psychological profiles of the two men that render their confrontation believable are developed in subtle ways by the mise-en-scéne throughout the film's first half.

The house where Bobby lives with his wife and parents comprises many small rooms, connected by narrow hallways. The sense of confinement creates a slow-burning tension before Bobby embarks on his rampage. Furthermore, every room in the house is painted blue. This was done to create a coldness, heightening Bobby's sense of isolation within his own home. Platt said, "I designed the interior of the house on stage, trying to make the ugly 60's décor so awful that it might provoke a young man to murder."[28] The use of blue in the house also exhibits how Platt and Kovács work together to deploy expressionist lighting that develops as Bobby mentally commits to his crime. Initial shots inside the house come in the light of day. Later shots occur in the evening by the glow of TV and electric lights. Finally, there are some extremely dark scenes late at night, which darken the blue of the walls to almost black. Suddenly, a shot in the bright light of the following morning announces the start of Bobby's rampage as he murders his wife and mother. Of vital importance is that until Bobby starts killing, the viewer is never explicitly shown what his plans are. He has guns in his car and appears to be stocking up on ammunition. He also aims his rifle at his father while the two are out target shooting. But there is no conversation or voice-over—no exposition—detailing what Bobby's actual plans are. Thus, the set design of his house is an effective indicator of his fragile, isolated state of mind.

In contrast, Byron Orlok's hotel suite—built on the same stage—consists of only two rooms, much more open and airier. The rooms are painted a light brown and accented with golds, yellows, and oranges. The decorations are ornate, as befits a Beverly Hills Hotel suite, for an overall effect much warmer and more inviting than the cold, tight interiors of Bobby's house. Platt took a similar approach to the film's costumes. In a letter to Karloff before production, she describes Orlok's clothes "in warm colors" and describes the mix of "warm brown" and "tweed" she has in mind.[29] Thus, while Bobby's sequences depict him descending calmly into madness, Orlok's show him surrounded by colleagues and friends who love him, who praise his talents, and encourage him to keep working during an emotional low point. This building up of the character is necessary to the dramatic impact of the climactic scene when Orlok and Bobby finally meet and the much older, frailer man slaps the killer down.

What's Up, Doc? further exemplifies Platt's understanding of the relationship between space, color, light, and emotion. While several of the film's set pieces were filmed on location in San Francisco,[30] most of the interiors were built on a Warner Bros. sound stage, all meticulously designed to convey various emotional and psychological states in tandem with the film's narrative development. One example, which again highlights the interplay of Platt's design and Kovács's lighting and framing, comes during and immediately after the film's banquet sequence, which is played for zany laughs. Ryan O'Neal's awkward musicologist Howard is vying for a prestigious grant when Barbra Streisand's Judy shows up, unplanned, and poses as his fiancé, horrifically unnerving him, but charming nearly everybody else in attendance. The scene's humor comes from its verbal wit, physical comedy, and prop work. The brightly lit, garish room heightens not only the sense of extreme wealth but also the vulgarity of its representatives deeming academics and artists "worthy" to receive a pittance of it. Later, though, after the banquet hijinks, the same room is relit and reframed to convey a sense of intimacy as Howard and Judy experience a moment of emotional connection that will propel much of the ensuing narrative.

Design that enhances character and narrative can also be found in location sets that Platt repurposed. For example, the entirety of *Paper Moon* was shot on location in and around the towns of Hayes, Kansas, and St. Joseph, Missouri, which were chosen because of their immense flatness and Depression-era sparseness. As Tatum O'Neal's Addie and Ryan O'Neal's Moze travel across Kansas, they visit a variety of small towns and cheap hotels, all of which were redressed or reset by Platt. In one key scene, while Moze sleeps, Addie slips into the bathroom and examines her secret stash of keepsakes, including a picture of her recently deceased mother. She tries on jewelry and perfume and poses like her mother in the photograph, examining herself in the mirror. This was shot in quite a large room, but Platt refit the space to make it cramped and confined, heightening the sense of Addie ensconced in her own private world.[31] She also rebuilt a storefront as a 1930s cinema marquee, which allowed for a stunning reflection shot and then a 180-degree cut—none of which is in the script. These designs convey the film's era, but they also reflect Addie's character including her early, contentious attitude toward Moze and her silent sadness over her recently deceased mother.

On both films, Platt also determined the setting and location. She chose most of the San Francisco locations for *What's Up, Doc?*, and it was her idea to move *Paper Moon* from the Alabama of the novel to the flat, wide open Kansas of the film. Thus, a great deal of what works about all of these films' visual palettes, both interiors and exteriors, derives from Platt's imaginative efforts to develop the relationship between each film's narrative and mise-en-scéne.

Later 1970s Films

As Platt began working on films with other directors, she continued to supervise location scouting and to design based on her conceptions of narrative, character, and theme. *The Thief Who Came to Dinner* follows Webster (Ryan O'Neal), a computer programmer in Texas who quits his job to become a jewel thief among the nouveau riche of Houston. Also starring Jacqueline Bisset, Warren Oats, and Ned Beatty, it features a snappy Walter Hill script, Philip Lathrop's cinematography, and a Henry Mancini score. As a film, it is a bit of a trifle, but O'Neal and Bisset have sexy chemistry and it looks fantastic. Platt suggested Houston rather than the source novel's Chicago, reasoning that the film's breezy narrative would benefit from being set within the new money Houston rather than the more traditional Chicago. She believed that Webster robbing the nouveau riche would keep his character sympathetic to an audience.[32] This move to Houston provides the film with its entire visual palette.

Platt scouted extensively for the film's varied settings, working closely with Frank Marshall.[33] Locations include the opulent homes of Webster's victims, the sparsely furnished house of Bisset's Laura, a down-on-her-luck, formerly wealthy socialite, and the many seedy exteriors where Webster meets the underworld fences who buy his jewels. These locations contextualize and complicate major character motivations. For example, Laura's decision to remain with Webster, even after she discovers he is a jewel thief, seems at first an unlikely decision.

The decrepit nature of her house, however, with its sparsely furnished rooms and a swimming pool emptied of water, is a visual signifier of all she has lost. This grounds her decision to take up with Webster in the reality of her economic situation.

In *Bad News Bears*, location is notable, in part, for what is not shown on film. *Bears* concerns a little league baseball team of ragtag, foul-mouthed kids with bad attitudes, who are frightful ball players. They are coached by Walter Matthau's Buttermaker, an equally foul-mouthed, washed-up drunk, attempting to supplement his pool cleaning job. Bill Lancaster's script delivers much of the film's exposition and profiles of the kids in scenes set in their individual homes,[34] which lend insight into their familial relationships and economic status. Platt found these scenes superfluous. In her reading of the script, the baseball diamond is the only home that matters, so she and director Michael Ritchie cut all the domestic scenes.[35] In the final film, aside from four scenes at other locations and a few in Buttermaker's car, the entirety of the action takes place on the field or in the dugout.

Platt designed the film's ballpark based on official Little League regulations. (She recounts how a "macho guy who was working on the movie kept saying, 'Why are you letting Polly Platt design this set? What does a girl know about baseball?'"[36]—ironic considering the film's major plotline concerns the team winning only after a girl starts pitching). Importantly, she laid out the diamond so that the sun would cross from third base to first, to avoid shading problems (about 65 degrees different from standard regulation) and providing cinematographer John Alonzo more opportunities to shoot during the magic hour, as he favored. Platt's location decision-making again plays a role in determining a film's visual style and narrative development.

However, Platt's primary role was again production design. As mentioned, she had refronted an entire street for *The Last Picture Show*, built a cinema facade for *Paper Moon*, and built four entirely different interiors on one small sound stage for *Targets*. For *Bears*, Platt designed not only the baseball field but also its accompanying structures: scoreboard, bleachers, backstop, and dugout. The structures have a worn feel, lending them an authenticity as the locus of summer after summer of kids gamboling over them and balls slamming into them. This realism is fundamental to Platt's vision of the baseball diamond as home. This is true especially of the team dugout. While the Bears share their very public defeats and their few triumphs on the field, in the dugout the kids and Buttermaker enact their more emotional dramas. Players tease each other and confess fears about the inadequacy of their play. They revolt against Buttermaker when his coaching decisions undermine their chances for victory. As with the other structures, Platt emphasizes the dugout's lived-in quality. The wood is scuffed, the paint chipped, and the protective fencing is bent out of shape, reflecting the many times that previous players gripped it anxiously or climbed it in frustration.

Significantly, the dugout is home to the film's thematic low point. While the major plotline treats the Bears' efforts to become a cohesive group of players who contend for the championship, a substantial subplot concerns the relationship between Buttermaker and Tatum O'Neal's Amanda. Previous to the film narrative, Buttermaker had been in a relationship with Amanda's mother that ended badly. After Buttermaker recruits Amanda to pitch for the team, she drops hints that she would enjoy having him back in her life. After the Bears win the semifinal, Amanda and Buttermaker have a one-to-one conversation in the dugout. Amanda ices her elbow and tries to convince Buttermaker that, after the season ends, they should continue to spend time together, perhaps with her mother. Buttermaker resists her increasingly desperate invitations, and she begins to implore him. Finally, he erupts in a fit of anger. He yells at her, cruelly explaining he wants nothing to do with her, then throws beer in her face.

This heartbreaking scene works because of a combination of talents: script, performances, direction, and cinematography. In fact, as with many of the best sequences of New Hollywood filmmaking, the design is practically invisible. However, keeping in mind that Platt suggested excising the script's domestic scenes, conceived of the diamond as the film's world, and built the confined space of the dugout wherein many of the film's emotional revelations occur, it becomes clear how her work allows for this climactic moment. The ballpark is a home, but a flawed home, bruised and mangled. The dugout, its unlikely hearth, the repository of this team's hopes, failures, disappointments, and, in this scene, heartbreak. Narratively speaking, the sequence prepares the audience for the Bears' failure to win the championship. Emotionally speaking, though, this is the crux of the movie, like many of the realistic films of New Hollywood, a cynical and sad puncture of American hope and sentimentality: there will be no championship, no reunited family, no happy ending. The production design in *Bears* may be unobtrusive, but it is also a vital component of the authorship of this deceptively complicated film.

Conclusion

Like many of her contemporary production designers—including Tavoularis and Sylbert—Platt recognized design not only as an extension of character and narrative but also as a motivator of them, a dialogic strategy in which all components of production complement each other. As a result, her work grounds her films in a realism so authentic that the hijinks of *Bears* or *What's Up, Doc?* are as equally at home as the stark existentialism of *Picture Show*. Her work deepens and extends her films' meanings. Consequently, the mise-en-scéne becomes a part of the narrative. Thus, returning to the discussion of auteurism that opened this chapter, it becomes clear that many of the production designers of New Hollywood contribute not only to their films' visual style but also to their thematic development, in which case, Platt, like many of her contemporaries, must be considered one of the authors of her films.

However, at least in terms of the scholarly and critical discourse on the era, such consideration has not been forthcoming. The auteur paradigm is so stringent in its celebration of directors that very few of the great practitioners of the 1970s have received scholarly analysis, let alone celebration.[37] Furthermore, historically the role of director has been so restricted to men that even when women do make dramatic creative contributions to Hollywood, they are marginalized or ignored. Statistics of women filmmakers in production or celebrated by awards continue to illustrate this clearly. For example, film fans around the world were excited in 2018 when Netflix acquired the rights to stream Orson Welles's final film, *The Other Side of the Wind*. There was much celebration about his devotion to the project over the years, as well as the dedication of people like Frank Marshall and Peter Bogdanovich who labored diligently to untangle the film's distribution rights. What went unremarked upon, however, with no reference in any of the news stories about the film's release, was Polly Platt's production design on the film within the film. Such developments seem likely to continue. Until scholars reapproach New Hollywood as something more than just a director's cinema, much of the creative labor of production designers and other crew, and especially women like Polly Platt, is destined for continued marginalization.

Notes

1   Like other scholars of the era, I recognize that terminology and dating are contested. Here, I use the term "New Hollywood" dating from 1967 (the release of *Bonnie and Clyde* and *The Graduate*) through 1980, for a variety of well-known reasons.

2   For example, Willis's ability to shoot in the dark and dramatically change the lighting within a scene; Kovács's lens flares and use of natural light; Zsigmond's flashing of film stock.

3   In keeping with past practice as well as the style of other scholars articulating multiple authorship, I eschew the standard formatting of placing directors' names in parentheses after a film title, in favor of production, and sometimes distribution company, and date. See C. Paul Sellors, *Film Authorship: Auteurs and Other Myths* (London: Wallflower, 2010); and Aaron Hunter, *Authoring Hal Ashby: The Myth of the New Hollywood Auteur* (New York: Bloomsbury, 2016).

4   Charles Tashiro, "The Auteur Renaissance, 1968–1980," in *Art Direction and Production Design*, ed. Lucy Fischer (London: I.B. Tauris, 2015), 99.

5   Peter Biskind, *Easy Riders, Raging Bulls* (New York: Touchstone, 1998), 121.

6   Ibid., 121, 131.

7   Geoff King, *New Hollywood Cinema: An Introduction* (London: I.B. Tauris, 2002), 41.

8   Robert Kolker, *A Cinema of Loneliness, Third Edition* (Oxford: Oxford University Press, 2000), 33.

9   Francis E. Stahl's sound design is of particular importance for its blending of realism and expressionism, including the birdsong in this scene, but also throughout the film.

10 Herb A. Lightman, "Raw Cinematic Realism in the Photography of *Bonnie and Clyde*," *American Cinematographer*, August 7, 2017, https://ascmag.com/articles/flashback-bonnie-and-clyde.

11 Mark Harris, *Pictures at a Revolution: Five Movies and the Birth of the New Hollywood* (New York: Penguin, 2008), 253.

12 Lightman, "Raw Cinematic Realism in the Photography of *Bonnie and Clyde*."

13 By all accounts, Guffey was miserable on-set and at one point quit the film for a few days. In the end, his work on the film earned him his second Academy Award. See Harris, *Pictures at a Revolution*, 253–4 and Biskind, *Easy Riders, Raging Bulls*, 48.

14 Harris, *Pictures at a Revolution*, 253.

15 Lawrence Webb, "The Auteur Renaissance, 1968–1979," in *Hollywood on Location: An Industry History*, ed. Joshua Gleich and Lawrence Webb (New Brunswick, NJ: Rutgers University Press, 2019), 124. Webb details the various historical, industrial, and technological factors that led to widespread location

shooting and the cultural conditions that made such on-screen representations desirable.

16 Fionnuala Hannigan, *Filmcraft: Production Design* (Lewes: Ilex, 2016), 184.

17 Vincent LoBrutto, *By Design: Interviews with Film Production Designers* (Westport, CT: Praeger, 1992), 51.

18 Polly Platt, *It Was Worth It* (unpublished memoir, typescript, collection of Antonia and Sashy Bogdanovich, undated), 68, 116.

19 Later in her career she would turn increasingly to screenwriting, including penning the scripts for *Pretty Baby* (Paramount, 1978) and the Academy Award winning short, *Leiberman in Love* (Chanticleer, 1995).

20 Often associated with this is the dramatic fallout of Bogdanovich leaving her for Cybill Shepherd, star of *The Last Picture Show*.

21 Platt first traveled to Europe by ship in the winter of 1946, arriving in early 1947, and during 1947–8 her father served as a judge at Dachau. She returned home in the summer of 1948 with her mother to attend to her ill grandmother and then returned to Germany. Later that year, the entire family returned to the United States. In 1949, the family moved to Bremerhaven, Germany, then later to Paris and then Orleans, in France. They returned to the United States for good in 1953. Much of the early portion of Platt's memoire, *It Was Worth It*, describes these travels and postings.

22 Platt, *It Was Worth It*, 17. Platt also recalls visiting the camps at Dachau in 1948, with her father telling her: "I don't want you to forget this because someday somebody will tell you that this never happened" (22).

23 Ibid., 27.

24 Ibid., 48.

25 Ibid., 57.

26 Ibid., 59.

27 In her historiographical account of how Platt's many contributions to 1970s Hollywood cinema have been overlooked, Samantha Herndon argues, "Platt had the skillset to be a director but the fact that she was unable to fulfil this particular goal does not mean that she was any less of a filmmaker." See Herndon, "Designer, Collaborator, Producer: What Polly Platt's Career Reveals about Gender and Authorship in New Hollywood," in *Women and New Hollywood*, ed. Aaron Hunter and Martha Shearer (New Brunswick, NJ: Rutgers University Press, forthcoming).

28 Platt, *It Was Worth It*, 130.

29 Polly Platt to Boris Karloff, Box 18, Bogdanovich mss., Lilly Library, Indiana University, undated.

30 Platt suggested San Francisco as opposed to early possibilities New York or Chicago because it would accentuate New Yorker Streisand as a "fish out of water."

Platt, *It Was Worth It*, 191–2. Peter Bogdanovich, "Director's Commentary," *What's Up, Doc?*, DVD, directed by Peter Bogdanovich (Warner Bros., [1972] 2010).

31 LoBrutto, *By Design*, 160.

32 Platt, *It Was Worth It*, 219.

33 Marshall assisted Platt on several of her 1970s films, with and after Bogdanovich, including with location and production design on the film-within-a-film portions of Orson Welles's *The Other Side of the Wind* (Netflix, 2018); Platt, *It Was Worth It*, 178–9; and Josh Karp, *Orson Welles's Last Movie: The Making of* The Other Side of the Wind (New York: St. Martin's Press, 2015), 87.

34 Bill Lancaster, *The Bad News Bears*, Box 54, Folder 37, Paramount Pictures Scripts, Margaret Herrick Library, Los Angeles, undated.

35 LoBrutto, *By Design*, 161. Michael Ritchie claims credit for the idea to cut these scenes. Michael Ritchie, interview by Jeremy Kagan, "Visual History Program," Chapter 1, Director's Guild of America, 2000.

36 LoBrutto, *By Design*, 160–1.

37 The recent archival turn in film scholarship has been shedding light on the ways that directors conceived of as single-author auteurs benefited from close collaboration on a much deeper and more creative level than previously assumed. See, for example: Philip Cowan, "Underexposed: The Neglected Art of the Cinematographer," *Journal of Media Practice* 13, no. 1 (2012): 75–96; R. Colin Tait, "When Marty Met Bobby: Collaborative Authorship in *Mean Streets* and *Taxi Driver*," in *A Companion to Martin Scorsese*, ed. Aaron Baker (Hoboken: Wiley-Blackwell, 2014), 292–311; and *Stanley Kubrick: New Perspectives*, ed. Richard Daniels, Peter Krämer, and Tatjana Llujic (London: Black Dog, 2015).

7

"The Ultimate Fusion of Commerce and Art": Waldo Salt and Screenwriting in the 1970s

Oliver Gruner

Speaking to the trade journal *Variety* in March 1970, screenwriter Waldo Salt reflected on what he termed a "cultural renaissance in films today." The creative freedoms afforded Hollywood filmmakers of recent years had, in Salt's view, laid the foundations for a politically conscious and thematically daring popular cinema—the "ultimate fusion of commerce and art."[1] Having just received an Academy Award nomination for his work on *Midnight Cowboy* (1969), Salt was enjoying something of a "renaissance" himself. Blacklisted in the 1950s for his political affiliations and the author of several critical and commercial failures in the early 1960s, his success with *Midnight Cowboy* signaled a career turnaround. Through the 1970s he would work on high-profile features such as *Serpico* (1973), *The Day of the Locust* (1975), and *Coming Home* (1978). As a screenwriter, as a collaborator, and as a prominent industry figurehead, Salt left an indelible mark on American cinema of this period. However, as is the case with so many screenwriters of the 1970s—an epoch still largely celebrated for its directors—his work is yet to receive sustained academic attention.

This chapter aims to recover Waldo Salt's screenwriting career during the 1970s. Elsewhere, I have explored his rise to prominence in the mid- to late 1960s, up to and including the release of *Midnight Cowboy*.[2] The following analysis, therefore, picks up the narrative in 1970, with an examination of draft scripts, correspondences, trade, and mainstream press reports produced over the next decade. If *Midnight Cowboy* was the film that revived Salt's career fortunes, his work through the 1970s established a strikingly coherent series of political and thematic preoccupations. Indeed, this chapter reveals the ways in which Salt—his screenplays and public persona—became entangled with wider debates on the counterculture and its legacy, nostalgia, and the screenwriter's status within Hollywood.

My analysis contributes to recent scholarship on the American New Wave that has sought to challenge the overwhelming focus on the director as key creative force. Aaron Hunter argues that "perhaps no single factor has influenced the construction of a New Hollywood canon more than the auteur cinema paradigm." Hunter's study of "multiple authorship" in films directed by Hal Ashby argues that a focus on various creative voices allows for "a more nuanced, dialogic analysis" of production.[3] While scrutinizing Salt's work, I am equally interested in placing it within a broader collaborative milieu. The chapter begins with a focus on Salt's career at the turn of the decade. Riding a wave of success on the back of *Midnight Cowboy*, his close affinity with the counterculture and visually and thematically innovative screenplays established him as one of the film industry's most well-known scribes. In this opening section, I explore the development of *The Gang That Couldn't Shoot Straight* (released in 1971, with Salt joining the project in 1969) and *Serpico* (which Salt started writing in November 1972) in terms of their countercultural themes and political content. Part Two considers Salt's career as a response to broader industrial transformations impacting screenwriters in the 1970s.[4] Here, I examine the aforementioned films, as well as *The Day of the Locust* (a project Salt joined in 1970). In screenplays and surrounding media discourse, we see a dialogue between "Old" and "New" Hollywood present throughout *Locust*'s development phase as Salt's biography—his arrival in Hollywood in the 1930s and blacklisting in the 1950s—becomes central to this film's identity.

Waldo Salt: "Oldtimer Youngster"

By the early 1970s, Waldo Salt was enjoying significant prestige in Hollywood. His screenplay for *Midnight Cowboy* had propelled him into the limelight as one of the industry's hottest talents. Produced on a budget of $3.2 million and generating $21 million in domestic rentals, *Cowboy* became the third highest grossing film of its year.[5] It not only won Salt an Oscar for Best Screenplay Adapted from Another Medium but also saw producer Jerome Hellman take home Best

Picture and John Schlesinger Best Director. Stars Jon Voight and Dustin Hoffman were both nominated for Best Actor. This downbeat interrogation of traditional masculine ideals was celebrated for its "progressiveness in cultural, political and aesthetic terms."[6] Everyone involved basked in the film's glory, their reputations burnished, their profiles raised within Hollywood. And everyone, it seemed, was writing about the 55-year-old Waldo Salt as if he were the counterculture incarnate.

"Dear Waldo," began one letter from *Cowboy*'s distributors United Artists, "kee-rist! Or should I say, shee-it! The one time in your young and lovely life you should be here! Where you is?" It continued in a similarly irreverent vein: "I know you don't give a shit, baby, after all the ugly years, but come Oscar time of 1970, I'll eat the 'midnight cowboy's' hat if you are not quite prominent in the voting."[7] Addressing the Academy on the night of his win, Salt—wearing oversize shades and sporting a shaggy haircut—thanked "all the beautiful people who helped to make *Midnight Cowboy* … [and] … all the beautiful people who went to see it." In *New York* magazine, the screenwriter's success was said to have coincided with his discovery of marijuana.[8] A piece in trade paper *Variety* described Salt as an "oldtimer youngster"; another in *Entertainment Weekly* introduced "a genial, hip Ben Franklin with longish hair and wire-rimmed glasses."[9] In the latter, Salt gave a playful reframing of his screenplay for swashbuckler epic *The Flame and the Arrow* (1950). Apparently, this Middle Ages-set action movie was "really supposed to be about a medieval Yippy [sic], an Abby [sic] Hoffman."[10] It has been argued that early films penned by Salt betray his liberal (or left-wing) values: anti-fascism in *The Flame and the Arrow*, and a critique of gender roles in *Rachel and the Stranger* (1948), for example.[11] But one would struggle to find much writing that argues they are precursors to the Yippies. Nonetheless, such rhetoric was encouraged by Salt himself, a writer repositioning himself at the turn of the 1970s. Known, at least until the late 1960s, as a "specialist in swashbucklers"—thanks to his work on films such as *The Flame and the Arrow* and *Ivanhoe* (1952)—a new identity as countercultural maverick was in the making.[12]

Work on his first screenplay credit of the decade, *The Gang That Couldn't Shoot Straight*, was well underway in the early months of 1970. An adaptation of Jimmy Breslin's comic novel of the same name had been in development since early 1969, with British actor and screenwriter Peter Ustinov down to write and direct.[13] However, in October of that year, Salt was approached by the film's producers Irwin Winkler and Robert Chartoff.[14] The novel is ostensibly about internecine conflicts within a mafia "family." The aging patriarch, Anthony Pastrumo (aka Baccala), sees his authority challenged by a young upstart, Kid Sally Palumbo. Attempts to assassinate Baccala become increasingly absurd as the hapless Kid Sally and his associates blunder at every turn. Preliminary notes give an indication of *Gang*'s appeal to Salt at this stage in his career. "Without belaboring the point," he wrote, "there is a credibility gap between Baccala's generation and Kid Sally's gang." And, continuing with a nod toward contemporaneous popular culture, he suggested that "the older generation could be cast with gangster stars of the thirties" and "Kid Sally's gang played by the Beatles."[15]

Salt envisioned *The Gang That Couldn't Shoot Straight* as emblematic of the broader "generation gap" so prominent in media debates of the late 1960s and early 1970s.[16] In the twisted world of *Gang*, Baccala and his older peers stand in for the American "establishment," while Kid Sally and the youngsters serve as an inverted mirror on the counterculture. Draft scripts and notes of 1970 announce that Baccala "is facing what might be called a generation gap in his family." We hear that "the Baccala family, like all establishments, suffers from age and success. Kid Sally's group has youth and greed on their side."[17] Throughout the screenplay completed between March and May 1970, the Kid Sally gang wages its own antiestablishment crusade. As they begin a violent assault on one of Baccala's cronies, Kid Sally calls for someone to turn on the jukebox (music will help drown out his victim's screams). "Something loud. Rock and Roll. The Beatles," he exclaims.[18] Foiled again, the idiotic sidekick chooses one of the Fab Four's less rambunctious numbers, "Let It Be"—hardly a scream-silencer. Inevitably, the attempted murder is as successful as the musical selection. Draft scripts contain references to various political and cultural touchstones of the late 1960s and 1970s (the Vietnam War, youth culture, student protests, Women's Liberation, etc.).[19]

The focus on "youth" certainly aligned with Hollywood's business practices at this time. Hit productions such as *Midnight Cowboy*, as well as *Easy Rider* (budgeted at $375,000 and garnering $19 million in domestic rentals), *Bob & Carol & Ted & Alice* ($2 million, $15 million), *M*A*S*H* ($3 million, $37 million), and *Woodstock* ($600, 000, $16 million) "led studios to speculate wildly in low-budget movies produced *directly* for the youth market."[20] Correspondences between Salt and others involved in the production suggest *M*A*S*H* as a model on which to base *Gang*. Both films, it was suggested, deal with an ensemble cast, loose narrative structure, social critique, and violent themes in an irreverent manner.[21] Throughout 1970—the year that Salt completed at least two drafts of *Gang*—*M*A*S*H* was storming the box-office charts; *Variety* declared that there was a "B.O. Dictatorship By Youth."[22] By 1972, a survey conducted by industry trade body the Motion Pictures Association of America (MPAA) found that "people under 30 accounted for 73 per cent of ticket purchases, while they made up only 39 per cent of the American population over 11."[23]

Salt's next screenplay credit of the decade, *Serpico*, was also replete with themes associated with this demographic. An adaptation of Peter Maas's biography of NYPD detective Frank Serpico, Salt joined the project in November 1972 (though the book was not published until 1973, Salt had access to the proofs). Preliminary notes on the screenplay indicate Salt's interest in Serpico's "hippie" credentials. The detective had, by 1972, become something of a cause célèbre in New York City, thanks to his high-profile role in bringing to light rampant corruption within the police force. As Maas's book makes clear, however, Serpico did not follow the stereotypical cop lifestyle.[24] With his long, shaggy hair, bushy beard, and eccentric, antiestablishment mentality, he was known as a rebel, or "crazy idealist and [Greenwich] Village character," as Salt observed.[25] Relentlessly abiding by a moral code that would see him become a pariah among his NYPD colleagues—willing to stand up to corruption even as it threatens his livelihood and his life—Serpico is conceived as a "quixotic" character, one whose quest for the truth borders on the "absurd."[26]

We might, here, draw connections between *Serpico* and Salt's earlier screenplays. In the mid-1960s Salt had adapted Cervantes's *Don Quixote*, though it never reached the big screen. It has been argued that quixotic themes prevail in his unproduced, hippie-themed screenplay *The Artful Dodger* (1967) and, later, in the Vietnam War drama *Coming Home*.[27] As William Childers argues, "it was in the process of creating his *Don Quixote* that Waldo Salt became the screenwriter who triumphed in the New Hollywood of the late 1960s and 1970s."[28] The "quixotic," as understood by the screenwriter, is not about abstract ideals but about commitment—political, moral, ethical—and a powerful desire to make "a real difference in this world."[29] The character of Don Quixote had, throughout the 1960s, enjoyed a revival as a countercultural hero with shows such as *Man of La Mancha* (1965) drawing parallels between his chivalric quest and the moral crusades undertaken by political movements of the period. Former communists—and, indeed, blacklisted writers like Salt—found in the Spanish setting and "Inquisition" themes a metaphor for their own plight at the hands of the House Un-American Activities Committee in the 1940s and

1950s.[30] In a more general sense, Salt mobilized an interpretation of *Don Quixote* "to support progressive movements in his society such as opposition to the war and the defense of a nonconformist lifestyle."[31]

Particularly notable is the way in which Salt's early drafts of *Serpico* attempt to connect their hero's personal narrative to a broader historical sweep. America's "sixties" experience becomes the mirror image of Frank Serpico's journey from innocence to enlightenment. The first draft begins with an introduction to the greenhorn cop: "Bright-eyed in his new uniform, Frank Serpico stares straight ahead into a life of childhood fantasy." From here, we cut between television footage of the "Police Commissioner" providing a commencement speech for the new group of police graduates and Serpico starting his job (undertaking basic roles like directing traffic, stopping a burglar, even delivering a baby).[32] The year is 1960 and we read of John F. Kennedy at the Democratic National Convention, declaring: "we stand today on the edge of a new frontier—the frontier of the 1960s."[33] A little later on and we join Serpico on a walk past "the folksingers" of Washington Square. He decides to take an apartment in Greenwich Village, thus beginning a new stage of his life as he adopts the eccentric, hipster characteristics that will come to define him throughout the screenplay. It seems apt that just as Serpico is settling into a Bohemian lifestyle, the first draft script suddenly cuts to an announcement of JFK's assassination. We read that "a crowd gathers around a TV set" and Serpico "watches for a moment, totally distracted, his imagination somewhere in Dallas."[34] As was the case with much popular culture of the 1970s and beyond, the Kennedy assassination, here, becomes a symbolic "coming-of-age" for young people of the time; young man or woman grows up in relative ignorance only to have America's glossy veneer ripped away by the events in Dallas.[35]

Serpico's moral crusade intensifies as he immerses himself in countercultural politics and lifestyles. Shortly after meeting a superior who refuses to act on Serpico's allegations, we read of "plainclothesmen ... watching the funeral of Martin Luther King."[36] The death of the civil rights leader, subsequent uprisings across major cities, as well as the assassination of Robert F. Kennedy become, in Salt's screenplays, representative of a broader descent into chaos and disillusionment.[37] As Serpico and his comrade David Durk approach the *New York Times* with their stories, television footage of radical group the Weathermen blowing up a New York apartment offers a symbolic commentary on events violently unraveling.[38] Not long after, Serpico himself is shot in the face. The remainder of the first draft screenplay focuses on the shooting's fallout,

Serpico's recovery and ultimate testimony in front of the Knapp Commission, the body charged with investigating his allegations, in 1971. At the script's conclusion, Serpico informs that he is leaving the police force. "I think what made my mind up," he says, is when "they announced that I was going to be given the department's highest award. The Medal of Honor. Not for my courage in fighting corruption—but because I was stupid enough to have been shot in the face."[39]

By the time Salt completed the first draft, events surrounding Serpico and the Knapp Commission had been playing out on the national news for more than two years. The revelations of a scandal that counted among its participants an ignoble assortment of crooked officers, public officials, gangsters, gamblers, drug dealers, and prostitutes were yet more evidence, in many people's view, of a United States in terminal decline. As Bruce Schulman notes, these sentiments were "everywhere to be heard and seen in the 1970s."[40] Numerous commentators lamented failed institutions—whether they be the US government, the military, the family, or, indeed, the police. In many ways, then, Salt's work on *Serpico* was another contribution to this debate. The screenplay's protagonist, like so many youthful (anti)heroes, had, to paraphrase the strapline for *Easy Rider*, gone looking for America but couldn't find it anywhere. Some of the historical context present in the first draft was ultimately cut from the finished film (discussed further below). But enough of Salt's work remained to suggest that *Serpico* was his first sustained effort to make meaning of the 1960s' impact and legacy. In its countercultural appropriation of the crime genre, the film was very much conceived in line with Hollywood's attempts to court the youth market. However, it is also worth considering the ways in which Salt's screenplays engaged with, and responded to, broader developments within the screenwriting profession throughout the 1970s.

Lost Illusions: Screenwriting in the 1970s

In his book *A History of the Screenplay*, Steven Price argues that, by the late 1960s, writers "were able to write their scripts in more idiosyncratic ways than would have been possible under the old order."[41] The years immediately following the Second World War and, in particular, the Paramount Decrees of 1948 are usually cited as heralding a new era in screenwriting.[42] With the closure of in-house story departments, writers were no longer contracted to a studio,

but would be approached on a film-by-film basis. The "package unit system"—
where creative talent was contracted for one-off projects—ushered in changes
to the ways in which screenplays were created and discussed.[43] Price notes the
importance of the "master-scene script" in Hollywood of the postwar years. This
format functioned as both a canvas upon which to experiment with innovative
subject matter and a promotional document for screenwriters themselves, one
which could entice potential employers. The master-scene script sits somewhere
between the traditional "treatment," a preliminary document that outlined key
scenes, characters, and narrative arcs, and the "shooting script," which was
developed with shot breakdowns and directions for camera angles, ultimately
serving as a final blueprint for production. More detailed than a treatment, less
specific than a shooting script, the master-scene script of the 1960s and 1970s
often contained vivid scene directions, visual metaphors, and literary flourishes.[44]
Salt himself secured the *Midnight Cowboy* job after director John Schlesinger
and producer Jerome Hellman had read his unproduced master-scene scripts
for *Don Quixote* and *The Artful Dodger*. Schlesinger and Hellman praised Salt's
ability to think visually and create interesting concepts through scene directions
(as well as his obvious sympathies for outsiders and countercultural values).[45]

Certainly, drafts for *The Gang That Couldn't Shoot Straight* were packed with
visual ideas and creative scene arrangements. Attention is paid to location details,
interiors, and character attire. In the first draft, an imposing mural "illustrating
the slaughter of French soldiers by the Sicilians in 1282" is visible within the
Baccala estate. It becomes a visual metaphor for the don's own sense of self-
importance and his reverence for Sicily's violent heritage.[46] In the draft of August
1970, this is removed in favor of an alternative image. Now we hear "operatic
overtures" as "six stone busts" come into view, each one a homage to Baccala.[47]
Such pomposity receives further illustration later in the screenplay, when we are
introduced to Baccala's office:

> Baccala enters, flicking on the light to reveal a sea of snake plants, lamps with
> ancient frilled shades, a large wooden desk—religious statues springing to life
> under multi-colored lights—a bank of red imitation candles glowing in front
> of Saint Anthony in the place of honor—directly behind Baccala's desk. Baccala
> removes his hat for Saint Anthony.[48]

From descriptions of clothing—chief hit man "Water Buffalo" is described as
being dressed in a "light blue suit in silver thread"; another mafioso sports "a
vast mohair jacket"—to an almost obsessive focus on the types of shoes worn by

each character, *The Gang* scripts are packed with visual detail.[49] Childers notes that Salt had developed an interest in visual art from a young age: "more than just a hobby, it was part of how he [Salt] was able to visualize film sequences so powerfully."[50]

One also gets the sense that Salt was considering visuals while writing *Serpico*. In the first draft references abound to the presence of a television screen. Everything from JFK's assassination, the Beatles' performance on *The Ed Sullivan Show* to "riots" in major cities is played out on television. In many ways, the ubiquitous television screen invests the film with a "newsworthiness." Late in the first draft, as Serpico and his Attorney Ramsey Clark prepare to speak in court, we are informed that "the hearings will be edited from actual film and tape coverage of the event." And furthermore, "at times we will be in the hall itself, at other times we will be watching on television."[51] Viewing *Serpico* will, therefore, become akin to watching television reports of these national events—a powerful and "authentic" collective experience.

There is also the occasional, more symbolic visual flourish, though, given the intention to create a gritty slice of city life, it is unsurprising that such devices are few and far between. Salt calls for a montage interweaving documentary footage of the corruption scandal and snippets of Serpico's life, as if the detective is now increasingly thrown on the winds of fate, a victim of political circumstance.[52] Subtle references to character behavior provide visual metaphors for broader themes within the film. For example, early scenes in Salt's updated screenplay of March 1973 feature references to Serpico and other police officers "polishing" their shoes and, more generally, smoothing out their appearances. These small additions become representative of the police's attempts to, as it were, put on a good show, a superficial demonstration of professionalism which, as Serpico soon discovers, is little more than a shiny front.[53]

Neither *Gang* nor *Serpico*, however, match *The Day of the Locust* for sheer richness in visual detail. Salt had been involved with the project, an adaptation of Nathanael West's novel of the same name, since 1970, when director and co-collaborator on *Midnight Cowboy* John Schlesinger approached him to write the screenplay.[54] Over the next four years, Salt and Schlesinger worked closely together on the screenplay. In interviews both would emphasize the collaborative relationship that produced this formally and stylistically inventive skewering of the Hollywood "Dream Factory."[55] Notes and correspondences between Salt, Schlesinger, and other creatives make clear that the draft scripts were produced not as blueprints for production but as *invitations to collaborate*.

This is a crucial point to bear in mind regarding so much screenwriting of the 1970s. As Price points out, the master-scene script was a work in progress, a canvas upon which various creatives could stamp their identities.[56] At a time when ideas of the "auteur" were gaining prominence across the US cultural landscape, contributing to the script (and publicly asserting that contribution) was a way of furthering one's career. On the one hand, the burgeoning of renowned writer-directors—figures like Francis Ford Coppola, Woody Allen, and Mel Brooks—helped to facilitate a broader understanding of screenwriters as "creative talents."[57] On the other hand, auteur criticism's standard recourse to the director also "elevated the reputation of the nonwriting director ... effectively devaluing the screenwriter."[58] Miranda Banks has demonstrated the extent to which arguments over possessory credits—that is, to ascribe a film to a single creator "A Film By ..." etc.—raged among the Writers Guild of America and Directors Guild of America throughout the 1970s and beyond.[59]

Discussions of auteurism's impact on screenwriters garnered some coverage in film criticism. Well-known challenges to director-centered analysis were penned by figures such as Pauline Kael and Richard Corliss.[60] In the Winter 1970–1 edition of *Film Comment*, Corliss declared it was time for screenwriters "to be remembered in film history."[61] As Tom Stempel has noted, however, barring the occasional publication, film criticism continued to focus predominantly on the director.[62] Perhaps because of this emphasis on directorial control, one can also note the extent to which screenwriters appeared to absorb some of the ideas associated with auteurism. In a January 1970 interview published in the Writers Guild of America West's *Newsletter*, the screenwriter Michael Kanin announced that "writing in our field is not really a whole profession" and "I would like to see *all* writers ... get off their asses, acquire the necessary technical know-how, and direct their own work."[63] Another article published in *Newsletter* stated that "we should no longer be content to turn our scripts over to the front office and let an army of misfits model a film from our brainchildren."[64] The fact of the matter was that, while screenwriters might well chastise popular auteurism as, at best, an incomplete account of a film's creative development and, at worst, a full blown travesty of criticism, there was no denying its importance for critics at the time.[65]

The Salt–Schlesinger collaboration on *Day of the Locust* was representative of these broader cultural debates, with the screenplay serving as a site of creative tension throughout its development. Story conferences took place before, after, and during each *Day of the Locust* draft. Much of the initial focus was on the central character, Tod Hackett, with a request that Salt draw upon his own experiences in order to put flesh and bones on a protagonist who, it was felt, was underdeveloped.[66] In notes that accompanied a 1973 story conference, Salt reflected on his own background as a young screenwriter in the 1930s. "Why do I have such difficulty remembering—being able to make dramatic use of— my emotional state of mind when I first went to Hollywood?," he pondered.[67] Hackett, who serves as the narrator in West's novel, is, as Joanna E. Rapf puts it, "hardly a thematic center or dominant character."[68] Or, as Salt himself observed, "Tod may be a successful editorial mouthpiece for West but he remains a cipher of a character."[69] And, for all of those involved in the film's early stages, the key to untangling the "cipher" Tod Hackett was Waldo Salt himself. The screenwriter's background in 1930s Hollywood, and blacklisting in the 1950s, became much-discussed aspects of his writing and public persona during *Locust's* production phase.

Waldo Salt joined MGM studios as a junior writer in 1936. In 1938, the same year as he received his first screenplay credit for romantic drama *The Shopworn Angel*, he joined the Communist Party. Historians have discussed his prominent status within the Hollywood Left throughout the 1930s and 1940s.[70] In 1951, after refusing to testify against fellow party members, he was cited for contempt and blacklisted. Thus, while other writers were struggling to build a reputation within the "package unit" production system, Salt, like his fellow blacklistees, was undertaking a very different kind of freelance work. He wrote under a pseudonym for television series such as *The Adventures of Robin Hood* (1955–9) and *The Buccaneers* (1956–7).[71] Not until 1962 did he enjoy another feature film credit (for the historical epic *Taras Bulba*). Throughout the 1970s, trade and mainstream press reports focused on the 1950s as wilderness years, when Hollywood's glossy veneer was peeled back to reveal a dark heart of paranoia, fear, and corruption. Salt's comeback in 1970 as an Oscar-winning screenwriter was celebrated as both a victory for the screenwriter and for antiestablishment voices more generally.[72] His scripts for *Day of the Locust*, *Serpico*, and *Coming Home* are not directly about the Hollywood blacklist. They all, however, are about lost illusions, critiquing superficial media-constructed images (of Hollywood, of the police force, of the military) to reveal a darker reality lurking beneath.

Day of the Locust's first draft (completed in 1971) begins with characteristic elaborateness. We meet the two young protagonists Tod Hackett, a scene painter, and Faye Greener, a wannabe actor, as they rampage through a Hollywood studio backlot. Tod is pursuing Faye on a frenzied dash "across the ages," careening through the set of a "crowded medieval street," King Arthur's court, the "Last Chance Saloon," ancient Greece, and a wealth of other far-flung, exotic locales. The scene's historical grandeur is undercut by references to the production process. We read that "trucks dump sand on a huge papier mache Sphinx" and actors eating "cardboard food" beneath a "cellophane waterfall." A screaming director brings the rampage to an end. "Tod turns back" writes Salt in the scene's colorful denouement, "under a dinosaur skeleton on a battlefield crisscrossed with barbed wire and sandbags—through a jungle of trees writhing with naked roots exposed, limbs bearing arms of pipe, fruit of spikes and swords."[73]

That Salt initially chose to introduce his key characters within this milieu is very much in keeping with his late 1960s and 1970s work as a whole. Joe Buck (Jon Voight) experienced his symbolic "birth" as the "Midnight Cowboy" surrounded by typical western film iconography. In the first draft of *The Gang That Couldn't Shoot Straight*, we are introduced to Kid Sally as he endeavors to imitate the movie mafiosos of classical Hollywood. Just as Joe Buck was tragically enamored with the John Wayne version of masculinity, the hapless gangster attempts to mimic screen legend Richard Widmark's mannerisms in *Kiss of Death* (1947). "All of Kid Sally's adult life," we read, "has been spent perfecting an imitation of [Widmark's character] Tommy Udo."[74] Like Buck and Kid Sally, Tod and Faye are symbolically "created" out of a heap of glossy Hollywood illusion. And, like their cinematic precursors, their lives will become inextricably intertwined with a broader narrative that sees this illusion come crashing down.

After the first draft's lively opening sequence, we cut to a scene of destruction: Tod's first assignment as a scene painter—the design of a shopfront—being taken down by a team of laborers. "Tod watches," the scene directions inform, "suddenly sad to see the shop dismantled and loaded onto a truck leaving only a skeleton wall against a sky backing." As the rest of Tod's work is torn down, the "Hollywoodland" sign comes into view.[75] The scene visually anticipates another key sequence later in the screenplay, when the set for the "Battle of Waterloo" begins to literally fall apart. Scaffolding collapses, paint is dumped on cast and crew, actors are injured—the chaos on set becomes harbinger of a Hollywood and Los Angeles about to go up in flames.[76] Unlike Nathanael West's novel, which avoided political exposition, the *Day of the Locust* screenplay incorporates contemporaneous (1930s) references. From the destruction of Tod's set, the screenplay cuts to a studio street. We are told that the art department where Tod works faces the "sound cutting" department and he can hear "music, sound effects, dialogue, newsreels, documentary voices of Roosevelt, Kaltenborn, Hitler."[77] As the next few pages progress, themes of illusion, decay and international crisis are woven together. Tod has been invited to his boss Claude Estee's swish party in Beverly Hills. Images of decadence are juxtaposed with those of death. At the party, as guests discuss the movies, beauty, sex, and the current political climate, a set of lights suddenly illuminate the swimming pool. Floating within the pool is a dead horse or, at least, a "realistic rubber reproduction." In a bizarre party activity, each of the guests then takes turns interpreting the horse's symbolic import. Some suggest it as an emblem of geopolitical decline, others declare it to be representative of "capitalism." Finally, Claude announces the dead horse to be "Hollywood. A grotesque illusion of reality."[78] This grim icon becomes, in the screenplay, a way of combining 1930s political/historical context, insight into various characters, and a reflection on Hollywood of the period.

Direct allusions to the Spanish Civil War and the run-up to the Second World War abound throughout. In early drafts, Tod announces his plans to fight in Spain when his contract in Hollywood finishes.[79] Given Salt's own background in left-wing causes one might read this addition to Tod's character as very much a case of him drawing on his personal experiences/viewpoints in the 1930s. Interestingly, by January 1972, this aspect of Tod's character had been changed. He now informs his boss Claude Estee that he is "not very political."[80] In many ways, as the script was developed, Tod's political commitment gives way to a greater focus on his psychological state. A personal narrative—a journey from innocence to knowledge, naivety to cynicism—is developed throughout. Small visual ideas, which were added to scripts in the wake of story conferences, serve to emphasize this tale of psychological and spiritual decline. For example, in April 1972, "sprinklers" become a prominent visual motif.[81] As Tom Symmons argues, water and "particularly the perpetual motion of sprinklers" serve throughout the finished film as metaphors for Los Angeles and Hollywood. On the one hand, water droplets glittering in the California sunshine invest scenes with an otherworldly, fantastical sheen; on the other hand, the very presence of sprinklers alludes to the region's "limited natural resources" and becomes another representative of "the artifice of Los Angeles."[82] A letter from Schlesinger to Salt and producer Jerome Hellman directly references sprinklers, suggesting the significance of this visual icon during script development.[83]

A key symbolic image introduced in the first draft, and developed throughout the production stage, is the painting on Tod's bungalow wall, something he works on throughout the narrative. Beginning life as little more than a few sketches and a "rather large but ambiguous phallic symbol," this ever-evolving image ultimately visualizes all the lost illusions, broken dreams, sexual frustrations, and tragedies to befall Tod and, indeed, so many of the people with whom he mixes.[84] Later on, we read that the mural has become an "apocalyptic view of Los Angeles in all its screwball splendor," complete with salacious advertising imagery, orange groves, "oilwells, temples and film studios."[85] The image swells with all the hucksters, salesmen, and corrupt executives with whom Tod becomes entangled in this tale of moral and spiritual decline.[86] References to the chaotic "Battle of Waterloo"—an important incident later in the narrative when a Hollywood set literally falls apart—are added, "clouds of smoke hang over lead soldiers, surrounded by motion picture equipment."[87] After the death and destruction of a sequence at a film premiere at Grauman's Chinese Theater—the film's chaotic denouement—we return one last time to Tod's mural. As houses, signs, shops, and other buildings collapse in flames all that is ultimately left is Tod's artistic representation: "a painting of the burning city left standing within the burning city itself."[88] While this visual icon was somewhat modified as *Locust* traveled from script to screen, it remained an important anchor to which key scenes and dramatic revelations are attached. In *Day of the Locust*'s last climactic sequence, images from the painting are intercut with the carnage at the film premiere and references to international crisis (allusions to Hitler, newspaper cuttings). In this way, Tod's personal narrative reaches a climatic end in an inferno of political, cultural, and industrial upheaval.

Conclusion

Throughout the 1970s, Waldo Salt undertook a careful balancing act. On the one hand, screenplays and publicity articles established him a strong identity as a countercultural maverick, as someone able to think visually and create work that "challenged traditional viewpoints."[89] But at the same time he promoted his screenplays as palimpsests upon which all number of creatives could establish their own ideas. Certainly, *The Gang That Couldn't Shoot Straight* and *Serpico* offer some evidence of this. His screenplays for the former were subject to various reports and suggestions, though to what extent they "improved" the script is debatable (*Gang* was roundly panned and was Salt's least successful credit of the 1970s).[90] With Sidney Lumet taking over *Serpico*'s directorial responsibilities from John G. Avildsen, Salt found himself removed from the project. Another scribe, Norman Wexler, undertook rewrites in the final months. If some of Salt's historical (1960s) references are cut and/or curtailed, the finished film remains a striking exploration of political and cultural issues associated with the era. Salt would share an Oscar nomination with Wexler for this work. With its themes of lost innocence/broken illusions, vivid literary scene descriptions, and political commentary it is easy to read *Day of the Locust* as part of Waldo Salt's oeuvre. However, like his previous collaboration on *Midnight Cowboy*, *Day of the Locust* was the product of a close working relationship between Salt and John Schlesinger.

By the time *Day of the Locust* was playing in cinemas, Salt was already at work on another project. The Vietnam War drama *Coming Home* was produced by long-time collaborator Hellman, starred Jane Fonda, Jon Voight, and Bruce Dern, and was directed by Hal Ashby (after the original director, again John Schlesinger, pulled out). This film synthesized ideas and issues with which Salt had grappled on both *Serpico* and *Day of the Locust*. Like the former it is an attempt to explore the legacy of the 1960s for contemporaneous (in this case late 1970s) America. Like the latter, it provides a coruscating assault on the power of illusions—the glossy, glorified, image of war that sends so many young men off to their deaths. Salt's early notes are packed with political commentary and references to 1960s popular culture (his initial treatment for the film was, in fact, structured around song lyrics by everyone from Bob Dylan to the Rolling Stones).[91] Story conferences indicate the script was once again influenced by various creatives throughout its developmental stage.[92] Furthermore, the screenplay would benefit from the significant contributions of Robert C. Jones, who joined the project when Salt became ill during production. *Coming Home* was Salt's last credited feature film screenplay and won him his second Oscar (shared with Jones and screenwriter Nancy Dowd, who wrote an initial draft and was given a "Story" credit). The Academy Award was both testament to this film's powerful critique of militarism and appropriate recognition for a screenwriter who had, for a decade, ridden the crest of Hollywood's New Wave. A recovery of Salt's career allows us, therefore, to reassess questions of authorship and the important role of screenwriters at this time, reflect on the political issues—past and present—that influenced these productions, move away from a director-centric approach to films of this era, and, indeed, emphasize the importance of close collaboration within the New Wave.

Notes

1 Addison Verrill, "Miscellany: Waldo Salt Fears 'Now' Liberty May Collide with New Reaction," *Variety*, March 25, 1970, 2, 61.

2 Oliver Gruner, "Hippie Superannuated Leprechaun: Waldo Salt, Screenwriting and the Hollywood Renaissance," *Historical Journal of Film, Radio and Television* 39, no. 2 (2019): 251–70.

3 Aaron Hunter, *Authoring Hal Ashby: The Myth of the New Hollywood Auteur* (New York: Bloomsbury, 2016), 42, 164.

4 Miranda J. Banks, *The Writers: A History of American Screenwriters and Their Guild* (New Brunswick, NJ: Rutgers University Press, 2016); Steven Price, *A History of the Screenplay* (Basingstoke: Palgrave Macmillan, 2013), 182–99; Kevin Alexander Boon, "The Auteur Renaissance, 1968–1980," in *Screenwriting*, ed. Andrew Horton and Julian Hoxter (New Brunswick, NJ: Rutgers University Press, 2014), 81–100.

5 Peter Kramer, *The New Hollywood: From Bonnie and Clyde to Star Wars* (London: Wallflower, 2005), 107.

6 Gary Needham, "Hollywood Trade: *Midnight Cowboy* (1969) and Underground Cinema," in *The Hollywood Renaissance: Revisiting American Cinema's Most Celebrated Era*, ed. Peter Krämer and Yannis Tzioumakis (New York: Bloomsbury, 2018), 130.

7 Valerie Douglas to Waldo Salt, June 10, 1969. Contained in the Waldo Salt Papers (WSP), Charles E. Young Research Library, UCLA, Los Angeles. Box 4, Folder 2 (4/2).

8 Catherine Breslin, "The Artful Dodges of a Very Hot Screenwriter," *New York*, April 26, 1971, 52.

9 "Tells College Kids: 'You're All Cop Outs,'" *Variety*, April 8, 1970, 2; Harry Klein, "Waldo Salt," *Entertainment World*, January 23, 1970, 14.

10 Klein, "Waldo," 14.

11 Jeffrey Richards, "The Politics of the Swashbuckler," in *The New Film History: Sources, Methods, Approaches*, ed. James Chapman, Mark Glancy, and Sue Harper (Basingstoke: Palgrave Macmillan, 2007), 123.

12 James Chapman, "*The Adventures of Robin Hood* and the Origins of the Television Swashbuckler," *Media History* 17, no. 3 (2011): 273–87.

13 "Hollywood Cross Cuts," *Variety*, March 19, 1969, 30.

14 "Breslin Novel to MGM," *Variety*, October 1, 1969, 3.

15 Waldo Salt, "Summary—Notes on 'Gang,'" undated, 1. WSP, 3/11.

16 Sharon Monteith, *American Culture in the 1960s* (Edinburgh: Edinburgh University Press, 2008), 88.

17   Waldo Salt, *The Gang That Couldn't Shoot Straight*, March 19–May 25, 1970, 1–2. WSP, 3/11.

18   Ibid., LL-3.

19   See, for example, Salt, *Gang*, March 19–May 25, 1970, U-1.WSP, 3/11; Salt, *The Gang That Couldn't Shoot Straight* (2nd Draft), May 27–June 10, 1970, 29. WSP, 5/2.

20   David Cook, *Lost Illusions: American Cinema in the Shadow of Watergate and Vietnam, 1970–1979* (Berkeley: University of California Press, 2000), 162, 163, 497. For a broader discussion of Hollywood's courting of the youth market, see James Russell and Jim Whalley, *Hollywood and the Baby Boom: A Social History* (New York: Bloomsbury, 2018), 102–21.

21   Russell Thacher to Irvin Winkler and Waldo Salt, July 21, 1970, 1. WSP, 5/4.

22   Quoted in Cook, *Lost Illusions*, 162.

23   Krämer, *New Hollywood*, 59.

24   Peter Maas, *Serpico* (New York: Harper Perennial, 2005).

25   Salt, "Notes on Approach," November 10, 1972, 5. WSP, 6/5.

26   Ibid., 4–5.

27   William Childers, "Surviving the Hollywood Blacklist: Waldo Salt's Adaptation of *Don Quixote*," in *Don Quixote: The Re-accentuation of the World's Greatest Literary Hero*, Kindle Edition, ed. Slav N. Gratchev and Howard Mancing (Lewisburg: Bucknell University Press, 2017).

28   Ibid., loc. 3434.

29   Ibid., loc. 3654.

30   Ibid., loc. 3683.

31   Ibid., loc. 3912.

32   Waldo Salt, *Serpico*, December 15–18, 1972, 1–5. WSP, 6/7.

33   Ibid., 5.

34   Ibid., 10–14.

35   Oliver Gruner, *Screening the Sixties: Hollywood Cinema and the Politics of Memory* (London: Palgrave Macmillan, 2016), 114–16.

36   Salt, *Serpico*, December 15–18, 1972, 26, 78.

37   Ibid., 80, 85.

38   Ibid., 116–17.

39   Ibid., 157.

40   Bruce Shulman, *The Seventies: The Great Shift in American Culture, Society and Politics* (Cambridge, MA: Da Capo, 2002), 48–52.

41   Price, *History*, 189.

42   Tom Stempel, *Framework: A History of Screenwriting in the American Film*, 3rd ed. (New York: Syracuse University Press, 2000), 155–85.

43 David Bordwell, Janet Staiger, and Kristin Thompson, *The Classical Hollywood Cinema: Film Style and Mode of Production to 1960* (London: Routledge, 1985), 330, 332.

44 Price, *History*, 184.

45 Gruner, "Hippie," 253–4.

46 Salt, *Gang*, March 19–May 25, 1970, 1.

47 Salt, *The Gang That Couldn't Shoot Straight*, August 10, 1970, 1. WSP, 5/4.

48 Salt, *Gang*, March 19–May 25, 1970, 11.

49 Ibid., 11, Q1.

50 Childers, "Surviving," loc. 3817.

51 Salt, *Serpico*, December 15–18, 1972, 150.

52 Salt, *Serpico*, December 15–18, 1972.

53 Waldo Salt, *Serpico* (Final Script), March 1973, 5, 7.

54 "Warner Bros. Forging Stronger Ties with Italo Industry's 'Creative Giants'," *Variety*, April 22, 1970, 4; Tom Buckley, "Waldo Salt Recalls *The Day of the Locust*," *New York Times*, December 7, 1973, 32.

55 Michael M. Riley, "'I Both Hate and Love What I Do': An Interview with John Schlesinger," *Literature/Film Quarterly* 6, no. 2 (1978): 111–13; Tom Buckley, "Waldo Salt Recalls *The Day of the Locust*," *New York Times*, December 7, 1973, 32.

56 Price, *History*, 193.

57 Boon, "Auteur," 82.

58 Ibid., 82.

59 Banks, *The Writers*.

60 Pauline Kael, "'Raising Kane I' and 'Raising Kane 2'," *New Yorker*, February 13, 1971 and February 27, 1971, https://www.newyorker.com/magazine/1971/02/27/raising-kane-ii; Richard Corliss, *Talking Pictures: Screenwriters in American Film* (Woodstock: Overlook Press, 1974).

61 Richard Corliss, "The Hollywood Screenwriter," *Film Comment* 6, no. 4 (Winter 1970–1): 7.

62 Tom Stempel, "Filling Up the Glass: A Look at the Historiography of Screenwriting," *Journal of Screenwriting* 5, no. 2 (2014): 183–98.

63 "A Quick Look at Michael Kanin," *Newsletter*, January 1970, 11.

64 "Renaissance Man '70 is Writer-Painter Ben Roberts," *Newsletter,* January 1970, 9.

65 For more on criticism of the period, see Shyon Baumann, *Hollywood Highbrow: From Entertainment to Art* (Princeton, NJ: Princeton University Press, 2008).

66 "*Day of the Locust*—Conference Notes," October 11, 1971, 2.

67 Waldo Salt, "The Central Problem." These are undated, handwritten notes, attached to notes for a story conference dated February 18, 1973. WSP, 9/7.

68 Joanna E. Rapf, "'Human Need' in *The Day of the Locust*: Problems of Adaptation," *Literature Film Quarterly* 9, no. 1 (1981): 22.

69 Waldo Salt, "Conference Notes," October 8, 1971, 4. WSP, 10/4.

70 See, for example, Patrick McGilligan and Paul Buhle, *Tender Comrades: A Backstory of the Hollywood Blacklist* (Minneapolis: University of Minnesota Press, 1997), 35–6, 407; Paul Buhle and Dave Wagner, *Hide in Plain Sight: The Hollywood Blacklistees in Film and Television* (New York: St. Martin's Griffin, 2005).

71 Steve Neale, "Pseudonyms, Sapphire and Salt: 'Un-American' Contributions to Television Costume Adventure Series in the 1950s," *Historical Journal of Film, Radio and Television* 23, no. 3 (2003): 245–57.

72 Buckley, "Waldo," 32; Warga, "Salt Survives," Part 4, 16; Klein, "Waldo Salt," 14.

73 Waldo Salt, *Day of the Locust*, June 26–August 3, 1971, 1–2. WSP, 9/8.

74 Salt, *Gang*, March 19–May 25, 1970, 6.

75 Salt, *Day of the Locust*, June 26–August 3, 1971, 2.

76 Ibid., 86–8.

77 Ibid., 3.

78 Ibid., 7–12.

79 Ibid., 54.

80 Salt, *Day of the Locust*, January 8–16, 1972, 21.

81 Salt, *Day of the Locust*, Revised 3rd Draft, April 1972, 2, 7, 10, 22.

82 Tom Symmons, *The New Hollywood Historical Film* (London: Palgrave Macmillan, 2016), 43–4.

83 John Schlesinger to Waldo Salt and Jerome Hellman, "*Day of the Locust*—Suggested Script Revision," July 25, 1973, 1. WSP 11/3.

84 Salt, *Day of the Locust*, June 26–August 3, 1971, 21.

85 Ibid., 23.

86 Ibid., 40.

87 Ibid., 99.

88 Ibid., 135.

89 Boon, "Auteur," 83.

90 Thacher to Irvin Winkler and Waldo Salt, July 21, 1970, 1.

91 Gruner, *Screening*, 14–16.

92 Peter Krämer, "When 'Hanoi Jane Conquered Hollywood: Jane Fonda's Films and Activism, 1977–81," in *The New Film History*, 111–13.

8

Expanding the Past: Julie Dash and Zora Neale Hurston, African American Women Filmmakers of New Hollywood and Early Cinema

Aimee Dixon Anthony

As much of my work in scholarship addresses the absence of African American women filmmakers in the archives of early film histories, this chapter attempts to recover that history by assessing the parallels between the lack of attention hitherto paid to the contributions and value of the African American female voice of early cinema, to that of the importance of that same demographic in New Hollywood. Race and gender shape this lack of history in a medium that has come to help define American culture. Therefore, this essay helps to flesh out a fuller picture of New Wave cinema as a film movement broader than the white male-centric period of cinematic innovation that it is often heralded to be. Furthermore, this essay, like the many essays on the younger generation of white male filmmakers of the New Wave movement, links the work and inspiration of early filmmakers to work of their descendants.

In early cinema histories, there has been a lack of attention to the film work of African American women filmmakers. Indeed, until the late twentieth century the focus of early cinema solely credited white men with the understanding, appreciation, and use of the nascent technology of motion pictures. Zora Neale Hurston, one of the African American women pioneers of film, was a celebrated writer of the Harlem Renaissance, but her inroads and attempts to penetrate Hollywood have been hidden in the archives until very recently. Similarly, Julie

Dash, an African American filmmaker from the L.A. Rebellion movement, embodied the desire to push back against Hollywood stereotypes in terms of both subject matter and style. Like many of her white female peers such as Barbara Loden and Claudia Weill, Dash had to take the independent route to make her films. Jonathan Kirshner and Jon Lewis state:

> The few women directors working at the time did not benefit from the commercial Hollywood financing that their male counterparts accessed and instead were relegated to indie micro-financing and playoffs at the art house, university film series, and museum showcases.[1]

More importantly for cinematic histories, women's films, like those of the L.A. Rebellion, have often been covered in dust in the film archives and undercelebrated by film historians and critics. But why should we care that African American women filmmakers' stories are undervalued in the film archives? Because the absence in the archives of the voice and labor of African American women filmmakers is a reflection on an unfinished American quilt—a quilt with holes in it of an impactful community of Americans who helped to shape this country in every way: economically, socially, and culturally.

Both Dash and Hurston explored the community of their roots from their unique vantage point as African American women. For these diasporic women artists of color, film offered them an opportunity to expand the past and reclaim their histories. In so doing, as Dudley Andrew aptly states in his analysis of critical approaches to film and history, their "alternative production practices ... point to a cinematic potential that the dominant paradigm denies or suppresses."[2] Hurston, too, saw her work as a means of communicating stories from the perspective of the unarticulated African American, or as she artfully states: "All these words from the seller, but not one from the sold."[3] Their intentions were not to discard what is currently understood regarding the known American stories but, as Ella Shohat and Robert Stam suggest, "seeing everything anew."[4]

With better appreciation for Dash and Hurston's goals in expressing through film the voice of African American women filmmakers as well as suppressed stories and perspectives of African Americans the next question would be: How do their films help to shape our present perspective of America? What do their contributions express about the past, present, and future? What has shaped their unique American voices? And while the African American women filmmakers' voice is not a monolith, why is it that Hurston and Dash created films through an anthropological lens? Through an assessment of the aesthetic and methodological lineages between Hurston and Dash, I will demonstrate how a fuller picture of the history of American cinema can be appreciated and understood. This is an investigation that reveals a richer narrative than the conventional story of a band of young, male maverick filmmakers who seized the reins from the patriarchs who ran the show until the late 1960s. It demonstrates how conceptualizations of Hollywood cinema's transition from "old" to "new" might be expanded to include the daring, experimental filmmakers who have toiled at the margins of the medium throughout its history to tell the stories Hollywood has not otherwise been interested in telling.

Recovered Filmmakers

Much of my work revolves around a theoretical discussion on the absence of a history of African American women in cinema, a history that has been dormant for many decades largely due to the mechanisms of power and knowledge as controlled through cultural hegemony and its by-products. My frustrations around this topic began with, as an African American female filmmaker myself, the discovery of a massive void in the early history of film on African American women behind the camera. The result of my inquiry led to a discovery of more writing and materials on Black women in early cinema who worked behind the scenes of filmmaking, despite a lack of scholarship. Some of these women are more well-known, like entrepreneur Madame C. J. Walker, considered by many to be the first Black millionaire through her enterprise of Black women's hair care products; Eslanda Goode Robeson, manager and wife of famed Renaissance man, Paul Robeson; and Drusilla Dunjee Houston of Oklahoma who, known for the first historical written account of the ancient Ethiopians, wrote a screenplay between 1902 and 1905 that constitutes a refutation of Thomas Dixon's *The Leopard's Spots* (1902) and/or *The Clansman* (1905).

Dixon was the author and inspiration for D. W. Griffith's well-known and infamous film *The Birth of a Nation* (1915) based on Dixon's second book, *The Clansman: An Historical Romance of the Ku Klux Klan* (1905). It was once my belief that most writing on African American women in film was about contemporary filmmakers as late in film's history as Julie Dash, whose first feature-length film production, *Daughters of the Dust* (1992), was still touted as the first feature-length film by an African American woman with a theatrical release.[5] Indeed, in contemporary times, there remains an emphasis in modern film history on male (predominantly white) filmmakers and their continued influence on contemporary cinema. Again, a void in history has been recognized. As the white male filmmakers of the old Hollywood were canonized as *auteurs* following Andrew Sarris's publication of "Notes on the Auteur Theory in 1962," the "New Wave" figures like Steven Spielberg, Martin Scorsese, Peter Bogdanovich, Francis Ford Coppola, and George Lucas (among others) were heralded as the important artists of The American New Wave. Their significance has been entrenched by the scholarly and popular preoccupation with their work to the extent that, in the twenty-first century, Hollywood's Academy, as reflected in #OscarsSoWhite in 2015 and repeated for the almost all-white nominations in 2020,[6] continues to determine that the "best" and "most important" works of an era are the films made by predominantly white men.

I believe I overestimated the acknowledgment given to modern-day women filmmakers like Dash in comparison to her white male counterparts. I, therefore, had to reconsider my earlier thoughts about the depth of scholarship on women in cinema as late as the end of the twentieth century. As such, I have garnered a new perspective on undervalued cinemas in the modern period of filmmaking, specifically, women in the era of New Hollywood. I am calling it the "era of New Hollywood" because I am, in part, arguing that the lack of focus or consideration for the importance of the work of women filmmakers, and in particular African Americans, is because of the subject of their films, not just because of their identity as women and women of color. In particular, L.A. Rebellion's Julie Dash can be compared to the early cinema pioneer Zora Neale Hurston: two women of accomplishment whose work explored life through an anthropological lens. Each focused on the quotidian qualities of the African American experience highlighting diversity within Black American culture. Their films depart entirely from the conventional models that characterized Hollywoods old and new, and thus have been largely written out of history.

If, as the story goes, "New" Hollywood offered more realistic engagement with political issues told through the stories of mostly young, rebellious men than an "Old" Hollywood which, after a long period of exceptional success in its "classical" iteration, had fallen into social irrelevance, where do Hurston and Dash fit in? These Black women, of very different eras, observed and explored communities ignored by mainstream histories and mainstream cinema. While the work of Hurston is literally anthropological, Dash's signature approach to the interrogation of the underrepresented Black world suggests her desire to almost scientifically study her culture despite the expectations of the Hollywood model. It is therefore fitting that Dash's seminal film is called *Daughters of the DUST*, as I have come to see my role as a film studies scholar as one who brushes off the "dust" from forgotten or ignored Black women in American film.

Recovered *Her*-stories

In comparing Julie Dash's oeuvre with the films of Zora Neale Hurston, I see parallels not only around their absence in the archives but also through the focus and themes of their work: recovering histories through an anthropological approach. Through their filmmaking, Dash and Hurston recognized the lack of attention to their *her*-stories. They used the medium of film to expand upon an often white male-centric history of America and acknowledged there were other points of view of the past to be told. As exemplified through Dash in her groundbreaking feature (the first theatrical release by an African American woman), *Daughters of the Dust*, and Hurston through her ethnographic films that studied the African American community of her Floridian hometown, each woman examines the past to recover it.

While the anthropological approach both women filmmakers utilized to make their films is similarly motivated, there are other aspects of their biographies that are important to point out when comparing their oeuvres. It must be recognized that Dash and Hurston lived in two very different eras under very different circumstances. Their films were ethnographic, literally in the case of Hurston and stylistically in the case of Dash. Hurston wanted to record visually an undocumented Black South for her anthropological research, and with the support of funds, a car, and a film camera through her white patron Charlotte Osgood Mason, she was able to make her first motion picture.[7] Dash, through her film work, wanted to capture her ancestral history not just through storytelling but also in energy, pace, and feeling. Moreover, as both women worked outside of Hollywood during periods of mainstream film history's golden eras—the Classical Hollywood of the 1930s into the 1940s and the "New Hollywood" of the late 1960s into the 1980s—they offered a fresh and different voice unfamiliar to the American film industry. Yet, the many decades of separation of time between these two women's filmmaking productions illustrates that not enough attention has been paid to African American women filmmakers of early cinema or of the New Hollywood era.

While "New Wave" Hollywood reflected the film industry's economic need to embrace a fresh, more international, and youth-generated film movement in order to rescue a "failed system,"[8] there were other movements outside of Hollywood afoot. Many new minority cinemas came into being during this period. In reaction to a lack of diversity behind the camera and lack of understanding on the screen of their communities, minority filmmakers, like their ancestors of the early cinema,[9] decided to tell their own stories outside the studio system through what had become a dominant mass cultural medium. David E. James sums up the motivation behind new independent minority cinemas:

> Realizing that the stereotypes of the dominant cinema had been complicit in their oppression, they conversely found their own filmmaking—cinemas of, for, and by themselves—to be necessary in the reclamation or construction of their identity.[10]

Moreover, beyond African American filmmakers' need to create films so they could tell stories of their own histories, Hollywood did not embrace African Americans as filmmakers. More than just an "old boy's network," Hollywood was an old white boy's network. The struggling American studio system forced to embrace new talent behind the camera did not use this opportunity to open its doors to a more diverse group of filmmakers. African American filmmakers had no choice but to be "independent" and industrious in their approaches to filmmaking.

The L.A. Rebellion

In the late 1960s, as the violence of Vietnam, the civil rights movements, and neighborhood riots like the Watts Uprising escalated tensions in America, UCLA was pushed to recruit more minority students and programming to explore these communities.[11] One result of this demand was UCLA's establishment of the Ethno-Communications Program that ran from the late 1960s to the mid-1980s (a period that aligns with the New Wave and New Hollywood periods). One of the most important cinematic movements of the time was the "L.A. Rebellion." Responding to Hollywood's unflattering attempts to make films about African Americans, the L.A. Rebellion group of filmmakers "strive[d] to perform the revolutionary act of humanizing Black people on screen."[12] Out of these decades came films produced by people of color about people of color. Led by professors Elyseo Taylor and Teshome Gabriel, an emphasis of these filmmakers was to create a new Black cinema that was political and inspired by their own community concerns.[13] Like their white male counterpart filmmakers identified as the "Film School Generation," their approach to filmmaking was significantly influenced by the work of the Italian Neorealists and the French New Wave. But, more importantly, the L.A. Rebellion filmmakers connected with the politically conscious approach of Third Cinema filmmakers like Tomas Gutiérrez Alea and Sara Gomez of Cuba, African filmmakers Ousmane Sembène from Senegal and Souleymane Cissé from Mali, and Brazilian filmmaker Glauber Rocha, to name just a few. There was, as Clyde Taylor, who created the moniker L.A. Rebellion, has described, a "revolutionary intensity"[14] to the work of the Black filmmakers from UCLA unlike other films out of America. They saw in these other cinemas of color voices that resonated with them in that they "provided a model of activist film as a medium that can bring about meaningful change in the minds and lives of its audiences."[15] Michael Chanan, in his analysis of Gabriel's writings on the Third World and Third Cinema, considers Gabriel's perspective as a film studies professor at UCLA at a time when there was an awakening within the United States to global issues.[16] As in the case of the Black film students that Gabriel taught at UCLA in the 1970s, Allyson Nadia Field, Jan-Christopher Horak, and Jacqueline Stewart discuss how Gabriel's philosophies influenced the work of the UCLA film students, and by doing so helped them to consider their films, with a focus on local issues of oppression, as part of a larger international struggle.[17] In the only edited collection on the movement, Field, Horak, and Stewart describe how

> L.A. Rebellion reflects the assemblage of these artists at a particular, politically charged place and time in which they attempted to speak truth to power—to address institutional racism manifested at UCLA and in the dominant film industry headquartered in Los Angeles.[18]

Within this group of Black UCLA filmmakers, there were many women. They include O. Funmilayo Makarah, Alile Sharon Larkin, Stormé Brightsweet, Melvonna Ballenger, Zeinabu Irene Davis, Barbara McCullough, Carroll Parrott Blue, Jacqueline Frazier, Gay Abel-Bey, and Shirikiana Aina. Among these women filmmakers, one stood out: Julie Dash.

Julie Dash's Oeuvre

Interviewed by Maori Karmael Holmes in 2016, when Dash was asked about her career and her interest in anthropology or folklore, she responded: "Yes. I think that if I weren't a filmmaker, I probably would have been an anthropologist with a focus on mythology or folklore."[19]

Born in Queens, New York, Dash studied film at several institutions both in New York City and Los Angeles, including the American Film Institute (AFI), before enrolling in UCLA's Ethno-Communications Program where she graduated in 1985. Dash immediately recognized a difference in her film education experiences, feeling more comfortable in the UCLA program where she worked with film students from both her ethnic and socioeconomic background, and international students from the African diaspora, versus the AFI where she felt out of place as a lone Black female.[20] Initially, Dash considered documentary filmmaking, but recognized a need for stories about women of color. Dash described her mission as a filmmaker to redefine how women of the African diaspora are seen in historical drama.[21] As such, she began to adapt films based on the writings of Black women authors like Alice Walker, whose short story became her short film, *The Diary of an African Nun* (1977), and musicians like Nina Simone who inspired her short film *Four Women* (1978).

Perhaps the most revealing of her desired message as a filmmaker was her short film *Illusions* (1982). Set during the Second World War, the film's main character, played by Lonette McKee, passes for white while she works in Hollywood at a major studio. During the course of the film McKee's character is challenged to tell the truth as she witnesses an African American woman dubbing the voice of a white actress. The film makes a statement not only because of Dash's decision to tell the story from the point of view of a main character who is a Black female, but it also directly critiques a history of Hollywood that has essentially left out images of positive Blackness. But *Illusions*, as Patricia Mellencamp aptly points out in her article "Making History: Julie Dash," through its powerful storyline also speaks to the cinematic apparatus as a manipulative tool to control images heard and seen in film. Further, Mellencamp suggests the film critiques the concept of American democracy for all Americans as the story is set during the Second World War. Overall, Dash's work, described by Mellencamp as "speculative fiction," shows the value of history by nurturing history, not diminishing it.[22]

Of Dash's oeuvre, the most recognized and lauded is *Daughters of the Dust*. It was in 1975 that Dash began to develop this story as a feature-length narrative about her father's heritage as a descendant of the Gullah peoples from an island off the southeastern United States. In her attempts to find funding for the project, Dash was turned down by the Hollywood studios. She described the experience as follows: "Mostly white men telling me, an African American woman, what my people wanted to see … deciding what we should be allowed to see."[23] Eventually she received support from PBS American Playhouse and the Corporation for Public Broadcasting with $800,000 toward funding.

The film, set in 1902, tells the story of the Peazant family who lived on the Gullah island off the coast of South Carolina and, devoid of the confines of white patriarchy and directed racism, survived on their own devices, values, and culture. The film is visually elegant and revisionist in its tone and style. Mellencamp describes the film as "striking portraits, the faces of beautiful African American women of all ages."[24] She further writes: "This is history as becoming, where the photographs are brought to life, made to speak, and surrounded by context."[25] Author and activist bell hooks describes Dash's film as "cultural appreciation" versus "cultural appropriation."[26] Dash in an interview with journalist George Alexander describes this inspiration:

> We wanted to do an authentic African American film that was truly a foreign film
> to the eyes of Americans because it was so not like Hollywood in terms of the
> story structure. It was very African in the way the story is revealed and unfolds
> slowly, like the way an African griot would tell a story and recount tales.[27]

And while *Daughters of the Dust* received great acclaim within arthouse circles, Dash never created another theatrically released feature-length film. She has made music videos, television and cable films, short documentaries, and recently directed episodes of shows like *Queen Sugar*[28] (an Ava DuVernay production on Oprah Winfrey's OWN channel). Fittingly, over the past decade, Dash has continued to develop a feature-length documentary film on the cultural anthropologist Vertamae Smart-Grosvenor, who helped Dash to research the Gullah culture for her film *Daughters of the Dust*. Again, Dash continues to demonstrate a desire to uncover an African American past and honor its richness and diversity.

I feel it important to point out that, most recently, *Daughters of the Dust* inspired musical icon Beyoncé in the production of her visual album *Lemonade* (2016).[29] In Beyoncé's goal to raise up the beauty of female Blackness, her film demonstrated what Dash called the "continuum" and cross-referencing of culture, which was a big component of the work of the L.A. Rebellion filmmakers. By establishing continuity, there also is an establishment of history of Black stories and Black lives.

African American Women in Early Cinema

In the early part of this century, film scholars focused much attention on the earliest histories of African American men in the film industry. They included William Foster of Chicago, the Johnson brothers, Noble and George, and Oscar Micheaux. They were considered "the most prolific and important African-American independent filmmakers in the first half of the twentieth century."[30] Similarly, scholarship is rich in the history of white women in the early history of film. In fact, women played a prominent role in the early film industry. Interviewed for an article on her work, film scholar Jane Gaines stated that "Between 1916 and 1923, women in the motion picture industry were more powerful than in any other business in America; in 1923, more women than men had their own independent production companies."[31] But, as the industry began to grow, even white women lost their power. As Gaines states,

> Could she have a husband and also run a film company? … It was a question that, like the films themselves, had a brief shelf life. In 1916, no one knew the outcome of the drama. But by 1925, the film industry had been thoroughly masculinized, and she was sent home.[32]

In large part, female filmmakers were sent home because the motion picture industry became more powerful and more lucrative. Wall Street was now involved as what motivated the studio heads shifted from "cultural legitimacy" where women were considered the model of morality to "financial legitimacy" where men were considered the ideal business*men*.[33] The studio system adopted an assembly-line model and converted into a vertically integrated business; as such, women's roles were marginalized, and the power behind the camera became gendered.

This masculinization, when married with the racialization of the industry, worked double-fold against African American women. Thomas Cripps in *Fade to Black: the Negro in American Film, 1900–1942* speaks to the dilemma for African Americans in Hollywood in the early days of cinema: "the only film role for African-Americans was to serve powerful whites and to act as models for screen characters. The resulting dependent class of blacks was never able to deal with the studios as equals. Blacks found they could not compete in this world."[34]

The Harlem Renaissance and Zora Neale Hurston

The L.A. Rebellion had its antecedents in an earlier period of African American filmmaking. One of its most significant periods was at the turn of the twentieth century. Like the tumultuous period from the late 1960s to 1980s when the L.A. Rebellion filmmakers created films motivated by "a particular, politically charged place and time in which they attempted to speak truth to power,"[35] the early twentieth century was an especially challenging time for African Americans. As W. E. B. DuBois stated, "for the problem of the Twentieth Century is the problem of the color line."[36] With the landmark decision of *Plessy v. Ferguson* in 1896— only a year after the Lumière brothers displayed their invention of the motion picture camera in France,[37] African Americans in the South were subjected to segregation and an (un)equal existence that affected their legal rights, social customs, and essentially shackled them in all aspects.[38]

African Americans, freed from slavery only decades before, eager to participate in the American dream, examined their circumstances and decided that in order to be accepted into white society, they needed to "uplift" their race.[39] "The New Negro"[40] was, in fact, a cultural renewal of African Americans symbolized in large part by a period in American history called the "Negro Renaissance" or more commonly referred to as "The Harlem Renaissance" for, as one of its artists, Langston Hughes states in his memoir: "Harlem was like a great magnet for the Negro intellectual, pulling him from everywhere. Or perhaps the magnet was New York—but once in New York, he had to live in Harlem."[41]

As the artistic ancestors of the L.A. Rebellion, the artists of the Harlem Renaissance were inspired to tell stories of their Black histories from a stronger understanding and appreciation of their roots that were encouraged by "recent European discoveries and appreciation of African culture and civilization."[42] Set in the 1920s, between the First World War and the stock market crash of 1929, one of the Harlem Renaissance's most illustrious figures was Zora Neale Hurston. Known as a core member of writers that were a part of this artistic and cultural movement, Hurston's interactions with influential people from both Black and white communities afforded her a broader understanding of opportunities in the world to push her creative talents and to discover the power of the medium of film.

Born January 7, 1891, in Notasulga, Alabama, but moving as a child to Eatonville, Florida, Zora Neale Hurston was one of the earliest Black female filmmakers.[43] While this side of her life has become, in the past few decades, a subject of great interest in film studies circles, Hurston is best known for her writings. Prolific, especially for a Black woman of her time period, she wrote over seven books and over one hundred short stories, plays, articles, and essays.[44] Best known for her two novels, *Their Eyes Were Watching God* (1937) and *Moses, Man of the Mountain* (1939), acclaimed author Alice Walker once described Hurston as "a genius of the South."[45] As a member of the Harlem Renaissance along with Langston Hughes, Claude McKay, Alaine Locke, and James Weldon Johnson, Hurston had the luxury of enjoying the company of other Black artists whose work spoke about the Black community and culture in a similar fashion to the L.A. Rebellion—a world characterized by what Babacar M'Baye calls "resistance against white racial and patriarchal dominance,"[46] a world that was far removed from the images portrayed by the while male dominance of Hollywood (and New Hollywood).

While Hurston became recognized for her literature, her education was deeply grounded in anthropology, specifically cultural ethnography. Studying at Columbia University under the renowned anthropologist Dr. Franz Boas, Hurston was encouraged by her professor to go back home and study the folklore of African Americans in the deep south of Florida. Eatonville, like the Gullah island of Dash's ancestral past, was an all-Black community where her father held a high presence as both minister and mayor. As is evidenced in her writing, she, like Dash, was deeply personal in her work that was largely inspired by her roots. Hurston's engagement with film began with her ethnographic studies. Not only is their extant film footage of Hurston's research now a part of the collection of the Library of Congress, but it is considered one of the earliest surviving motion pictures by an African American woman.

Hurston was groundbreaking as an anthropologist as well. She became the first African American woman anthropologist to study African Americans.[47] Hurston wrote in her book *Mules and Men* (1935) that she "prowled about the countryside, living in turpentine camps, railroad camps, a phosphate mining village. Everywhere she went, she cajoled people into telling her all sorts of tales, 'big old lies,' a townsman called them."[48] Hurston's work was funded by a white patron, Charlotte Osgood Mason, also the benefactor for some of Harlem's most gifted writers, artists, and musicians. Osgood supplied her a salary of two hundred dollars a month for a year, an automobile, and a motion picture camera.[49] Osgood was also an amateur anthropologist but given her health issues, could not do field work herself. Mason saw in Hurston an opportunity to stay active in the field. She required Hurston to sign a contract that obligated her to turn over all of her fieldwork as Osgood retained exclusive rights. But Hurston cleverly gathered some material for herself.[50] Even in this milieu, white power and capital trump the talent and labor of the undervalued African American Hurston.

While Hurston's film footage is scientific in nature, I argue in studying her work the nature of the film suggests the presence of a director as the action seems more staged than not.[51] In fact, Boas encouraged Hurston to focus on "manner rather than matter, style rather than substance."[52] Other footage of Hurston's ethnographic film work, a part of the "Margaret Mead Film Collection" at the Library of Congress,

> suggest a narrative: each take of the film shows action and space. The subjects
> of the films move about the frame purposefully, and it is suggested, through
> title cards [that are difficult to read] that Hurston did direct the actions of her
> subjects more than not.[53]

In spite of Osgood, who was concerned about Hurston's use of the footage for commercial purposes, writings by Hurston speak to her longing to become a part of the motion picture business. While one argument for why Hurston became curious about Hollywood could be her own anthropological desire to document her work in film, another could be her exposure to other artists within the Harlem Renaissance group that explored adapting their work for cinema. But more than likely her desire to transition into writing for the film studios was her witnessing the success of her white female writer peers. Both of her friends Marjorie Kinnan Rawlings and Fannie Hurst broke into Hollywood with the adaptation of their novels into feature films like *The Yearling* (Clarence Brown, 1946) and the two versions of *Imitation of Life* (John M. Stahl, 1934/Douglas Sirk, 1959) respectively.

Hurston's curiosity to make pictures is further supported by letters she wrote about a stint at Paramount Pictures as story consultant. While the work bored her,[54] she did get some buzz from the major studios MGM and Warner Bros. who both seriously considered the adaptation of her novel *Seraph on the*

Sewanee (1948). Ironically, as Hurston desperately wanted commercial success in Hollywood, after her works about the Black life in the South were rejected, she pitched her only novel centered around poor white characters.[55] While the gift of Hurston was to articulate with such vivid acuity the essence and soul of the African American southerner she knew so well, she felt pressured to write about, as she describes them, "white crackers."[56] As she wrote:

> Having been on the writing staff at Paramount for several months, I have a tiny wedge in Hollywood, and I have hopes of breaking that old silly rule about Negroes not writing about white people. In fact, I have a sort of commitment from a producer at RKO that he will help me to do it. I am working on that story now.[57]

Hurston's work encapsulated a style of writing that authentically captured the voice of the people of Florida, specifically the African Americans of her childhood hometown of Eatonville and its environs. Her unapologetic use of vernacular distinguished her from her literary peers. This passion for authenticity and telling stories related to her roots spread into all of her work, including her ethnography. In fact, the film footage that is extant of Hurston's studies of South Florida document a specific community of African Americans and their daily activities. The storyteller, that she was well known to be—is suggested through these notes—perhaps also a desire to direct.

As research by scholar Elizabeth Bingelli indicates, Hurston did pursue a career in Hollywood.[58] Hurston worked as a writer on the lot of Paramount Studios, as well as shopped a screenplay at Warner Bros. And while in Hollywood, she tried to pitch several other story ideas for film production, including a story about Madam Walker, her daughter A'Lelia, and Annie Pope Malone (another Black millionaire who built her business selling Black women's hair care products).[59] A letter that Hurston wrote in responding to Eslanda Goode Robeson indicates some discussion of the adaptation of a screenplay on the life of Paul Robeson to be submitted to Hollywood producers.[60]

Without much success in Hollywood, Hurston continued to write. After years of travel around the country and in the Caribbean for her anthropological studies and for gigs to support her writing career, Hurston moved back home. Sadly, in 1960, she died alone and penniless.

Comparison: Dash and Hurston

Daughters of the Dust in so many ways is a perfect metaphor not only for a discussion on the film work of both Julie Dash and Zora Neale Hurston, but it also is fitting for my scholarship as a whole: a lack of access to capital which, in turn, reflected a disregard for the value of these Black women's stories and histories. The earliest years of the film industry were reflective of its time when racial segregation was commonplace; money was controlled by white men, and the film industry of the United States was run by white men. Therefore, the stories Hollywood made on film reflected an America they knew or imagined. And yet, sixty-plus years later, in the "New Hollywood" not much changed in what types of people managed or made the movies despite the desperate situation the old studio system was in.[61] The white male executives of the fading studios of old passed the baton, and most importantly studio-backed financing, to younger white men who, while inspired by European cinema and its more realist approach to narrative and style, continued to focus on subjects of their own white male-centric histories. Films that represented a female and Black point of view were (and are) underappreciated in Hollywood from its origins through to the period of the "New Wave" in American cinema. And, as I argue, the work of both women—their films, subjects, and style of analyzing specific worlds within African Americana—was often the biggest obstacle to their success. But fortunately, I think both women aspired to make films for greater reasons than material gain. Both were filmmakers as well as anthropologists on a search for the unearthed bones of their culture and their past that had been ignored or undervalued. Dash explored the Gullah peoples as a celebration of their beauty and unique culture by structuring a film like a tableau vivant that allows the viewer to gaze respectfully at the Blackness onscreen. Hurston, who used words to articulate the diversity and strength of the Black community of the South, also understood the value of the medium of film and utilized the camera as a tool to show evidence of this culture.

Therefore, African American women *did* make motion pictures in the early years of film and *did* make films during the New Hollywood period. Despite the challenges of race, gender, capital, or subject matter of their work, many women found agency and created films that reflected a perspective of their own. The "faux universality of Western man, a universality that posited him as the basis of all life, labor and language"[62] merits pushback through the exposure of other voices. Absence is too a construction. As Gloria Gibson, one of the first film scholars to write on the contributions of African American women in early film, eloquently says:

> As archeologists unearth bones, they do not discard them because they don't add up to a complete, intact skeleton. Every fragment, no matter how small, helps reconstruct evolutionary history. And every frame of film, no matter how fragile and incomplete, helps scholars to understand the history of our relationship to culture and ultimately to ourselves.[63]

While Gibson is directly referring to her analysis of early films by pioneer African American filmmakers Zora Neale Hurston and Eloyce King Patrick Gist,[64] her words resonate when speaking of the work of African American women filmmakers and, in particular, the work of Hurston and Dash.

As Barbara Christian argues of African American female writers in "The Race for Theory,"[65] African American women filmmakers are not voiceless, merely shelved. Given that the films of African American women in the early years of film are extant, as exemplified by the work in the Library of Congress on Hurston, it is likely that many other films are filed away, somewhere within the deep corners of archives, with layers of dust to be blown away. Equally so, Dash's work has also been shelved in a compartmentalized space within film history, that of art film or independent cinema. Like many of her contemporaries within the L.A. Rebellion, her work was political in nature—not to be essentialized as a critique of the mainstream American film industry but to be an alternative voice that could and should have broadened it. The focus of the L.A. Rebellion as a whole—ethnographic and political in nature as encouraged by their UCLA educators who embraced their fresh and underrepresented voices of people and women of color—offered an alternative voice to the "New Wave" of Hollywood—and therefore should be a natural part of that celebrated period of film history. Julie Dash exemplified this perspective as did her filmic ancestor Zora Neale Hurston who through her ethnographic studies exemplified a need to expand our understanding of American histories and stories. It is refreshing to know that in this moment of film scholarship we can reexamine the New Wave period of Hollywood and expand its scope to consider the films of Dash and her contemporaries of the L.A. Rebellion. Perhaps by doing so, we will be able to write a more inclusive and expansive history of American cinema and disturb the by now ossified mythology of Hollywoods old and new.

Notes

1   Jonathan Kirshner and Jon Lewis, *When the Movies Mattered: The New Hollywood Revisited* (Ithaca, NY: Cornell University Press, 2019), 8.

2   Dudley Andrew, "Film and History," in *Film Studies: Critical Approaches*, ed. John Hill and Pamela Church Gibson (New York: Oxford University Press, 2000), 182.

3   Zora Neale Hurston, *Barracoon: The Story of the Last "Black Cargo,"* 1st ed. (New York: Amistad, an imprint of HarperCollins, 2018), 6.

4   Ella Shohat, *Unthinking Eurocentrism: Multiculturalism and the Media*, Sightlines (London: Routledge, 1994), 7.

5   Shannon Kelley, "L.A. Rebellion/Filmography/Daughters of the Dust," UCLA Library Film & Television Archive, 2014, https://www.cinema.ucla.edu/la-rebellion/films/daughters-dust, accessed January 3, 2018.

6   Reggie Ugwu, "The Hashtag That Changed the Oscars: An Oral History," *New York Times*, February 6, 2020, https://www.nytimes.com/2020/02/06/movies/oscarssowhite-history.html?smid=em-share, accessed February 9, 2020.

7   Robert E. Hemenway, *Zora Neale Hurston: A Literary Biography*, ed. Illini books (Urbana: University of Illinois Press, 1977), 109.

8   Kirshner and Lewis, *When the Movies Mattered*, 9; Kelley, "L.A. Rebellion/Filmography/Daughters of the Dust," 4.

9   Many of the early African American filmmakers were motivated to make motion pictures and start their own studios after the releases of D. W. Griffith's highly racially charged blockbuster film *The Birth of a Nation* (1915). While there were some African Americans who had established film studios prior to Griffith's celebrated epic, most in the Black community were responding to negative portrayals of their race onscreen by the white-dominated film industry.

10 David E. James, *The Most Typical Avant-Garde: History and Geography of Minor Cinemas in Los Angeles* (Berkeley: University of California Press, 2005), 297.

11 "The Story of L.A. Rebellion," 2014, https://www.cinema.ucla.edu/la-rebellion/story-la-rebellion, accessed January 3, 2018.

12 Allyson Nadia Field, Jan-Christopher Horak, and Jacqueline Najuma Stewart, "Introduction: Emancipating the Image—The L.A. Rebellion of Black Filmmakers," in *L.A. Rebellion: Creating a New Black Cinema* (Oakland: University of California Press, 2015), 1.

13 Kelley, "L.A. Rebellion/Filmography/Daughters of the Dust."

14 Field, Horak, and Stewart, "Introduction: Emancipating the Image—The L.A. Rebellion of Black Filmmakers," 1.

15 Ibid., 3.

16   Michael Chanan, "The Changing Geography of Third Cinema," *Screen* 38, no. 4 (1997): 380.

17   Field, Horak, and Stewart, "Introduction: Emancipating the Image—The L.A. Rebellion of Black Filmmakers," 23.

18   Ibid., 2.

19   Maori Karmael Holmes, "Invisible Scratch Lines: An Interview with Julie Dash," *Film Quarterly* 70, no. 2 (2016): 49–57, https://doi.org/10.1525/fq.2016.70.2.49, accessed January 3, 2018.

20   Ibid., 54.

21   Ibid., 57.

22   Patricia Mellencamp, "Making History: Julie Dash," *Frontiers (Boulder)* 15, no. 1 (1994): 76, https://doi.org/10.2307/3346614, accessed January 10, 2018.

23   Ibid., 86.

24   Ibid., 90.

25   Ibid.

26   Ibid., 94.

27   George Alexander, *Why We Make Movies: Black Filmmakers Talk about the Magic of Cinema*, 1st ed. (New York: Harlem Moon, 2003), 237.

28   Julie Dash, "Yet Do I Marvel," *Queen Sugar* (OWN, October 3, 2017); Julie Dash, "Drums at Dusk," *Queen Sugar* (OWN, October 4, 2017).

29   Beyoncé, *Lemonade. Visual (2016)*, [Explicit version] [Visual album edition], CVD 171126 (New York: Parkwood Entertainment, 2016).

30   Pearl Bowser, *Writing Himself into History: Oscar Micheaux, His Silent Films, and His Audiences* (New Brunswick, NJ: Rutgers University Press, 2000), xvii.

31   Beth Potier, "Radcliffe Fellow Explores Early Female Film Pioneers," *Harvard Gazette*, November 6, 2003, 6 edition, news.harvard.edu.

32   Potier, "Radcliffe Fellow Explores Early Female Film Pioneers."

33   Karen Ward Mahar, *Women Filmmakers in Early Hollywood*, Studies in Industry and Society (Baltimore, MD: Johns Hopkins University Press, 2006), 7.

34   Thomas Cripps, *Slow Fade to Black: The Negro in American Film, 1900–1942* (New York: Oxford University Press, 1993), 90–1.

35   Allyson Nadia Field, *Uplift Cinema: The Emergence of African American Film and the Possibility of Black Modernity* (Durham, NC: Duke University Press, 2015), 2.

36   W. E. B. Du Bois and Brent Hayes Edwards, *The Souls of Black Folk* (Oxford: University Press USA – OSO, 2009), 2.

37   Charles Musser, *History of the American Cinema: The Emergence of Cinema: The American Screen to 1907* (Berkeley: University of California Press, 1990), 91.

38   Henry Louis Gates, *Stony the Road: Reconstruction, White Supremacy, and the Rise of Jim Crow* (New York: Penguin, 2019), 186.

39   Field, Horak, and Stewart, "Introduction," x. "Uplift" was an ideology by African
     Americans at the beginning of the twentieth century, most notably led by
     Booker T. Washington and W. E. B. DuBois, who felt that if they could not fight
     white patriarchal apparatuses of the law, then they could elevate themselves in
     society as individuals as well as "self-sufficiency of the race" through "material
     improvements."

40   Alain Locke, *The New Negro*, 1st Touchstone ed.; Touchstone Books
     (New York: Simon & Schuster, 1997), xxv.

41   Langston Hughes, *The Big Sea* (New York: Hill and Wang, 1993), 240.

42   Ibid.

43   Gibson, "Cinematic Foremothers," 206.

44   Mary E. Lyons, *Sorrow's Kitchen: The Life and Folklore of Zora Neale Hurston*, 1st
     Collier Books ed., Great Achievers (New York: Collier Books, 1993), ix.

45   Alice Walker, "Foreword: Those Who Love Us Never Leave Us alone with Our
     Grief: Reading *Barracoon: The Story of the Last Black Cargo*," in *Barracoon: Story of
     the Last "Black Cargo"* (New York: HarperCollins, 2018), ix.

46   Babacar M'Baye, "African Influences in Atlantic World Culture: Julie Dash's
     Daughters of the Dust," *Literature Compass* 13, no. 5 (2016): 283, https://doi.
     org/10.1111/lic3.12307, accessed January 3, 2018.

47   Aimee Dixon, "The Historiography of Early African-American Women in Film"
     (M.A., New York: Columbia University, 2009), 6.

48   Valerie Boyd, *Wrapped in Rainbows: The Life of Zora Neale Hurston*
     (New York: Scribner, 2003), 280.

49   Hemenway, *Zora Neale Hurston*, 109.

50   Virginia Lynn Moylan, *Zora Neale Hurston's Final Decade* (Gainesville: University
     Press of Florida, 2011), 21–2.

51   Aimee Anthony Dixon, "Early African-American Female Filmmakers," in *Silent
     Women: Pioneers of Cinema* (Twickenham: Supernova Books, 2016), 52.

52   Hemenway, *Zora Neale Hurston*, 91.

53   Dixon, "Early African-American Female Filmmakers," 53.

54   Ibid., 55.

55   Moylan, *Zora Neale Hurston's Final Decade*, 43.

56   Anna Lillios, *Crossing the Creek: The Literary Friendship of Zora Neale Hurston and
     Marjorie Kinnan Rawlings* (Gainesville: University Press of Florida, 2010), 160.

57   Zora Neale Hurston, *Zora Neale Hurston: A Life in Letters*, 1st ed.
     (New York: Doubleday, 2002), 46.

58   Elizabeth Binggeli, "The Unadapted: Warner Bros. Reads Zora Neale Hurston,"
     Cinema Journal 48, no. 3 (2009): 1–15, https://doi.org/10.1353/cj.0.0109.

59   Hurston, *Zora Neale Hurston*, 602–3.

60   Ibid., 99.

61   Kirshner and Lewis, *When the Movies Mattered*, 44.

62   Roderick A. Ferguson, *The Reorder of Things: The University and Its Pedagogies of Minority Difference*, Difference Incorporated (Minneapolis: University of Minnesota Press, 2012), 32.

63   Gloria J. Gibson, *Cinematic Foremothers: Zora Neale Hurston and Eloyce King Patrick Gist* (Bloomington: Indiana University Press, 2016), 196.

64   Ibid., 206.

65   Barbara Christian, "The Race for Theory," *Cultural Critique* 6, no. 6 (1987): 51–63.

9

Lost in the Landscape: The Legacy of Barbara Loden's *Wanda* (1970) on the Contemporary American Independent Female Road Movie

Aimee Mollaghan

The late 1960s and early 1970s proved a fertile period for creativity and innovation in American cinema. Moving film production from the confines of the film studio to the highways and byways of America, a number of now iconic road movies such as *Two-Lane Blacktop* (Monte Hellman, 1971), *Five Easy Pieces* (Bob Rafelson, 1970), *Badlands* (Terence Malick, 1973), *Vanishing Point* (Richard C. Sarafian, 1973), *Scarecrow* (Jerry Schatzberg, 1973), and *Easy Rider* (Dennis Hopper, 1969) were produced, which directly engage with the topographical specificity of the American landscape. This body of work is associated almost exclusively with male directors. Yet, in 1970, Barbara Loden, perhaps better known at the time for her work as an actress and her marriage to director Elia Kazan, wrote and directed her erstwhile road movie *Wanda* (1970). Although *Wanda* was awarded the Critic's Prize at the Venice Film Festival and lauded by European intellectuals such as Marguerite Duras, it enjoyed release at only a single cinema in New York and was subject to some excoriating reviews by American critics such as Pauline Kael, who described it as "such an extremely drab and limited piece of realism that it makes Zola seem like musical comedy."[1] It was arguably for a time written out of the history of American Independent Cinema until its limited rerelease on DVD in 2004. Since then, the film's historical and cultural position within American New Wave cinema has been subject to reassessment by critics and academics such as Richard Brody and Bérénice Reynaud.[2] Moreover, the year 2018 saw a digitally restored version of the film released on DVD by the Criterion collection. This chapter extends this reassessment of the film in two ways. First, to interrogate *Wanda's* rendering of the American landscape and second, to reflect the position of marginalized women within postwar American society. Further to this, it investigates the legacy of Loden's film in the road movies of contemporary female directors such as Kelly Reichardt and Andrea Arnold, exploring the manner in which the landscape in these films serves to represent and scrutinize the aesthetic, existential, and political representation of female figures stranded within the topography of the American landscape.

Context for New Hollywood Road Movies

The road has typically held a fascination within the American psyche, as symbolic of a source of freedom. Although the journey narrative has been woven throughout the history of Hollywood cinema, it arguably became a vital trope during the New Hollywood period. Rather than offering the goal-orientated narratives of road movies made during the studio system, they instead served as loose narrative devices offering metaphors for the contemporary "American experience."[3] David Laderman asserts that most of the New Hollywood road movies fall into two predominant, but often overlapping, categories of the quest road movie or the outlaw road movie. While he traces the lineage of these films back to *Easy Rider* and *Bonnie and Clyde* (Arthur Penn, 1967), he points out that the road movies of the 1970s evolved from these initial 1960s offerings to enshrine a more pessimistic worldview as characters journey through the American landscape on roads to nowhere.[4] Although earlier road movies did not necessarily have specific destinations set out, they arguably enshrined a sense of active determination, excitement, and freedom that seems to dissipate formally and thematically by the 1970s. This was a period marked by disillusionment and malaise with prevailing political and social structures; the war in Vietnam was raging, Richard Nixon's administration was unraveling, and the country was divided over the rise of the civil rights and feminist movements. Rather than simply serving as countercultural critique of American society, these films turn inward, using the journey as a way in which to explore more existential and personal concerns. This is apparent in films such as *Five Easy Pieces*, *Badlands*, *Scarecrow*, and *Vanishing Point*, which are imbued with a deep sense of loneliness and alienation, reflective of the social and political estrangement felt by many Americans during this period.

In *Five Easy Pieces*, for example, protagonist Bobby Dupea (Jack Nicholson) escapes his privileged background to work a succession of menial jobs. He drives north from the oil fields of California to his family home in Washington state with his pregnant working-class girlfriend, Rayette (Karen Black), to reconcile with his father who has had a stroke. When the trip proves unsuccessful, he abandons Rayette, his car, and belongings at a gas station to hitch a ride on a truck traveling north, the opposite direction to that in which he and Rayette are traveling. Bobby's drifting is a metaphor for his inner turmoil, and his frequent violent expressions of anger are a manifestation of his discomfiture in the world. He does not conform to the rarefied milieu of his family, nor does he fit into the domain of the working-class manual laborer. This ambiguity of the ending is characteristic of the road movie of this period. Rather than serving to close the film, the ending demonstrates that we have merely been privy to a snapshot of Bobby's life. He will continue to drift across the country indefinitely.[5]

Wanda can certainly be located within this 1970s shift in the road movie toward the existential. However, I suggest that the rendering of the journey within the American topography in *Wanda* also draws on a European tradition of realism in order to address personal cogitation peculiar to Barbara Loden: the positions of women within the American social and political economy. This is something that is extended by Reichardt and Arnold in the films under consideration here. Inspired by a newspaper article about a woman who passively thanked the judge sentencing her to 20 years in prison for her role as accomplice to a bank robbery, *Wanda* was the only feature film directed by Loden, who died from breast cancer at the age of forty-eight. Wanda, the eponymous protagonist of the film, played by Loden herself, is the estranged wife of a Pennsylvanian coal miner and mother to two small children. She is an acquiescent character who allows her husband to divorce her and gain sole custody of her children. She thanks the factory boss who turns her down for more work. She meanders aimlessly through the scarred industrial American landscape until meeting her lover, the criminal Mr. Dennis (Michael Higgins), who she aids on a crime spree. She countenances him telling her how to dress. When their final robbery goes awry, resulting in the death of Mr. Dennis, she is again left drifting, devoid of goal and destination. Unlike the male protagonists in many of the road movies of the early 1970s, the road in Loden's film does not signal an open road to freedom nor conversely does it solely signal the manifestation of a psychological crisis. Rather, Wanda is imprisoned wandering within the landscape with nowhere to go. She cannot actively choose to drop out like Bobby in *Five Easy Pieces*. Rather, she is passively drifting, unwanted, her place nowhere.

In more recent years, Kelly Reichardt's predominantly female protagonists also find themselves trapped within the confines of a seemingly expansive landscape. Cozy (Lisa Donaldson), the heroine of her 1994 film *River of Grass*, is a housewife who, bored with her suburban existence in Florida, goes on the run with drifter Lee (Larry Fessenden) believing that they have committed a crime. Referred to by Reichardt as "a road movie that never gets on the road,"[6] they end up drifting to a motel. Similarly, Wendy (Michelle Williams), the main character in *Wendy and Lucy* (2008), finds her journey to secure work in Alaska curtailed after her car breaks down and she is trapped in small town Oregon. Further to this, the characters in *Meek's Cutoff*, Reichardt's 2010 articulation of the western, feature three settler families wandering lost on the Oregon trail. Subjectively, we follow the plight of the female characters. More recently, British director Andrea Arnold's 2016 episodic road movie *American Honey* follows Star (Sasha Lane), a teenager who joins a marauding mag crew, crisscrossing the American Midwest to hawk magazine subscriptions.

Landscape as a Mode of Signification

If we approach landscape from the perspective of cultural geography, interrogating the evolution of the form and its cultural contents, we can consider landscapes in a number of ways that are useful for the moving image. Landscape, as a socially constructed concept, implies a physical environment that is composed or manufactured, a shaping of the natural environment, something ideological that potentially informs the manner in which we see or experience the world. Geographers such as James and Nancy Duncan[7] and Denis Cosgrove[8] position landscape as a sociopolitical concept, writing that the history of landscape can only be understood as part of a wider history of economy and society. It has its own implications that represent the way certain classes of people have signified themselves and their world through their imagined relationship with nature, and through which they have underlined and communicated their own social role and that of others with respect to the external environment. As James Duncan asserts, landscape acts as a "signifying system through which a social system is communicated, reproduced, experienced, and explored."[9] If landscape is something that can be fabricated, then it is something that can be subject to multiple readings or interpretations. In a similar fashion, film as a constructed text has the power to fashion cinematic landscapes through the creation of audiovisual narratives imposed on a geographic locale.

This idea that landscape can function as a system of signification and communication has implications for the body of films discussed in this chapter, which in addition to bearing some hallmarks of the psychological and "down-to-earth"[10] realism of the 1970s New Hollywood Cinema road movies also resides within an aesthetic and philosophical tradition of a realist or vérité mode of cinema. Indeed, Richard Brody suggests *Wanda* is closer in tone to the films of John Cassavetes than those associated with New Hollywood cinema.[11] This is something that Raymond Carney also highlights, writing that American filmmakers such as Loden, Elaine May, and Michael Rappaport explore "the vexed transactions between the imagination and the forms of expression available to it."[12] Carney also points out that outside of this American tradition, this work has similarities with those of European filmmakers such as Jean Renoir or Vittorio De Sica who worked within a realist or neo-realist filmmaking tradition.[13]

This mode of filmmaking is tied intimately to the ideological representation of space. In his article "Space, place, spectacle," Andrew Higson asserts that there is quantifiable tension in which the landscape exists in realist filmmaking. Although Higson is specifically referring to the British realist filmmaking tradition of the late 1950s and early 1960s, his reading of the landscape is nonetheless relevant to the positioning of landscapes and construction of female characters within the films examined here. The landscapes in realist films must construct a narrative space in which actions related to the plot can be performed. Furthermore, they must enjoy the iconography of what Higson refers to as *surface realism*, to be read as real or authentic places in order to legitimate the fiction.[14] Thomas Elsaesser highlights something similar in relation to New Hollywood film settings, asserting that the inherent realism of these films is authenticated by the "realized physical presence" of the American landscape.[15]

Loden, Reichardt, and Arnold's films, like many of the New Hollywood films, can certainly be read in terms of their surface realism. Loden made the conscious decision to hire Nicholas Proferes, a director and cinematographer associated with the Direct Cinema movement, to capture the verisimilitude of the Pennsylvanian landscape, blemished by the craters of coal mining and poverty. Consequently, the film enjoys much of the realism of a documentary due to its mode of production. It is shot on 16mm reversal film, a format used extensively by Proferes in his work as a cameraman and editing assistant for documentaries produced by Drew Associates, the independent documentary production company founded by Robert Drew during the 1960s. It appropriates the handheld shooting style of Direct Cinema, utilizing natural light and pushing the film average shot length (ASA) when necessary to lend it a gritty aesthetic associated with a vérité style of documentary filmmaking. Loden eschewed a storyboard and rehearsals, which resulted in a high shooting ratio that Proferes wrestled into shape at the editing table. This style of filmmaking also allowed Loden and Proferes to improvise performances and incorporate unexpected situations and local people they encountered during the shoot, further lending these films an air of realism. This surface realism of both a European and New Hollywood tradition is also apparent across Reichardt and Arnold's body of work.

These films, however, resist Higson's contention that this iconography can potentially be fetishized into what he deems to be the spectacle of the real. It is significant that, unlike many film directors, Loden and Arnold did not grow up in salubrious surroundings. Loden was born to an impoverished family in North Carolina and raised by her grandparents, while Arnold grew up on a council estate in England. Reichardt's parents were police officers in Florida: her father a crime scene investigator, her mother an undercover narcotics agent. There is a distinct humanism inherent to their realism that is not necessarily present in the pessimism of much New Hollywood cinema. One can therefore posit that they also inhabit a tradition of humanist American documentary photography in the manner of Dorothea Lange's Farm Security Administration photographs documenting the migration of displaced agrarian workers across the country during the Great Depression. Rather than uphold the myth of the farmworker as an American hero, Lange's photographs demonstrate the reality and hardship of their lives. Loden seems to have approached the documentation of her figures within the landscape through a similarly humanist lens, referring to Proferes's cinematography in the following terms in a 1971 *New York Times* interview: "Sometimes you see a film, and they make people look ugly, and then [with] another cameraman ... they're human beings, and you don't have the feeling that they're ugly. I guess it's just the soul of the cameraman."[16] If one considers these films as belonging toward the poetic end of the realist spectrum, it is possible to understand that the constructions of landscape in these films are politically engendered. This is perhaps not as overt as the British Social Realist films of Ken Loach or Tony Richardson, but the landscapes in these films provide voices to female characters who do not have voices within society. The central characters in these films are disenfranchised women and often lack the verbosity to express their inner desires and ambitions. The landscapes in these films speak for them.

As Higson points out, a way of transcending the tension inherent in the construction of narrative spaces in realist films is through the sublimation of the landscape into the narrative and by allowing the landscape to become a signifier of character or a metaphor for the state of mind of the protagonists. Rather than using landscape as a material site for the locus of action, these representations allow for an engagement with the aesthetic effects of the geographical landscape as a reflection of the psychological states of the protagonists. Landscape functions metaphorically within the narratives of these films through what Higson refers to as a "geography of the mind,"[17] or what Harper and Rayner call "landscapes of the mind,"[18] psychologizing rather than historicizing the space to allow for the rendering of psychological or emotional concerns. Higson further suggests that the relationship between character and landscape is psychological, positing that "it is not just that the character is *in* the landscape, but that the landscape becomes part of the character."[19]

This is evident in one of the longest shots in *Wanda*. Early in the film, a camera zooms into the grounds of a coal processing plant, settling on a tiny female figure, luminous in her light-colored clothing and headscarf as she slowly winds her way through the expansive gray landscape. The camera slowly pans to follow the woman, later revealed to be Wanda, keeping her centered within the frame as she becomes at times semi-obscured behind piles of coal. The shot, which lasts approximately 90 seconds, intimates Wanda's social and interior position. She is simultaneously of the landscape and yet not of it, her journey dictated and arrested by the shifting coal mounds that constitute her surroundings. In a similar fashion, the characters in *Meek's Cutoff* are frequently positioned as small figures traversing the increasingly burned out Oregon desert, moving forward and yet never progressing; when we meet them, their planned two-week journey to the "Eden" promised by Meek (Bruce Greenwood) has now become a five-week drift through an unmerciful landscape that refuses to help them.

Although more often associated with the idea of *the white man walking*, these female directors draw on a psychogeography of landscape to lend structure and meaning to their work. There has been a certain repurposing of the meaning of psychogeography within the context of the moving image from the way in which the Situationists originally conceived the concept. The Situationist

International, a Marxist left-leaning organization consisting of artists and intellectuals, developed under the de facto leadership of Guy Debord in Paris during the 1950s. Drawing on a long tradition of wandering stretching back to Charles Baudelaire, this was primarily an urban movement. The group became increasingly concerned with the politicization of geography and the psychological effects of the geography of Paris and conceived a number of strategies related to the psychogeography of the city. One of these strategies involves a dérive or drift through the urban landscape. These subconscious drifts, guided by the flow of architecture and geography, became the Situationists' principal technique for exploring the psychogeography of an area in their search for new and authentic experiences. Although more typically associated with an urban milieu, the idea of an allegorical psychogeography has a unique guise when transposed to an American geographical context linked to a female *flâneuse* as opposed to the male Baudelairean *flâneur*, who enjoyed access to urban spaces that wandering women often did not. The notable exception in twentieth-century cinema can be found in Agnès Varda's 1962 film *Cléo de 5 à 7*, in which protagonist Cléo (Corrine Marchand), a well-known actress, wanders through the streets of Paris as she contemplates her own mortality while awaiting the results of medical tests.

Barbara Klinger suggests that New Hollywood road movies from the 1960s offer a cultural and social critique of contemporary American society,[20] and certainly one can assert that many of the New Hollywood road movies from the 1970s serve a comparable function. However, not only do Loden, and more recently Reichardt and Arnold, use the journey as an extended metaphor in order to reveal something about the country and the people who live in it, they like Varda also expressly use it to comment on their female characters. These films do not enjoy the spectacular rendering of the American landscape of *Easy Rider*. They often lack the expansive open roads of *Vanishing Point*, which provide a canvas for its frenetic chase scenes. There are signs of poverty and deprivation scarring the landscapes and people who live in them throughout these films.

Wanda was set and filmed in the Northern Anthracite Region of Pennsylvania, a location known for its deep coal mining, which had, in the wake of the Knox Mine Disaster of 1959, virtually faded away by the mid-1960s, resulting in severe poverty in the area. This is visible as Wanda travels through the landscape of the region. Near the beginning of the film Wanda meets a man called Tommy who is collecting coal with a pail, who she asks for money. We are unsure what their relationship is to each other, but it is obvious that Tommy is also grappling with the vicissitudes of the collapse of the industrial economy. Tommy makes clear that he does not have much but as he informs Wanda, if he had more, he would give her more. Tommy's pleasures in life are simple ones, in the face of economic struggle. Once he has collected one more pail of coal, he will go fishing in the afternoon for a few hours. It will take up his time and he will enjoy himself for a while.

Similarly, when we first meet Star in *American Honey*, she is dumpster diving for food with her half-siblings. Later in the film, Star enters a house in Rapid City while trying to sell her magazine subscriptions to find a family of impoverished young children with a mother lost in a haze of meth, their fridge empty except for bottles of Mountain Dew. Further to this, Reichardt has overtly asserted that *Wendy and Lucy* is a comment on the economic situation in America.[21] In *Wendy and Lucy* we are made continuously aware of the precariousness of Wendy's situation through her constant calculation of money, her shoplifting, her lack of a mobile phone, her collecting of cans by the side of the road, how grateful she is on receiving $6.00 from the Walgreen's security guard she encounters—all the money that he can spare. The guard tells her that there is a dearth of jobs in the town. He doesn't know what people do all day since the collapse of the mill. He despondently tells her that you can't get a job without an address anyway, or a phone: "you can't get an address without an address, you can't get a job without a job—it's all fixed."

In this respect, these films also owe a certain debt to the Situationists. These women function like *flâneuses* enjoying *dérives* through the cinemascape. However, their journeys are not directed by the undulating geography of the film and they do not displace the male wanderer as they have limited capacity for movement. Unlike the male drifter of New Hollywood cinema who has the freedom to pass through the landscape, these women are lost or trapped by unseen boundaries. They have nowhere to go, nor can they effect change on the landscape. Loden, Reichardt, and Arnold share a distinctive aesthetic approach to the rendering of landscapes. While landscapes in film are often deified and positioned as spectacular objects for sublime contemplation through the use of widescreen aspect ratios, Loden, Reichardt, and Arnold's often trembling cameras employ academy ratio that creates a sense of enclosure without walls in the often seemingly limitless environments through which their protagonists move. This means that the landscapes essentially become psychologized subjective points of view of the landscape, producing and imposing meaning at what Higson refers to as "*the level of representation*."[22] The audience is rarely privy to the vastness of the American landscape in these films.

One can posit that landscape painting and photography were never objective experiences through a process of framing. Figures were often used in landscape painting and photography as a reference point to articulate the scale and vastness of a space. This is apparent in *Wanda*, when Wanda is positioned as diminutive against the landscape. It is also apparent in Reichardt's films. In *Wendy and Lucy* for example, there are frequent long shots of Wendy walking out of frame from behind, often outside the focus of the camera. Conversely, although *American Honey*, for example, is an erstwhile road movie, it does not mythologize the American landscape, nor does it conform to P. Adam's Sitney's fundamental modes of emphasizing landscape in film: the long shot, the panoramic sweep, and the moving camera.[23] Films typically employ the long shot to establish the terrain or location of the film, emphasizing human dominance or diminishing the human scale in relation to the landscape. This is something that Arnold rarely does in her films unless it is rooted, however loosely, in the subjective experience of her protagonist.

In *American Honey*, the camera tightly follows Star's subjective experience of the American landscape. When Star and her mag crew stop for a bathroom break, urinating by the Grand Canyon, we are never privy to the spectacle of its immense grandeur, rather the canyon is in shallow focus as the handheld camera moves around to offer us Star's inscrutable experience of it. In *Meek's Cutoff*, the bonnets of the female characters mirror their point of view. They are unable to physically observe the immensity of the landscape through which they move, dependent on a frontier guide lacking in competence, and a Native American guide who does not speak their language. Subjectively, we are with the female characters trying to make sense of hushed conversations that the male characters have at remove from them. There is the idea that the potential of what lies outside the frame is not available to these female characters. Wendy and Wanda are frequently filmed through windows or partially obscured by passing cars. This is in contrast to the manner in which the landscape is experienced by the male protagonists in films such as *Easy Rider*. We watch a montage of Billy, Wyatt, and a hitchhiker cruising through Monument Valley, another of America's mythological landscapes, for over two minutes, while the entirety of song "The Weight" (1968) by The Band plays. The audience is encouraged to pause and indulge in the majesty of the landscape through a series of traveling shots, moving point-of-view and 360-degree panoramic shots, which subsume us into the characters' experience and enjoyment of the landscape. In contrast to the denatured, washed out cinematography of *Wanda*, *Wendy and Lucy*,

River of Grass, and *Meek's Cutoff*,[24] these shots are drenched with rich colors, the landscapes so luminous it dazzles the camera. Klinger points out that there is a sense of reverence to the presentation of the landscape, tying it to a sense of American history.[25]

Ambiguity and Dispossession

Wanda shares much of the ambiguity and pessimism of 1970s New Hollywood films, but this ambivalence and hopelessness also extend to the contemporary films of Reichardt and Arnold. However, rather than simply reflecting an ennui or social malaise, Loden, Reichardt, and Arnold are instead keenly highlighting the disenfranchised position of their female characters. With the exception of Cozy from *River of Grass*, who is provided with the device of a voice-over, we are only offered small snapshots of these female protagonists' lives outside of what we see onscreen. Wanda has no discernible goal or motivation in her drifting. In *Wendy and Lucy*, we understand that Wendy's motivation for driving north from Indiana to Alaska is to earn some money, but we learn little about her background or life through exposition. There is a single telephone call to her sister, which serves to elucidate the precariousness of Wendy's financial situation and loneliness of her life. Wendy's sister is herself struggling financially and, irritated that she would ask, cannot help her.

Like *Wanda* and many of the New Hollywood road movies of the 1970s, these films employ unresolved endings. *Wanda*, recalling the final shot from *Les Quatre Cents Coups* (François Truffaut, 1959), culminates on a freeze-frame. *River of Grass* finishes with a shot of heavy traffic on the highway, the seemingly endless promise of travel down the open road curtailed by a tailback of cars. The ending of *Meek's Cutoff* is comparably obtuse. We are subsumed into protagonist Emily Tetherow's (Michelle Williams) perspective to watch as their Native American guide, a tiny figure in the center of the harsh desert landscape, walks away from the camp as the shot fades to black. *Wendy and Lucy* ends with Wendy jumping onto a moving train without her beloved dog Lucy to travel north, the final shot her view of the passing trees, blanketed by her humming. *American Honey* also ends on an enigmatic note. In the final scene, Star attends a bacchanalian lakeside bonfire with the members of her mag crew. She slips away in the twilight, entering the lake and resurfacing loudly as the music cuts suddenly, like Wanda, Emily, Cozy, and Wendy before her, left to contemplate the reality of her situation. We never find out what happens to these women and they are left to wander indeterminately.

Moreover, these stories are built around the geography of space, spaces in which moral uncertainty is rife. There is an ambiguity to motivations in *Wendy and Lucy*. As in *Wanda*, one is never sure how pure people's intentions, specifically male intentions, are. We do not know whether the garage owner is trying to take advantage of Wendy in his assessment of her car. When Wendy picks up cans from the side of the road, taking them to be recycled at the bottle return alongside the down and out men, we are not certain whether the offer from the male figure in a wheelchair is genuine or not. As there is a long queue, he offers to take the cans for Wendy and find her later to give her the money. In the end, she just gives them to him and leaves. In *Meek's Cutoff*, we like Emily are unsure whether Meek is ignorant and delusional or "just plain evil." In *American Honey*, we are irresolute whether the charismatic Jake (Shia LeBeouf) seduces Star in order to recruit her to the mag crew, as Krystal (Riley Keogh) the leader of the crew asserts, or whether he in fact enjoys a genuine attraction to her. While figures such as the charming, directionless Jake share many characteristics of the alienated New Hollywood male protagonist, Loden, Arnold, and Reichardt do not celebrate these characters or cast them as the main protagonists in their road movies. Rather than concentrate on a male character such as Bobby in *Five Easy Pieces*, these directors shift their focus to the plight of female figures such as the deserted Rayette, who often serve as peripheral characters in New Hollywood road movies. Instead, they present the effects of male ambivalence, malevolence, and selfishness on their female characters.

These women are stuck without identities of their own. They are, however, made active agents in their interaction with the geography only in moments of crisis, which detract from the futility of their daily existence. To paraphrase Loden, Wanda is running away from everything. She doesn't know what she wants but she knows what she doesn't want and she doesn't have the equipment to get out of her problems and her life. Life is a mystery to her and all she can do is drop out and become a passive figure.[26] Wanda is, however, momentarily given agency through her meeting of Mr. Dennis and her involvement in his crime spree. On his death, she is once again left drifting directionless across the landscape. Cozy in *River of Grass* is given impetus through her encounter with Lee and the crime that they think they have committed. In *American Honey*, Star's meeting of Jake in a supermarket leads her to abandon the care of her younger half-siblings; Jake's subsequent "rescue" of her at gunpoint from some middle-aged cowboys precipitates a raw sexual encounter for her, one that affects the very fabric of the film, which seems to shake and shudder in response to Star's experience. On becoming disillusioned with Jake's intentions toward her, she passively takes her place in the mag crew van, continuing to traverse the country, her life no longer an adventure. Wendy is given some purpose and structure to her day when her car breaks down and Lucy her beloved dog is missing but is ultimately forced to leave Lucy behind in a foster home due to a lack of money to support them both. In a slightly different fashion, Emily in *Meek's Cutoff* is given some modicum of agency in crisis through her appropriation of the camp's gun, which serves to bolster her skepticism of Meek's ability as a guide. She has an increased hand in guiding the direction of the trail as the film progresses even if their journey ultimately does not.

An interesting aspect of the wanderer in American cinema is the reliance on the myth of going *west* for a better life that stretches back to the seventeenth century. From this period to the twentieth century, pioneers of European origin began to extend the boundaries of the American frontier as they colonized and shaped the previously wild landscape, ascribing it a narrative of a "wide-open land of unlimited opportunity for the strong, ambitious, self-reliant individual to thrust his way to the top."[27] This frontier mythology is explored and critiqued in *Meek's Cutoff*. Rather than conquering the landscape and "The Great American Desert," the families following the contours of the Oregon trail are at the mercy of their guide and the vicissitudes of the brutal landscape. In the twentieth century, the myth of the west came to be associated with the automobile as an instrument of locomotion. Stretching back to the Dust Bowl Migrations of the Great Depression, predominantly poor white Americans drove west toward California in search of work and prosperity. This was a mass displacement of people facilitated by the car, a provider of both transportation and shelter. Moreover, the Federal Aid Highways Act of 1956 authorized the construction of 41,000 miles of the American Interstate Highway System over a period of 10 years, allowing for faster transcontinental travel and providing some members of American society with increased autonomy for travel. Interestingly, the female protagonists under consideration here are largely not in operational control of moving vehicles, vehicles that would render these highways or trails accessible to them. This is in contrast to New Hollywood road movies such as *Vanishing Point*, *Two-Lane Blacktop*, and *Easy Rider*, which fetishize vehicles, speed, and the open road as symbolic of freedom from the status quo for the male driver. In *Wanda*, Wanda is frequently found walking through the landscape. The only time that she is in control of a car is at the bidding of Mr. Dennis as part of his plan for a bank robbery, when she momentarily gains purpose and direction in her life. Ultimately, she gets stopped by police on her way to the bank to meet her criminal beau. She is delayed in reaching the bank and thus is too late to partake in the robbery, resulting in her fleeing on foot destined to continue her wandering. Wendy's car, her vessel to the utopian space of Alaska,[28] breaks down, stranding her in a dying Oregon town. Star is a migrant in the white van driven by one of the teenage boys in her crew and, as Krystal reminds her, always in danger of being left behind if she does not pull her weight. Each of these female characters is disempowered in their freedom to move through the American landscape. They cannot move to a "mythical" west to improve their lot. They cannot select to travel at leisure or at a time of their choosing.

Conclusion

Although the road movie has traditionally been a notable genre of American cinema, it took on a more pessimistic or existential guise during the late 1960s and early 1970s period of New Hollywood Cinema. Principally associated with male directors, these films afford their male protagonists the autonomy to move through the distinctive American landscape, allowing for an engagement with the idiosyncratic geography of a country stratified and demarcated by vast networks of roads. Further to this, there is an evolution within the genre from an emphasis on quest or outlaw road movies such as *Bonnie and Clyde* and *Easy Rider* in the late 1960s to films such as *Scarecrow* and *Five Easy Pieces*, which provide space for fatalistic comment on the state of contemporary America and more interior ruminations. *Wanda* reconciles both of these aspects of the New Hollywood road movie. It is on a superficial level an outlaw road movie as Wanda hitches herself to a criminal on the run for much of the film, but it also embodies much of the ennui and psychological anxieties of early 1970s releases, marrying them with expressly female concerns.

As a social construction, landscape implies a physical shaping of the natural world, which has ideological consequences for how one approaches or experiences a given environment. Furthermore, although landscape can serve as a canvas for narrativization within cinema, it can also serve a metaphorical role, allowing for a psychological embodiment or reflection of the emotions of the characters within the fabric of the film. While this is generally apparent in New Hollywood road movies, it is particularly palpable in *Wanda*, which draws on both a surface and psychological realism. This allows it to comment concurrently on the state of the nation and the position of disenfranchised working-class American women, while also allowing for more personal preoccupations.

Drawing on this idea, this chapter has explored how *Wanda* and its idiosyncratic articulation of the American landscape in road movies can be placed within a lineage of subsequent female directors such as Kelly Reichardt and Andrea Arnold. It has considered the way in which their largely poor white female protagonists, like Wanda, are aesthetically, politically, and existentially positioned as "lost" within this landscape and the psycho-geographical connection they enjoy with the topography of this cinematic geography. As Wanda tells Mr. Dennis, "I don't have anything. Never did have anything, never will have anything." He responds by telling her that if she doesn't want anything, she is nothing and "may as well be dead" because she is "not even a citizen of the United States." Wanda and her screen sisters are not in the position to share in or reject the American Dream. This dream, open to the male wanderers of New Hollywood cinema, was never open to them.

Notes

1   Pauline Kael, "The Current Cinema," *New Yorker*, March 20, 1971, 136.

2   See Richard Brody, "Wanda," *New Yorker*, January 26, 2010, https://www.newyorker.com/culture/richard-brody/wanda, accessed August 6, 2020; Richard Brody, "Bringing Wanda Back," *New Yorker*, August 30, 2010, https://www.newyorker.com/culture/richard-brody/bringing-wanda-back, accessed August 6, 2020; and Bérénice Reynaud, "For Wanda," in *The Last Great American Picture Show: New Hollywood Cinema in the 1970s*, ed. Thomas Elsaesser, Alexander Horwath, and Noel King (Amsterdam: Amsterdam University Press, 2004).

3   Thomas Elsaesser, "The Pathos of Failure: American Films in the 1970s: Notes on the Unmotivated Hero," in *The Last Great American Picture Show: New Hollywood Cinema in the 1970s*, ed. Thomas Elsaesser, Alexander Horwath, and Noel King (Amsterdam: Amsterdam University Press, 2004), 227.

4   David Laderman, *Driving Visions: Exploring the Road Movie* (Austin: University of Texas Press, 2002).

5   Unlike the vast majority of New Hollywood Films, the screenplay for *Five Easy Pieces* was written by a female screenwriter, Carole Eastman, working under the

pseudonym Adrien Joyce. In a number of ways, it is aesthetically, philosophically, and ideologically the closest in tone to the road movies of Loden, Reichardt, and Arnold of any of the other New Hollywood road movies. Kelly Reichardt has stated that her attempts to write a narrative for her first feature film *River of Grass* were influenced by deconstructing the narrative of films such as *Five Easy Pieces* (Kelly Reichardt interview in James Mottram, "Kelly Reichardt: Small Scale, Big Picture," *Film Ink*, April 12, 2017, https://www.filmink.com.au/kelly-reichardt/, accessed October 4, 2020.

6 Kelly Reichardt qtd in *Spike, Mike, Slackers & Dykes: A Guided Tour across a Decade of American Independent Cinema* (Austin: University of Texas Press, 1996), 307.

7 James and Nancy Duncan, *Landscapes of Privilege: The Politics of the Aesthetic in an American Suburb* (Cambridge: Cambridge University Press, 2003).

8 Denis Cosgrove, *Social Formation and Symbolic Landscape* (Madison: University of Wisconsin Press, 1984).

9 James Duncan, *The City as Text: The Politics of Landscape Interpretation in the Kandyan Kingdom* (Cambridge: Cambridge University Press, 1990), 17.

10 Elsaesser, "The Pathos of Failure," 227.

11 Richard Brody, "Wanda," https://www.newyorker.com/culture/richard-brody/wanda.

12 Ray Carney, *The Films of John Cassavetes: Pragmatism, Modernism, and the Movies* (Cambridge: University of Cambridge Press, 1994), 146.

13 Ibid., 284.

14 Andrew Higson, "Space, Place and Spectacle," *Screen* 25, nos. 4–5 (July 1, 1984), 2–21.

15 Elsaesser, "The Pathos of Failure," 236.

16 McCandlish Phillips, "Barbara Loden Speaks of the World of 'Wanda,'" *New York Times* (March 11, 1971), 32.

17 Higson, "Space, Place and Spectacle," 8.

18 Graeme Harper and Jonathan Raynor, "Introduction—Cinema and Landscape," in *Cinema and Landscape: Film, Nation and Cultural Geography*, ed. Graeme Harper and Jonathan Raynor (Bristol: Intellect Books, 2010), 21.

19 Higson, "Space, Place and Spectacle," 12.

20 Barbara Klinger, "The Road to Dystopia: Landscaping the Nation in *Easy Rider*," in *The Road Movie Book*, ed. Steven Cohen and Ina Rae Hark (London: Routledge, 1997), 181.

21 Kelly Reichart. "Decade: Kelly Reichardt on 'Wendy & Lucy,'" interview by Peter Knegt. *Indiewire* (December 30, 2009), https://www.indiewire.com/2009/12/decade-kelly-reichardt-on-wendy-lucy-246069/, accessed August 6, 2020.

22   Higson, "Space, Place and Spectacle," 12–13.

23   P. Adams Sitney "Landscape in the Cinema: The Rhythms of the World and the Camera," in *Landscape, Natural Beauty, and the Arts*, ed. Salim Kemal and Ivan Gaskell (Cambridge: Cambridge University Press, [1993] 1995), 103–6.

24   *American Honey* is in some ways the exception to this. Although it certainly enjoys much of the surface realism of Loden and Reichardt's film, the colors are vibrant and densely saturated. The camera is almost constantly moving, constantly quivering, constantly shifting in and out of focus. It is repeatedly drawing attention to the fact that these images are mediated through lens flare and blown out colors, a heightened sense of reality. This is particularly apparent at moments where Star has active agency in events. At one point the ferocity of Star and Jake's desire for each other is so overwhelming that it begins to affect the body of the film. The sounds of rustling leaves and sprinklers become heightened, the brightness of the sun burning white through tree branches. One could posit that we experience the landscape subjectively through Star. We see what she sees. We hear what she hears. We feel what she feels, and we touch what she touches during these moments.

25   Klinger, "The Road to Dystopia," 189.

26   *The Mike Douglas Show* (1961–82). Episode #11.122. Aired February 15, 1972.

27   Richard Slotkin, *Regeneration through Violence: The Mythology of the American Frontier, 1600–1860* (Middleton: Wesleyan University Press, 1973), 5.

28   Interestingly, Palm and Terry, the two female hitchhikers that Bobby and Rayette pick up on their journey to Washington State, are heading for Alaska. Palm's diatribe on the politics of American consumerism positions Alaska as a "clean" Arcadian space based on a picture she has seen. Bobby pessimistically shatters her illusions by informing her that it was "white" and "clean" until "the big thaw." At the end of the film Bobby himself hitches a lift on a truck heading north to Alaska, demonstrating a tension between his fatalism and an optimism for a place in which he too might belong.

10

The New Wave in the New Millennium: *Joker*, *Taxi Driver*, Nostalgia, and Trumpian Politics

Karen A. Ritzenhoff and Hannah D'Orso

In Fall 2019, when the DC Comics supervillain origin story *Joker* (Todd Phillips, 2019) was released in theaters, Martin Scorsese debuted his new film. *The Irishman* represented for Scorsese a return to the gangster movie, a genre in which he has worked consistently over his fifty-year career in Hollywood, ever since his second film, *Mean Streets* (1973), attracted considerable critical approval as an emblem of the stylistic flair and gritty realism of the American New Wave. Scorsese is one of the only auteurs associated with the American New Wave still alive and working regularly today, coming to prominence in a period when American cinema was thriving and vital, politically charged, and formally and aesthetically experimental. However, to get *The Irishman* made, Scorsese collaborated with Netflix and, while it enjoyed a limited release on the big screen, the main portals through which it was seen were tablets and smartphones. Netflix stated that more than 26.4 million accounts had streamed the movie during the first week of its release in November 2019.[1] Meanwhile, in movie theaters, *Joker* made over $1 billion in global revenue.[2] Thus, these two movies were competing for audiences in different formats. While Scorsese himself utilized the new technologies available to him to realize his creative vision in the twenty-first century, Phillips took the genre that defines the contemporary cinematic *zeitgeist*, the superhero film, and looked backward, seeking to draw a genealogical link between *Joker* and Scorsese's totemic New Wave output, looking for a nostalgic recall of an earlier cinematic era. Phillips did so not only by casting Robert De Niro—who, through his performances as Johnny Boy in *Mean Streets*, Travis Bickle in *Taxi Driver* (1976), and Rupert Pupkin in *The King of Comedy* (1982), among others, is indelibly associated with the American New Wave generally and Scorsese in particular but also by recreating the style and tone of Scorsese's films of the New Wave era.

This chapter considers the legacy of the American New Wave in the twenty-first century through an analysis of the parallels between Todd Phillips's DC superhero film *Joker* and Martin Scorsese's classic and formative films of the period, particularly *Taxi Driver* and *The King of Comedy*.[3] Phillips adopted the look of a crumbling mid-1970s New York during the heat wave and infamous garbage strike to connect *Joker* to *Taxi Driver*. He constructs Arthur Fleck (Joaquin Phoenix), an aspiring though untalented comedian whose delusions ultimately lead to violence, in the mold of Rupert Pupkin in *The King of Comedy*. In considering *Joker* in relation to these films, this analysis will evaluate how and why Phillips mimics the style and tone of Scorsese's earlier work and how the politics of the New Wave era might speak to the issues alive in the age of Trump. In a roundtable discussion about *Joker* preceding the publication of a special issue of *New Review of Film and Television Studies*, Caroline Bainbridge suggests that while it is difficult to view the film as a "harbinger of our experiences in 2020," it can certainly be seen as "useful cipher through which to read the writing that was clearly on the wall."[4] In the same issue, Sean Redmond explains the timeliness of *Joker* in a time marked by political turmoil: "Alongside Trump's fictionalization of the real was an appeal to alienated and disenfranchised (white) men, fueling and flaming the toxicity that sought to poison the democratic well."[5] This chapter looks to establish the political resonances between the end of the New Wave era—after Watergate, Nixon, and Vietnam, when a sense of decay and decline planted the seeds of a reactionary movement that would flourish in the subsequent decade—and the age of Trump, which has witnessed its own violent upheavals and similar revanchist tendencies.

***

However, *Joker* would not necessarily enjoy the blessing of the cinematic father figure that inspired it. Scorsese famously criticized superhero films in an interview with *Empire* magazine in November 2019 as fundamentally at odds with what he understands as the essence of cinema. He said,

> I don't see them … I tried, you know? But that's not cinema. Honestly, the closest
> I can think of them, as well-made as they are, with actors doing the best they

can under the circumstances, is theme parks. It isn't the cinema of human beings trying to convey emotional, psychological experiences to another human being.[6]

As if in response, journalist Bilge Ebiri explained the allure of superhero movies in the post-9/11 film world:

> As our world has become increasingly more complicated and unsettling—or, perhaps more accurately, as we've become increasingly aware of how complicated and unsettling our world has always been—the films we consume have become ever more infantilizing. ... Comic-book movies understandably, maybe even unwittingly, maybe even *thankfully*, took advantage of this circumstance and gave us what we wanted.[7]

Scorsese's comments, in conjunction with the assessment of superhero films as childish escapism, suggest that closer scrutiny of *Joker* will help us establish what Phillips hoped to gain from dressing his superhero film in the style and tone of the American New Wave.

Realist, psychologically complex, politically charged, and formally inventive, Scorsese's New Wave films are arguably the antithesis of the shiny, rollercoaster rides of the contemporary blockbuster cinema of the type Ebiri describes here. As a director better known for lowbrow entertainment such as *The Hangover* trilogy (2009–13), Phillips's credentials as a filmmaker able to bring the style and tone of the American New Wave to a comic book movie were inauspicious. As if to confirm this, on its release, critics considered *Joker* to lack the nuance and complexity of Scorsese's films. Journalist Alissa Wilkinson discusses this issue in her 2019 article in the popular trade magazine *Vox*: "Scorsese's *Taxi Driver* and *The King of Comedy* are two sides of a story that *Joker* doesn't get." She continues, "by mashing the two together in one tale—and removing most of their films' humor and irony—we're left with a movie that can't quite get a handle on its protagonist the way Scorsese's two films managed to do."[8] Wilkinson concludes that "sadly for Fleck and his eventual Joker evolution, the resulting character is just a pathetic victim, and we know what we're supposed to feel for him: pity. That's signaled throughout the movie, loud and clear. He is beaten up, abandoned, mocked, and mistaken."[9] In her reading, the lack of complexity of the Joker character does not allow the audience to reflect on violence or the ambiguity of the hero status assumed by the protagonists in Scorsese's tales of failed masculinity.

***

Jon Lewis situates Scorsese among the directors of the "first wave of new Hollywood auteurs" in the early 1970s, along with Francis Ford Coppola and

Robert Altman.[10] Where traditional Hollywood entertainment, such as big-budget musicals and heroic westerns, no longer commanded the box office as it once did, the new auteurs changed the fortunes of Hollywood in the late 1960s and 1970s, sidestepping escapist fantasies to focus on the realities of America in this period. Socially and politically engaged, and aesthetically experimental, it was, as the title of Jonathan Kirshner and Jon Lewis's 2019 collection suggests, when the movies mattered.[11] That's when the young directors of the New Wave were celebrated as true artists, experimenting with form and style in a fashion to which Hollywood was unaccustomed, and pushing the envelope following the collapse of the Production Code to produce cinema for adults. For Heather Hendershot and J. Hoberman, *Taxi Driver* represents the peak (and perhaps end) of this New Wave.[12] Since then, American cinema has been dominated by the kinds of child-friendly blockbuster that has resulted ultimately in the dominance of the superhero genre. It is an era that was ushered in by Steven Spielberg and George Lucas, who would emerge spectacularly on the scene in the period around the time of *Taxi Driver*. *Joker* is unmistakably for grown-ups not just in its violent and explicit content but in its desire to connect to a glorious cinematic past, deliberately reconstructing the mise-en-scène of Scorsese's New York, the gritty, decaying "mean" streets of Times Square, and Manhattan. In so doing, Phillips wants *Joker* to "matter" in the same way as *Taxi Driver*, perhaps the last time that American cinema did.

In order to connote seriousness and thematic heft, Phillips deliberately co-opts *Taxi Driver*'s grimy aesthetic, recreating the look of 1970s Manhattan as, in J. Hoberman's description, a decaying "Malignopolis."[13] The New York of *Taxi Driver* and the Gotham City of *Joker* are emblematic of themes of corruption, decay, and moral decline that characterize both films. Phillips drew his aesthetic of a defunct Gotham City from the collective visual memory of New York in the 1970s, extensively represented in Scorsese's body of work. In the period *Taxi Driver* was released, New York was on the verge of bankruptcy, and the film was shot during the infamous 1975 garbage strike that soiled the streets, an event Phillips includes in *Joker*. *Taxi Driver* also captured the political malaise and sense of decline in the period following America's defeat in Vietnam. Scorsese's film was preoccupied with the legacy of the Nixon era, after years of civil unrest, protest, and a sense of inevitable national decline symbolized by a crumbling New York. Indeed, Hollywood's New Wave directors were fascinated by the depiction of the urban cultural spaces and decaying cityscapes, populated by the disenfranchised and disillusioned working-class white male. Similar to *film noir*'s visual allegories with their doomed male lead who spirals out of control, or the oeuvre of French director Robert Bresson, Scorsese is seen as a master of situating his protagonists in a bleak mise-en-scène and as the center of a narrative depicting toxic masculinity.

America's malaise in the aftermath of Nixon's resignation is palpable in *Taxi Driver*, as a fetid, moral decay sets in, a situation the angry white male resists through excessive violence. As Hendershot explains,

> we can see how New York City, which came to symbolize all that was wrong with America in the troubled 1970s, functioned as a driving narrative force, a character in and of itself, in the films of the New Hollywood years. If the old Hollywood had been based in the City of Angels, New York would become the City of Losers, symbol of the shattered fallout remaining in the wake of Attica, Vietnam, Mayor Daley, Nixon, and Watergate.[14]

One of the most significant features of *Taxi Driver* is the idea of the cab as a self-contained unit. Bickle watches this decaying, dystopian New York from the vantage point of his taxi, his reality captured by the frame of the car window[15] (see Figure 10.1). He projects his anger and disgust about an urban population, which he describes as being "scum," on the passers-by in the different neighborhoods he services. As Amy Taubin describes, "the figure of Travis Bickle is an emblem of that masculine anxiety, and, as such, exerts enormous influence on the films

Figure 10.1 Travis Bickle in his cab in *Taxi Driver* (Columbia Pictures, 1976).

Figure 10.2 Arthur Fleck in the police car in *Joker* (Warner Bros. Pictures, 2019).

of the next two decades, particularly those of the 90s, a decade in which 'white male backlash' and 'white male paranoia' became prime media topics."[16]

The city streets of New York are depicted as a "nightmare narrative" through the eyes of the protagonist who is increasingly alienated from civilian life and portrayed as a "male anxiety dream of castration and death."[17] Scorsese starts the movie with a slow-motion close-up of the cab as it emerges from the dense fog like a hellish demon.[18] The connotation of menace and doom is further established in this opening scene by the glowing red and yellow street signs of Times Square that illuminate the city at night. The haunting soundtrack supports the idea that something has come from the underworld to take revenge. Taubin explains that "if *Taxi Driver* owes something to the French film of the 50s and 60s, it's even more influenced by American film noir, the genre the French New Wave adored."[19] The imagery is blurred once the shot changes to the inside of the cab and the subjective point of view depicts the rain-drenched windshield where the lights dance as the car drives. The first impression of Bickle is haunted: Scorsese shows an extreme close-up of his eyes, looking out restlessly, drenched in red colors from the night lights, reflected on his face.

This is very similar to the final scene in *Joker* when Fleck looks out the police car window onto the streets where protesters are looting downtown Gotham (see Figure 10.2). Like Bickle in his cab, Fleck gazes at the world from a moving vehicle, trapped in his own world and somehow detached from the outside. The

Figure 10.3 Fog emerging from the sewers in *Taxi Driver* (Columbia Pictures, 1976).

Figure 10.4 The chaos and destruction at the end of *Joker* (Warner Bros. Pictures, 2019).

glow of fires and the rotating lights from the police car he is in illuminate his smiling face. The fog from tear gas creates an identical effect of doom that is reminiscent of the apocalypse and hell at the outset of *Taxi Driver*, creating a visual continuity of the mise-en-scène between both movies (Figure 10.3 and Figure 10.4).

Fleck grins with joy as he watches the burning storefronts, the looting of shops, incinerated cars, and flocks of protestors who wear clown masks, honoring his legacy as a murderer and domestic terrorist, as he is driven in a police vehicle through downtown Gotham. He is fascinated as street gangs wave guns and destroy real estate to take revenge on the elites. In the final moments, he stands on top of a police car, dancing in euphoric bliss while the downtown area of Gotham burns (see Figure 10.8). He looks like a devil as he moves in a triumphant pose, cheered on by civilians in clown masks. The film's ending mirrors the beginning of *Taxi Driver* by showing a dystopian world in flames, although the reasons for the urban decay and the protagonists' responses are different. Scorsese is fascinated by a "new anti-hero, with his pathological relation to violence as the answer to the castration anxiety he barely troubled to hide,"[20] therefore attacking others as a way to feel better about his social isolation in a reclusive, poor environment. Fleck is an antihero who thrives on chaos, anarchy, and murder as a form of societal destruction.

The obvious similarities between the protagonists Arthur Fleck, Travis Bickle, and Rupert Pupkin are an important aspect of how Phillips attempts to draw a link between his film and Scorsese's work. Bickle is a key figure in the New Wave, not only because he is a nonconformist but also because he is disenchanted with domestic life after returning from the war in Vietnam, suffering from posttraumatic stress disorder. Both Bickle and Fleck are psychotic loners who are supposedly emblematic of a period when white males were disempowered by society.[21] Both characters sustain a deep hatred for the people in their cities, which stems from the interactions they have had with them. Fleck is outraged by the wealthy people who benefit from the system while poor and sick people like him are walked all over. Bickle is sickened by the "whores, skunk pussies, buggers, queens, fairies, dopers, junkies, sick, and venal" of his city, but seems to have the greatest hatred for prostitution. To rescue a sense of masculine strength, vitality, and centrality they obsess about women they want to rescue—in Bickle's case, the teenage sex worker Iris (Jodie Foster), and in Fleck's, his neighbor, the African American single mother Sophie (Zazie Beetz). Both Bickle and Fleck live on the edge of poverty. They are both victims of a system that has abandoned and abused them. Phillips goes to even further lengths than Scorsese to show how Fleck has been victimized and punished by society: he is not only fired from his low-income job as a clown-for-hire, and maligned and beaten in the streets by teenage bullies, but also cut off from social services by a corrupt government and laughed at on national television as a failed comedian. Fleck is the victim of childhood abuse, suffering from mental illness, consistently ignored, derided, and dismissed by a brutal, uncaring society quite willing to discard him like the garbage that litters the streets in the film. His mother lives with him on social welfare in a decrepit apartment complex and his father figure rejects him as an abject nuisance.

Indeed, this aspect of Fleck's characterization invites comparison with both Bickle and Pupkin. All three look up to male mentors who ultimately betray them: while Bickle watches Charles Palantine (Leonard Harris), the political candidate running for American president on TV, Fleck looks at his TV screen to monitor Gotham's mayoral candidate Thomas Wayne (Brett Cullen) and admire Murray Franklin's (Robert De Niro) showmanship. Pupkin watches the showman Jerry Langford (Jerry Lewis) on TV in his mother's basement and decides that he could be a better comedian. Sick of rejection in *The King of Comedy*, he kidnaps Langford and forces him to get a spot on his show. Where Bickle fails to assassinate the presidential candidate Palantine, Fleck succeeds in executing Franklin, a TV celebrity like Langford, live on television. Each of these decisions comes on the heels of the main characters being mocked or pushed aside by their idols. Another important similarity between the films is how each of the main characters fantasizes about achieving their goals or getting something they want but cannot have. Throughout *The King of Comedy*, Pupkin imagines himself as a successful comedian alongside Langford. Pupkin seems to convince himself that these fantasies are real: his fantasy of being invited to Langford's home is so realistic that he convinces himself it happened and shows up at his house. Ultimately, Pupkin releases Langford and goes to prison, eventually returning as a notorious celebrity. In Fleck's case, he manufactures a vivid impression of himself in a tender relationship with his neighbor, Sophie, which is revealed later to be a sad illusion. He also spends a lot of time in his apartment coming up with imaginative scenarios based on other aspects of his life. For example, he practices going on Franklin's show, projecting himself as a confident person with a bright future in comedy. Like Pupkin, Fleck realizes that his idol is uninterested in him. Pupkin is obsessed with Langford until he realizes that he does not care about him at all: "So that's what it's like when you're famous, huh? … Now I know how people like you are." After this insight, Pupkin takes drastic, criminal measures, as both Bickle and Fleck do.

Bickle sees the world of urban New York as a threat. He recognizes that crime, drugs, and prostitution lead to war zones, quite different from the affluent world that some of his clients, including Palantine, come from. He sees himself as disenfranchised, leaving the streets that are drowned in vibrant colors and sound to pull up to a grand hotel where his rich passengers who might be unaware of the "other side of the tracks" socialize and move around. Similar to Fleck, the clown-for-hire in low-income Gotham neighborhoods, who holds up signs and performs for children in the hospital, Bickle has access to different sides of the city as a cab driver, where he sees the poor and the rich and takes in the spectrum of social class. He is also aware of the "white man's rage," impersonated by Martin Scorsese himself in a cameo as a vigilante husband who wants to murder his wife and her Black lover. The passenger's vulgar and racist rants entice Bickle to buy several guns from an illicit arms dealer to take the law into his own hands.

Bickle practices drawing his newly acquired guns in the mirror and instigating fights through conversation, as we see in the infamous "you talkin' to me?" scene. Elaborate montages are shown of Bickle creating devices, such as the quick-draw sleeve gun system, to aid him in a fight. These scenes underscore Bickle's violent, aggressive behavior. In *Joker*, Fleck obtained his gun through his coworker, Randall (Glenn Fleshler), who talked him into it as a means of self-protection, as Fleck would frequently receive beatdowns from random people on the streets. In the scene where Fleck kills the three bankers, it seemed at first as though the gun served him well for self-defense. As the men were beating Fleck relentlessly, he pulled out the gun and shot two of them to save himself. The last man was murdered execution-style, suggesting Fleck has snapped and become fully psychotic. These violent acts play into a fantasy of omnipotence for the marginalized, disenfranchised, and ignored white males in the American urban landscape. Fleck takes revenge for being mocked and belittled.

There are several important visual allusions to *Taxi Driver* in *Joker*. Bickle's violent rampage against Iris's pimps culminates in him sitting on the couch, barely conscious and weak from his injuries. Three police officers arrive moments later, their guns pointed at him. Bickle raises his head to look at the officers, then puts a finger gun to his temple, daring them to pull the trigger. His hand is completely covered in blood, with additional spots on his face. The scene cuts right from the close-up of Bickle to a bird's-eye view shot that moves through the building, displaying the excessive blood-drenched corridors of the brothel, several guns, the dead and mutilated body of Iris's pimp who has collapsed on the floor, and the overall damage from the shootout. This creates a somber assessment of the violence, caused by Bickle's access to guns before the shoot-out. When the camera passes over the officers, they stand perfectly still with their guns still trained on him, who is slumped on the couch, barely conscious.

In *Joker*, the suicidal finger gun gesture is initially mimicked by Sophie, who is stuck with Fleck in a malfunctioning elevator with her young daughter. She

Figure 10.5 Sophie puts a finger to her head in *Joker* (Warner Bros. Pictures, 2019).

Figure 10.6 Arthur Fleck uses Bickle's classic hand gesture in *Joker* (Warner Bros. Pictures, 2019).

lifts her hand to her temple, just like Bickle did over forty years earlier, and pulls the imaginary trigger (see Figure 10.5). Audience members familiar with *Taxi Driver* will recognize this gesture as it has become one of the most recognizable images in the repository of the New Wave. The same gesture is repeated several times by Fleck, who obsesses about the single mother in the same way Bickle fantasized about Iris and Betsy (Cybill Shepherd) (see Figure 10.6).

In both *Taxi Driver* and *Joker*, the use of the finger gun motif is a symbol for the violence and aggression of the male protagonists as an outlet for their frustration with the people in their communities. This motif becomes another visual connection between the films to remind the audience of the influence Bickle's character had on the creation of Fleck. The use of the finger gun in these films has several implications for both characters. The deployment of the gesture appears to speak to their nihilistic, self-destructiveness, as well as representing a symbol of the thirst for power that contributes to their violent and aggressive personalities.

The scene where Fleck is on *Live! With Murray Franklin* in *Joker* can be compared to the scene in *Taxi Driver* in which Bickle drives Palantine in his cab. In each of these scenes, Bickle and Fleck spill all the hostile thoughts about the people in their city that they previously kept private. Although Bickle has not personally taken any action, his conversation with Palantine seems to further convince him that "washing the garbage off the sidewalks" is the right move. Fleck, on the other hand, has already begun to take revenge on the wealthy by killing the three finance workers on the subway and inadvertently starting a widespread movement of protestors dressed up in clown masks. The structure of these two scenes is considerably different in many ways, although they are alike in the important role they play in each character's development. Fleck's assassination of Franklin speaks to some of the themes in *Taxi Driver*, as well as its bloody conclusion. Fleck tells Franklin during the talk show that he wants to be seen: "I want people to see me," he states. "Have you seen what it is like out there," he asks Franklin on the set. Fleck then points his handgun at the talk show host and pulls the trigger. Franklin throws his head back and a huge splash of blood covers the wall of the studio. Fleck fires another bullet into the lifeless body, drops the gun, and starts dancing as if in a trance. Killing brings him satisfaction and joy. For the first time, he is indeed being seen by everybody. To heighten this moment, Fleck grabs a television camera and speaks directly into it. Similarly, Bickle was invisible before he committed the murders at the end of *Taxi Driver*. He gains social notoriety through an act of excessive violence.

Franklin's murder is repeated and multiplied in a long segment where Phillips displays concurrent television windows that all show different news feeds.[22] Several of them replay the actual killing, while others show the street protests and burning facades (Figure 10.7). A third of the monitors show different news anchors. Surprisingly, many monitors display mundane ads for alcoholic drinks or other consumer goods, conflating news coverage with advertising. Phillips

Figure 10.7 The bank of televisions broadcasting Franklin's murder in *Joker* (Warner Bros. Pictures, 2019).

contrasts the violence with television monitors that magnify and replay the violence, thereby reducing the shooting to another television event, like the supposedly lawless protestors and the reference to corporate America. Murder becomes entertainment for the evening news (see Figure 10.7).

However, Phillips's representations are distinctly different from Scorsese's choices. Where the killer rampage at the climax of *Taxi Driver* has a grand, operatic quality, the mayhem that erupts at the conclusion of *Joker* does not fit this mold. *Taxi Driver* shows the shoot-out and Bickle's killing spree with the exaggerated high-angle shots that display the carnage with a caustic soundtrack. However, contrary to political activists who resort to armed struggle as a form of protest, Fleck kills out of pleasure.

While the comparisons between *Joker* and Scorsese's work in terms of aesthetics and character are numerous, there is the sense that, in keeping with the criticisms of Phillips's film that accompanied its release, it lacks the seriousness, nuance, and complexity of the New Wave films to which it so clearly invites comparison. In *Joker*, the scene most clearly reminiscent of the concluding bloodbath in *Taxi Driver* occurs when Fleck murders one of his former colleagues who had bullied and taunted him. Fleck sits slumped against the wall in his apartment, his white clown face covered in blood. Fleck, unlike Bickle, is not catatonic. On the contrary, he shortly afterward gets up and even kisses his friend Gary (Leigh Gill) on the head, thanking him for having been his only trusted ally. Gary is a little man who also worked with him in the clown business. Contrary to *Taxi Driver*, the killing is almost justified, and its seriousness is undercut through a reversion to infantile, politically incorrect humor, perhaps more in keeping with Phillips's financially successful forays into frat boy comedy: Gary cannot reach the lock of the door because he is too short and has to ask Fleck to come and help him, adding a queasy, comic effect to the scene that stands in marked contrast to the grandiose horror of the massacre at the end of *Taxi Driver*.

***

Phillips's nostalgia for the New Wave's 1970s urban mayhem, projected in decrepit tableaus that resemble the style of Scorsese's neo-noir, also leads to an eerily timely misconception of social protests in the Trump era and the administration's battle cry to reestablish a "law and order" government.[23] This has led some to argue that *Joker* fundamentally reinforces some of the core tenets of Trump's rhetoric.[24] Indeed, the destructive ending of the film could be mistakenly understood as reminiscent of the images of violent demonstrations in the summer of 2020 when the police killing of George Floyd in Minneapolis led to widespread peaceful protests for Black Lives Matter (BLM). In the wake of the protests, Trump's lawyer, Rudy Giuliani, former mayor of New York from 1994 to 2001, promoted a renewed call for "law and order" as part of his online five-minute speech at the 2020 Republican National Convention, insinuating that the BLM movement was inherently violent and will destroy the major, Democrat-controlled American cities. He told his audience that BLM protests had been "hijacked" by violence.[25] Trump and Giuliani's reactionary "law and order" rhetoric is indeed reminiscent of white supremacist rhetoric of the late 1960s. Framing BLM in this fashion is eerily similar to Richard Nixon's "law and order" messages that so successfully mobilized the "Silent Majority" of white voters who, angered by and afraid of the protests for civil rights and against the war in Vietnam, delivered him a victory in the 1968 presidential election. Bickle's anger, though channeled through the barrel of a gun rather than the ballot box, is born of the same impulse to clean up the streets and to protect the nation from what he perceives to be a rapid descent into an immoral, chaotic cesspool.

However, despite his stated claim to be in favor of "law and order," Trump spent his four years in office trying to destroy the institutions of American democracy, culminating in an attempted violent coup in his final days in office. "Isn't it beautiful," Fleck states while sitting in the back of a police car. While Bickle looks out at the city from the windows of his taxi with disgust, Fleck admires the destruction he witnesses (Figure 10.2). The police officer in front tells him that he is the cause of the uprising. "The City is on fire because of what you did," he is being told. Fleck presses his face against the grid that separates him from the policemen. They are his enemies as institutional representatives of a "law and order" government, led by Wayne, that Fleck has come to distrust. Shortly afterward, the police car is in an accident, the police officers are killed behind the wheel, and Fleck is carefully (almost gently) helped out of the car by vigilantes who wear clown masks as he used to as a clown for a talent agency. They set him free and place his body on the hood of the vehicle where Joker initially spits blood and then awakens. Even though Fleck is the murderer of three men, has strangled his mother, stabbed one of his coworkers to death, and then assassinated Murray Franklin on live television, he becomes a hero.

When the insurrectionists stormed the Capitol in Washington, DC on January 6, 2021, Trump watched their actions on television screens, at a safe distance. Several observers reported that he was delighted. In the evening after the siege, Trump encouraged the mob to "go home" but also stated that he loved them. Trump's status as hero and savior among his supporters is therefore comparable to the treatment afforded Fleck at the conclusion of *Joker*. Moreover, Fleck's delight finds eerie comparison with the scenes of celebration and pride witnessed outside the Capitol Building in January 2021, as Trump fanatics sought to overturn the results of the presidential election through violence and intimidation of lawmakers. They were pictured giving each other high fives after the attack had concluded and told journalists reporting on the incident that they were proud to have participated. The terrorists who invaded the Capitol are reminiscent of the protesters in Gotham, whom Phillips depicts as lawless rebels without an obvious cause who defy the police and disturb social order, celebrating a serial killer who has taken the law into his own hands. Where Bickle seems in some respects to embody the extreme end of the electoral coalition that supported the New Right in the 1980s, Fleck's expression of disenfranchisement can be linked to the appeal Trump makes to the economically marginalized and forgotten working-class white males in the United States. Indeed, Fleck's embrace of anarchy is disturbingly reminiscent of the "Proud Boys," the neofascist group that has risen to prominence during Trump's presidency and which was involved in the invasion of the Capitol Building. So, rather than compare Fleck's violent rebellion to the protests that followed the murder of George Floyd, it is perhaps more accurate to consider them as akin to the white supremacist actions of someone like Kyle Rittenhouse, a seventeen-year-old who shot two BLM activists in Kenosha, Wisconsin, in September 2020 and has since been charged with murder. Bickle's rants about the "scum" on the streets of Manhattan have an eerie resemblance to the rhetoric of contemporary right-wing groups and the correlation between violence and fascist ideology to which white supremacists such as Rittenhouse ascribe.

However, it is not easy to determine the political motivations of Phillips's film. While Bickle is treated as a hero by the press after murdering pimps and clients of teenager Iris, the film does not appear as confirmatory of his actions as *Joker* is of Fleck's. *Joker* appears to revel in Fleck's ascent to hero status at the very conclusion of the film, as he dances in slow motion out of the psychiatric ward to the tune of "That's Life," trailing bloody footprints behind him following the apparent murder of his social worker. This conclusion suggests that *Joker* is at best ambivalent about the violence its protagonist unleashes, seemingly both reveling in, and recoiling from, the chaos and destruction we see on screen. Indeed, it could therefore be argued that the seriousness of *Joker* is largely superficial, co-opting the façade of the New Wave but failing to interrogate the moral complexity of the characters that feature in these films. While *Taxi Driver, The King of Comedy*, and *Joker* all demand of their audiences some identification with their troubled protagonists, Scorsese's critique of social dysfunction in the post-Nixon United States in *Taxi Driver* does not ask us to enjoy the spectacle of destruction that concludes the film in the same way. If Scorsese offers us a bird's-eye view, Phillips offers a wide-eyed one, the look of Fleck as he gazes out of the police car window in a state of awe at the chaos he has inspired. Perhaps we should see *Joker* as he sees himself: as Fleck plainly states to Franklin before he shoots him in the head, "I'm not political, Murray. I'm just trying to make people laugh."

***

Nixon, Vietnam, Watergate, New York in decline. Trump, continuous political scandal and corruption, BLM protests and far-right, antidemocratic, violent insurrection in Washington, DC. Two periods of political chaos and upheaval. Two films that speak to their contexts by telling stories of disenfranchised, psychotic white men who resort to violence and revel in chaos and destruction. The American New Wave is revered somewhat misleadingly as a brief moment in which American cinema made works of cultural, political, and aesthetic significance where its makers were free of commercial constraint. Conglomerate Hollywood of the twenty-first century is derided almost as simplistically as a period in which none of its films matter except as diverting though insubstantial spectacles. *Joker*, born of the latter period but seeking to don the costume of the former, sits uncomfortably between the two.

Politically, both *Taxi Driver* and *Joker* emerged in an interregnum, the former after the end of the Vietnam War and the Nixon era but before conservatism reestablished its hegemony, and the latter in the long period of political instability after the financial crisis of 2008 that still shows little sign of abating despite the Democratic victories in 2020. Indeed, as this chapter has demonstrated, *Joker* speaks even more loudly to its political context in 2021 than it did on its release in 2019. The insurrection at the Capitol Building on January 6, 2021, is reminiscent of the riots concluding the film. Fleck's wide-eyed admiration of the chaos and destruction he has inspired demands comparison with the reports that President Donald Trump was delighted with what he was seeing as his supporters ransacked the Capitol and threatened elected officials with violence. Fleck, the impoverished, mentally unstable white male who feels neglected, ignored, and discarded by a vicious society, turns to violent pseudo-fascism to demand attention and recognition. The same can be said for Bickle's violent rampage concluding *Taxi Driver*. Both men, in keeping with the belief structure that underpins white male vigilantism, believe there to be no other option than violent chaos and retribution to reassert a semblance of control and authority. As Fleck so viciously asserts before he shoots Franklin through the head, "What happens when you cross a mentally ill loner with a society that treats him like trash? … You get what you fucking deserve." Both characters, created by periods of political upheaval and uncertainty, are emblematic of the belief that society is in inexorable decline, an unsalvageable cesspit of immorality and misery, deserving of a ritualistic cleansing through cathartic ultraviolence.

Through mise-en-scène, character, and politics, *Joker* deliberately recalls *Taxi Driver*, *The King of Comedy*, and, more widely, Scorsese's work in the period commonly described as the American New Wave. While there are clear and observable instances in which *Joker* does so, it takes a rather superficial approach, failing to understand its protagonist in the way that Scorsese did with Bickle and Pupkin, and in more than one instance betrays both its unserious comic book origins and Phillips's own past as a director of juvenile, politically incorrect comedies. However, what matters here is that it does so at all. It demonstrates that the American New Wave remains a critical touchstone for contemporary American filmmakers looking to produce cinema that "matters."[26] Why? Because, as Kirshner and Lewis contend, "much of what's good about modern American cinema … is rooted in [the New Wave] era."[27] Kirshner and Lewis are unashamedly nostalgic for the New Wave and, as this chapter has shown, so is Phillips. To give his superhero film a "serious" sheen, he mimics the style of the earlier period. *Joker*, therefore, occupies an uncomfortable, liminal position between being a blockbuster of the type that American cinema has specialized in since the mid-1970s, while at the same time yearning for the moment that immediately preceded it. The critics who derided *Joker* themselves betrayed their nostalgic feelings toward the New Wave, viewing Phillips's film as an inferior copy of the great works of the earlier period. What *Joker*'s very existence demonstrates, however, is not only how the New Wave remains something of a "year zero" when it comes to our considerations of aesthetically and culturally significant American cinema, but also our continued fascination with movies about troubled white men who, because they feel they are deserving of more power and control than they are afforded, would prefer to destroy everything (Figure 10.8).

Perhaps *Joker*'s political resonances, like those of *Taxi Driver*, will only become clearer in the years to come. What *Joker* achieves through its stylized mise-en-scène and central performance is the reinforcement of the critical significance of the American New Wave in contemporary film discourse. Simultaneously, however, its superhero garb forces us to recognize that the New Wave has long since ceded the floor to a different type of filmmaking. The really serious and important stuff is, as Scorsese's foray into the world of streaming demonstrates,

Figure 10.8 Arthur Fleck admires the destruction he has wrought in *Joker* (Warner Bros. Pictures, 2019).

happening elsewhere, an eventuality likely to only continue as a consequence of the pandemic.

Notes

Thanks to the students at the University of Hartford and Central Connecticut State University in spring 2020 who alerted us to many details in the visual comparison.

1   David Itzkoff, "Martin Scorsese Is Letting Go." *New York Times.* January 2, 2020. https://www.nytimes.com/2020/01/02/movies/martin-scorsese-irishman.html, accessed January 4, 2021.
2   Travis Bean, "Box Office: Why $1 Billion Doesn't Make 'Joker' Joaquin Phoenix's Biggest Film." *Forbes*, January 6, 2020. https://www.forbes.com/sites/travisbean/2020/01/06/box-office-why-1-billion-doesnt-make-joker-joaquin-phoenixs-biggest-film/?sh=49a1a0724e0d, accessed January 4, 2021.
3   Peter Krämer and Yannis Tzioumakis talk about this phase of Hollywood filmmaking not as the "New Wave" but as a form of Renaissance in American Cinema. Their 2018 coedited collection is entitled *The Hollywood Renaissance: Revisiting American Cinema's Most Celebrated Era* (New York: Bloomsbury). The editors contrast the fiscal realities of Hollywood studios in the 1960s and 1970s, losing revenue, with the "high esteem" that was associated with the movie releases by auteur directors. Among the innovations in filmmaking that have been attributed to this Renaissance, Krämer and Tzioumakis point out that film styles were changed, thereby

> inviting audiences to understand films as works of art (in turn to be understood in relation to the directors making them); protagonists (mostly male and young and often rebellious) who, due to their characterization and actors' performance styles, could be at times unsympathetic and difficult to relate to; the loosening of the cause-and-effect chains of the stories being told (in favour, among other things, of self-contained spectacle of the foregrounding of artistic elements associated with a particular director) and also on occasion ambivalent endings, which might encourage audiences to actively interpret the film, looking for hidden meanings; and, last but not least, a more explicit depiction of sexuality and violence. (Introduction, 2018)

4   Caroline Bainbridge, "White Riot: A 'Joker' Roundtable," *New Review of Film & Television Studies*. Special Issue 19.1. March 2021. Guest edited by Sean Redmond. https://nrftsjournal.org/white-riot-a-joker-roundtable/, accessed January 25, 2021.

5   Sean Redmond, "Introduction" to "That Joke Isn't Funny Anymore: A Critical
    Exploration of *Joker*." *New Review of Film & Television Studies*. Special Issue
    19.1. March 2021. Also see: Sean Redmond (ed.), *Breaking Down Joker: Violence,
    Loneliness, Tragedy*. Routledge Advances in Film Studies, forthcoming.

6   Nick De Semlyen, "*The Irishman* Week: Empire's Martin Scorsese Interview."
    Empire. November 6, 2019, https://www.empireonline.com/movies/features/
    irishman-week-martin-scorsese-interview/, accessed January 4, 2021.

7   Bilge Ebiri, "Okay, Fine, Let's Talk about Marvel." *Vulture*. October 23, 2019,
    https://www.vulture.com/2019/10/ok-fine-lets-talk-about-marvel-vs-martin-
    scorsese.html, accessed January 4, 2021.

8   Alissa Wilkinson, "Scorsese's *Taxi Driver* and *The King of Comedy* Are Two Sides
    of a Story That *Joker* Doesn't Get. Todd Phillips's Movie Pays Homage to the
    Unsettling Classics, but Misses Their Point." *Vox*. October 14, 2019, https://www.
    vox.com/culture/2019/10/14/20908734/joker-taxi-driver-king-of-comedy-de-niro-
    scorsese, accessed January 4, 2021.

9   Ibid.

10 Jon Lewis, "The Perfect Money Machine(s): George Lucas, Steven Spielberg, and
    Auteurism in the New Hollywood," in *Looking Past the Screen: Case Studies in
    American Film History and Method*, ed. Jon Lewis and Eric Smoodin (Durham,
    NC: Duke University Press, 2007), 61–85.

11 Jonathan Kirshner and Jon Lewis, eds., *When the Movies Mattered: The New
    Hollywood Revisited* (Ithaca, NY: Cornell University Press, 2019). Also see the
    latest publication by Jim Cullen, *Martin Scorsese and the American Dream* (Rutgers
    University Press, 2021).

12 J. Hoberman, "The Spirit of '76: Travis, Rocky and Jimmy Carter," in *When the
    Movies Mattered*, 149–63.

13 Ibid., 153.

14 Heather Hendershot, "City of Losers, Losing City: Pacino, New York, and the New
    Hollywood Cinema," in *When the Movies Mattered*, 86–100.

15 Jon Lewis characterizes Martin Scorsese's cinematic style in *American Film: A
    History* (2008) as originating in the director's confined childhood. "Scorsese's
    ability to capture real life on camera—especially the gritty reality of the streets
    of New York—was rooted in a childhood spent watching the world pass by his
    window. Scorsese was a sickly child, a sufferer of asthma, forced to linger in his
    apartment as other children played outside in the streets" (Lewis, 305).

16 Amy Taubin, *Taxi Driver* (New York: Palgrave Macmillan, 2009), 15.

17 Ibid., 14.

18 "Scorsese's *Taxi Driver* (et al. …) uses camera movement and slow motion to
    extend the emotional impact of a scene," write David Bordwell and Kristin

Thompson in *Film Art: An Introduction* (2009, 480). "Stylistically, no single coherent film movement emerged during the 1970s and 1980s. The most mainstream of the young directors continued the tradition of classical American cinema. Continuity editing remained the norm, with clear signals for time shifts and new plot developments. Some directors embellished Hollywood's traditional storytelling strategies with new or revived visual techniques." Ibid., 480.

19 Taubin, *Taxi Driver*, 14.
20 Ibid., 15.
21 Barton R. Palmer, "Allegory of Deliverance. Class and Gender in Scorsese's Bringing Out the Dead," in *Millennial Masculinity: Men in Contemporary American Cinema*, ed. Timothy Shary (Detroit: Wayne State University, 2013), 123.
22 Other directors of the New Wave have established similar visual references between entertainment and murder in the 1970s by depicting a wall of television sets visible in department store displays like Sidney Lumet's *Serpico* (1973).
23 Linda Hutcheon coins the role of nostalgia in postmodern cinema. "The aesthetics of nostalgia might, therefore, be less a matter of simple memory than a complex projection; the invocation of a partial, idealized history merges with a dissatisfaction with the present" (250).
24 CNN journalist Jeff Yang writes in October 2019 when *Joker* is released in a CNN opinion piece that Phillips's movie is "a political parable for our times." He states: "While many reviewers have focused on Fleck as an 'incel' hero—his status as a sexless loner who turns to violence—the true nature of the movie's appeal is actually broader: It's an insidious validation of the white-male resentment that helped bring President Donald Trump to power." Jeff Yang, "Joker—a political parable for our Times." October 6, 2019. https://www.cnn.com/2019/10/06/opinions/joker-political-parable-donald-trump-presidency-yang/index.html, accessed January 19, 2021.
25 Excerpt from the speech of former New York Mayor Rudy Giuliani during the 2020 Republican National Convention speech on August 28, 2020. https://www.axios.com/rudy-giuliani-rnc-speech-151780bd-6c7d-4947-892a-4b08ecf68778.html, retrieved October 28, 2020.
26 Wilkinson, "Scorsese's *Taxi Driver and The King of Comedy* Are Two Sides of a Story That Joker Doesn't Get."
27 Jonathan Kirshner and Jon Lewis, eds., *When the Movies Mattered: The New Hollywood Revisited* (Ithaca, NY: Cornell University Press, 2019), 16.

11

Indie Courtship: Pursuing the American New Wave

Kim Wilkins

American indie cinema is difficult to categorize. Geoff King writes that it "only ever really has meaning as an essentially *relative* quality."[1] That is to say, indie cinema is a category whose identifying characteristics are most observable when placed in contrast to others—particularly, or most commonly, the perceived mainstream commercial output of Hollywood. Michael Newman makes this sentiment explicit in his characterization of "indie" as an American film culture whose nexus between film and spectator, text and audience share a set of three overlapping viewing strategies, the third of which lays bare the critical importance of indie's oppositional positioning as a discursive practice: "When in Doubt, Read as Anti-Hollywood."[2] According to Newman,

> In many quarters, difference from Hollywood itself can be a mark of significant value. Indie film profits from its alterity, which sustains it and has the potential to be politically progressive and counter-hegemonic. At the same time, this same culture functions to reproduce social class stratification by offering an elite, culturally legitimate alternative to the mass-market Hollywood offering of the megaplex. The audience for specialty films ... is generally urban, affluent, well-educated, and fairly narrow by comparison with the audience for studio pictures. By positioning itself as artistic and sophisticated in comparison to mainstream cinema, indie culture functions as an emergent formation of high culture—or perhaps more accurately, high-middlebrow culture.[3]

As Newman's comments elucidate, there is a hierarchical cultural cachet associated with American indie cinema. This cultural cachet is underpinned by Pierre Bourdieu's concept of distinction, where acts of cultural consumption are demarcated by preferences and expressions of taste and, as such, selections made by individuals are concomitant with their social position and respective accumulation of cultural capital. While the demographics of any actual audience is impossible to know, indie cinema is often directed toward niche audience markets as markers of distinction.[4] As Janet Staiger correctly asserts, "the reason this matters is that implicit declarations are being made that this sort of film is ideologically better or more worthwhile than what it is not: a classical Hollywood film."[5] This statement is as instructive as it is clear—critical discourse does not simply seek to position indie cinema in level opposition to Hollywood but culturally above it. Staiger's excellent work sits among a wealth of scholarship on indie cinema that has sought to interrogate the political implications of its cultural cachet.[6]

My intention is not to repeat these important interventions in film discourse but to demonstrate how such cultural cachet has shaped the critical construction of two specific periods and traditions in American film history—the American New Wave and the Sundance-Miramax indies. I argue that critical, and scholarly, accounts of the Sundance-Miramax indies often court a quasi-genealogical relationship to the American New Wave that capitalizes on its persistent position as a nationally important moment in American film history, predicated on its legacy of independence. Problematically, these comparisons are rarely accompanied by analysis or comment on the type and function of independence perpetuated by the American New Wave legacy. In this chapter, I reassess the American New Wave legacy in light of its use as a mechanism for cultural elevation.

According to Newman, the Sundance-Miramax era that ran between 1989—the year that Steven Soderbergh's *sex, lies, and videotape* debuted at the Sundance Film Festival—and 2010—the year that saw the demise of Miramax alongside many mini-major indie studios and specialty divisions—is synonymous with the term "American indie cinema."[7] Although I contend that indie cinema continues to be produced by filmmakers like Wes Anderson and Noah Baumbach, it is unquestionable that the period identified by Newman saw an increase in popularity of a specific type of non-Hollywood cinema. This particular brand of filmmaking employed a set of aesthetic and formal strategies—for instance, quirky or ironic tonality, heightened degrees of formal play and referentiality, overt stylization—and encouraged modes of reception that have come to be associated with American indie cinema.

Part of the encouraged modes of reception promoted in both popular histories and scholarship is predicated on framing the Sundance-Miramax era as an unusual period in American film history. Against the backdrop of monotonous late 1980s and early 1990s Hollywood blockbusters, a band of "indie-auteur" filmmakers, including Quentin Tarantino, Steven Soderbergh, Richard Linklater, the Coen brothers, and Wes Anderson, emerged. Their films offered more thematically, stylistically, and aesthetically interesting alternatives to the generic fare on offer at the megaplexes and, in doing so, temporarily shook American film culture. This is a familiar narrative, even to those not versed in American indie film history, for it loosely mirrors the culturally legitimating discourse of a "new wave." However, unlike the famous "new waves" of postwar Europe, the Sundance-Miramax indies were not bound by a manifesto, nor did they represent any coherent political position.[8] Rather than looking across the Atlantic, Sundance-Miramax adherents have courted cultural elevation through comparison to the dominant American New Wave narrative of rebellion and revolution despite many, and increasing, scholarly accounts that indicate the hypocrisy of its racial and gendered elisions and overreach of claims to a period of Hollywood-made "art cinema." As such, employing the American New Wave as a framework for legitimation is a fraught critical act with revealing complications.

This chapter is underpinned by three intersecting provocations. First, that celebrating the American New Wave as a socially, politically, and culturally engaged moment aligned with countercultural politics of revolution and rebellion relies on specific omissions and exaggerations. Second, the gendered and racial nature of these elisions and overstatements are antithetical to the politics proffered. Third, that the spirit of rebellion and revolution at the heart of the American New Wave myth is "deeply American" because it reflects individualist ideals, both narratively in its canonized films and through the celebration of the romantic renegade auteur figure. In doing so, it sustains the white patriarchal hierarchies bound to the auteurist tradition. As such, employing American New Wave mythology as an elevation mechanism in "indie" rhetoric is culturally colonizing as it reaffirms these frameworks and hierarchies. I ask which cultural creeds are upheld when comparisons to the American New Wave are made, and whom do they serve in the contemporary moment? What does it mean that in 2019, Quentin Tarantino, the most notable alumnus of the Sundance-Miramax era, released *Once Upon a Time … in Hollywood*, a film that not only nostalgically evokes Hollywood during the American New Wave era but also reimagines the era saved by an aging, conservative television Western actor?

The American New Wave Myth

Few periods in Hollywood's history have received as much critical and scholarly attention as the American New Wave. Nick Heffernan pithily summarizes the era as "a brief flowering of politically and culturally radical film-making that blossomed with the decline of the traditional movie mass audience in the mid-1960s and withered with the arrival of the big-budget blockbuster in the mid-1970s."[9] In fact, the American New Wave narrative is a myth, in the terms defined by Julie Levinson as, "ritually retold consensus narratives that exemplify cultural creeds, and that are marked by recurring conventions of plot, characterization, and causality."[10] Peter Biskind's *Easy Riders, Raging Bulls* typifies this myth, characterizing the American New Wave as a youth culture of creative genius entangled with megalomania, sex, drugs, and violence. Although few have quite matched Biskind's sensationalist tenor, many have echoed his narrative formulation.[11] Tellingly, over twenty years after its original publication, *Easy Riders* has never been out of print.[12]

Part of the popular appeal of accounts like Biskind's is the characterization of now-famous filmmakers and actors as a band of youthful visionaries like Dennis Hopper, Francis Ford Coppola, Hal Ashby, and Peter Bogdanovich as auteurs-in-waiting. That such accounts tend to support their assertions through anecdotes and direct quotation confirms their commitment to an artist-centric narrative aligned with broad-scale cultural revolution.[13] It may seem obvious that accounts of Hollywood would naturally be preoccupied with star personas given its prominent role in promoting celebrity culture since its foundation. Yet, despite their occasional intimate details, Biskind and others do not merely provide exciting behind-the-scenes encounters with Hollywood's celebrity figures. Instead, their narratives correspond to what Richard Maltby describes as Hollywood's mythological history, which proposes that the history of Hollywood must conform to the conventions of its own narratives.[14] The story of misfits or outcasts who—against all odds—save a public inadequately served by inflexible bureaucratic systems and stifling old-world prejudices, and in the process prove individualism is desirable, is as old as the Hollywood hills. It governs the logic of the western tradition and the current superhero cycle as much as it does the history of United Artists' establishment and the American New Wave.[15] Considered in this light, it is unsurprising that the American New Wave follows a tale of revolution executed by "rebels" who "took back Hollywood" and in doing so created American cinema's last "Golden Age" precisely because it is at once seductive (in part due to its sheer unlikelihood) and yet completely familiar. After all, the American New Wave myth is not only a story about but authored by Hollywood.

While scholarship on the era largely eschews the sensationalism and gossip that color the popular histories, the dominant New Wave narrative is generally attributed critical significance as a unique era of politically engaged auteurist cinema within Hollywood's commercial history. As such, American New Wave films have been afforded the status of national or art cinema rather than mass entertainment in scholarly writing. As Thomas Elsaesser elegantly put it, during the American New Wave

> a whole new America came into view ... there, one came across rural backwaters, motels, rust-belt towns and Bible-belt communities, out-of-season resorts and other places of Americana, whose desolation or poignancy had rarely been conveyed with such visual poetry, enriched by oddball characters, a love of landscape and a delicacy of mood and sensibility, even in scenes of violence or torpor.[16]

Elsaesser's appreciation is indicative of the many scholars for whom the American New Wave was a period marked by artistic, cultural, and political intervention in Hollywood history.[17] Indeed, the collection in which Elsaesser's essay appears, *The Last Great American Picture Show: New Hollywood in the 1970s*, is at once an exploration of the American New Wave as a pivotal moment in American film history and, as the title suggests, an examination of its perceived end and legacy. Noel King's chapter, "The Last Good Time We Ever Had," similarly holds the American New Wave up as a nationally important bygone cinema. He explicitly posits that the era "might be the last good predominantly *American* time American cinema had" that in turn "challenged film criticism to find a critical language appropriate to the [American New Wave's] cinematic achievements."[18] In the same collection, David Thomson's provocatively titled essay "The Decade When Movies Mattered" concludes with this impassioned lament:

> In the 1970s, for a few years at least, our movies spoke to us with unaccustomed candour. For that moment, not just the audience, but the business responded

... So many kids wanted to put everything on film; so many people reckoned anything could work there. For a few years it was all one could do to wait for the next startling picture.[19]

Thomson's words illustrate the new language King suggests befits American New Wave cinema where nostalgia is both romantic and self-aware, "real and justified."[20] As such, it is particularly telling that Thomson's essay serves as the impetus for Jonathan Kirshner and Jon Lewis's 2019 collection, unironically titled, *When the Movies Mattered: The New Hollywood Revisited.* In their introduction, Kirshner and Lewis similarly grieve the passing of the American New Wave as a time when film was "embraced with an intellectual energy unthinkable with regard to [newer periods in Hollywood]."[21] They regard their anthology as a reexamination of the American New Wave but one that "is not without a degree of nostalgia for a better, smarter film culture."[22] Leaving aside the question of whether or not it is academically scrupulous—or even possible—to *reexamine* a celebrated period while maintaining from the outset that its elevated cultural position is justified, the dubious suggestion made is that the American New Wave was a naturally occurring formation.

Generally speaking, New Waves position themselves—in the event of those with manifestos (nouvelle vague, New German Cinema)—or are critically positioned (American New Wave, Cinema Novo) in opposition to the perceived outmoded traditions of an unrepresentative "old guard" within a given national or regional context.[23] While the distinctions between "old" and "new" cinemas are invariably a combination of historical, political, social, and industrial realities, once a corpus is established, "new waves" tend to be evaluated according to the political and cultural conditions discernible in their films' aesthetic and formal projects. Canons are subsequently formulated around those works that best service the articulation of these projects. Nicholas Godfrey makes this notion explicit when he states that the American New Wave "is an historically specified industrial phenomenon transformed into an ahistorical critical category."[24] Indeed, delineating any "new wave" is a critical act, whereby films selected as part of its corpus are automatically assigned national (if not international) and cultural importance. The term "New Wave" also connotes transience. Although their impact may result in potentially lasting alterations to film culture—be that national or international—consider the exemplary legacy of Italian neorealism and auteurism through the nouvelle vague—the "wave" itself must subside or be subsumed into a newer aesthetic and formal system or modes of production.

That these "waves" end (even if their start and end dates are almost always contested) facilitates narrativization, nostalgia, and, potentially, mythology. The evocation of "new waves" as neat descriptors, or even acknowledged imprecise shorthand, belies the contested and complex nature of their emergence.[25]

As Godfrey explains of the American New Wave,

for a brief period of time in the late 1960s and early 1970s, unique production circumstances were at play in Hollywood. However, the extent to which these industrial conditions permitted an American art cinema renaissance to bloom was far from certain at the time. Nor was it the aesthetic or commercial norm for the period. Nevertheless, a select body of films would be lionized in the critically constructed [American New Wave ...] The same privileged critical community that determined the fortunes of these films also ultimately galvanized the historical narrative of their purported radicalism, despite the film's ultimate inability to respond to the more tumultuous upheavals of the surrounding culture. Critical and commercial reception in turn influenced subsequent production trends, foreclosing the aesthetic and thematic adventurousness of the period while retrospectively lionizing atypical works. This process has gradually shaped our historical understanding of the period, as some films passed into the canon and others passed from view.[26]

Unfortunately, it seems few have heeded the cautions implicit in Godfrey's mindful explanation.[27] Kirshner and Lewis, for instance, maintain the American New Wave canon is indicative of "a decade of terrific filmmaking [... that was], alas, too good to last."[28] As such sentiments indicate, viewed from a contemporary position where American film culture has been altered by the technological impacts of digitalization (including modes of production, distribution, and exhibition associated with the uptake of streaming services, such as Netflix and Amazon Prime), debates about diversity, and political discourse shaped by the rise of populism, the American New Wave is still considered a uniquely *important* cinema.[29]

In drawing attention to the celebratory rhetoric employed in American New Wave scholarship, I am not implying that American New Wave films are unworthy of critical or scholarly attention, nor am I suggesting that they are not "deeply American." How am I to read the figure of the compromised frontiersman, entwined with unethical practice, prostitution, violent crime, and capitalist greed in films such as *Midnight Cowboy* (1969) or *McCabe and Mrs. Miller* (1971) as anything other than comments on the failure of American founding principles?

Certainly, the canonized films of the American New Wave are introspective about a distinct type of American identity in the face of perceived unfulfilled promises. However, perhaps what is most "deeply American" about the New Wave is not the films but rather the era's status as a nationally important cinema in light of the nature of its openly acknowledged mythologized history. Yet, if this proposition holds water, what does it mean for American film culture—and indeed culture itself—that the American New Wave continues to function as a framework for legitimation over half a century later?

The Tensions behind the Myth

The American New Wave myth is predicated on a series of overstatements and elisions. There are the obvious postulations about a universally "new" ideological, thematic, and aesthetic push across Hollywood, but such claims are easily refuted. That 1971—a year often considered the New Wave's aesthetic high and historical midpoint—was the year of release for both now-consecrated New Wave films such as Bogdanovich's *The Last Picture Show* and Altman's *McCabe & Mrs. Miller*, as well as the commercially successful *Fiddler on the Roof*, *Diamonds are Forever*, and *Bedknobs and Broomsticks* alone gestures toward the myth's overreach.[30] However, these romantic generalizations are—at least on face value—fairly benign untruths. The more insidious inaccuracies lie in the gulf between the American New Wave's touted virtues and its omissions or misrepresentations, particularly in relation to gender and race.

In addition to Godfrey's work, Aaron Hunter's *Authoring Hal Ashby*, Maya Montañez Smukler's *Liberating Hollywood: Women Directors and the Feminist Reform of 1970s American Cinema*, and Tzioumakis and Krämer's *The Hollywood Renaissance: Revisiting American Cinema's Most Celebrated Era* are among a push to unpick the gendered and racial biases at the core of the American New Wave through reassessments of authorship. In the introduction to their brilliant collection, Tzioumakis and Krämer rightly observe the American New Wave canon "deal[s] almost exclusively with films made by white, male directors born between the early 1920s and the late 1940s" whose films focus on white, male protagonists.[31] While there has been work, such as Robert Kolker's thoughtful *A Cinema of Loneliness*, that has sought to locate this distinctly male experience as a politics or ideology evident within its key auteur's oeuvres, there is still an overwhelming desire to link the specificity of this politics to a broader understanding of American cultural identity. How can it be that an era celebrated as a reflection of—and participant in—the various political and cultural revolutions of the 1970s is, in reality, fundamentally preoccupied with a narrow set of concerns pertaining to the anxiety and anomie of white men? Molly Haskell suggests:

> The demand for equality from the emerging women's movement was simply too threatening ... Easiest to avoid the subject altogether, a solution facilitated by the newfound freedom from traditional marketing and storytelling demands. Now the Young Turks were under no obligation to use women at all, or make movies for that once-crucial audience. They were free to go the limit with language and nudity, a privilege geared toward the delectation of the male viewer. In other words, the sexual revolution turned out to be more about fucking than feminism.[32]

It is curious that Haskell's chapter appears in Kirshner and Lewis's collection, given their introduction only goes so far as to acknowledge that the "cultural constraints of the time" resulted in a number of "imperfections." These "imperfections" are briefly discussed in a subsection titled "Marginal and Marginalized Voices,"[33] which effectively cordons off the myth's hypocrisies from its lauded accomplishments. I find it difficult to see this section as anything other than a disclaimer—a note to reassure the reader that the homogeneity of the canon has not gone unnoticed—but that such acknowledgments should not hinder or alter the fact that the American New Wave is still "better" and "smarter" cinema than anything that has emerged since.

Yet, it is, as Haskell suggests, not just that the American New Wave auteurs are all white men. It is hard to argue that the American New Wave canon does not trade in sexism or even at times misogyny when canonized films like *Easy Rider* (1969) and *Five Easy Pieces* (1970) display open disdain for female characters, while others, like *Straw Dogs* (1971), present indulgent portrayals of rape and torture as plot points in the characterization of men.[34] Women's plights are frequently used to elucidate the complexities of the male psyche. The women behind the cameras have fared little better. Until recently, women's careers in the American New Wave have been largely confined to footnotes in discussions of the male auteurs with whom they worked. Polly Platt is often framed as Peter Bogdanovich's creative (ex)wife rather than the set-designer responsible for his most successful films. Director Elaine May is occasionally mentioned as the exception that proves the all-male auteurist rule and Barbara Loden's *Wanda*

(1970) is remembered, ironically, as a "forgotten masterpiece."[35] Despite claims to supporting the civil rights movement, African American voices share a similarly disheartening position in the New Wave canon and criticism, which as Charlene Regester notes, "marginalize[s] films representing the African American experience."[36] African American performers were rarely cast in main roles and so Black characters remained on the peripheries, if in frame at all. Instead, as Adilifu Nama points out, racism was addressed through "foreground[ing] casual racism by whites."[37] It is true that in films like *The French Connection* (1971), or *The Godfather I* and *II*, white characters imbued with racist attitudes displayed an ongoing ugly reality. Yet, Nama's suggestion that these films "at the least [did not avoid racism] as an ongoing presence in American society" sets the bar extremely low for an era intensely celebrated for its political and social concerns. Aside from the occasional inclusion of Melvin Van Peebles's *Sweet Sweetback's Baadasssss Song* (1971), no films by African American filmmakers are included in the canon.[38] American New Wave cinema may have reflected racism as part of the sociopolitical and cultural climate of 1970s America but from a uniformly white, male perspective without retort or counterpoint.

To sustain its elevated status, the American New Wave must also preserve its auteurist agenda. After all, it is far neater to attribute a film's intelligence to a single artistic vision than to unpack the intricacies of collaborative creativity. Given that the gendered passion that the original *politique des auteurs* bestowed on specific "men of the cinema," auteurism was undeniably inaugurated as a tradition of largely white, male genius and as such, the American New Wave myth's foundation is exclusive along racial and gendered lines.[39] Assigning the privileged position as the artists of "truly American" cinema to the most powerful and privileged demographic in American society is undoubtedly a politicized act of exclusion that (intentionally or otherwise) reinforces the white, patriarchal structures that the New Wave myth's claims to cultural and political revolution seek to challenge. Thus, while American New Wave films are "deeply American" the gendered and racial hierarchies they maintain are an integral aspect of this "Americanness."

Courting Importance by Association

Noel King writes that the American New Wave has become "a benchmark against which developments in contemporary Hollywood cinema could be measured, invoked either to confirm a continuing decline from a time of adventurous commercial cinema or to constitute the most appropriate analogy for any current instances of adventurous American cinema."[40] And why not? Given its continually elevated cultural status, it makes perfect sense that comparison to the American New Wave is an aspirational touchstone for some filmmakers and a mechanism of cultural legitimation for adherent critics and scholars. King illustrates this point with a characteristically bold statement made in 1991 by a young Quentin Tarantino. In the lead-up to the release of his debut feature film, *Reservoir Dogs* (1992), Tarantino claimed the burgeoning 1990s indie scene was "the most exciting time in Hollywood since 1971. Because Hollywood is never more exciting than when you don't know."[41] In this statement, "1971" is almost certainly a synecdoche for the American New Wave.

That Tarantino made this claim ahead of the rise of the indie divisions that would alter the Hollywood landscape may appear prophetic.[42] Sure enough, the following decade saw a band of indie-auteurs heralded as the "spiritual descendants" of the American New Wave, among whom were Steven Soderbergh, David Fincher, Spike Jonze, Wes Anderson, Alexander Payne, P. T. Anderson, David O. Russell, Richard Linklater, and, on occasion, Sofia Coppola—depending on the delineator. Comparisons between this collection of young "indie" auteurs and the American New Wave were laid on thick and fast in favorable film criticism. Alongside Newman's "Sundance-Miramax" indies, categorizations such as Jesse Fox Mayshark's "American Eccentrics" and Derek Hill's "(New) American New Wave" all claimed the new band of indie-auteurs as analogues, or inheritors, of the American New Wave. James Mottram, for instance, credits the "Sundance Kids" (a group largely comprised of the filmmakers mentioned above that he associates with an increased importance of the Sundance Festival, rather than actual attendees) as a second coming of the American New Wave. To him, these were filmmakers with idiosyncratic visions who "still believe, even if nobody else does."[43] Although Mottram does not state what these filmmakers believe *in*, the suggestion that they "believe" in *something* promotes an auteurist ideal—a suggestion that personal, visionary cinema was still made within America's overwhelmingly commercial film context.

Despite the vagueness of Mottram's linkages, there certainly are discernable connections between the cinema created by some of the "indie-auteur" filmmakers listed and the canonized films of the American New Wave, many of which are textual. Anderson's *Rushmore* (1998), for instance, clearly recalls *The Graduate* (1967) in its narrative, thematic, and occasionally stylistic strategies.

Yet, other comparisons, such as Edward Norton's claim that *sex, lies and videotape* (1989) was his generation's *The Graduate*, are far less distinct. Norton's rationale, that *sex, lies* expresses "this generational energy" of reluctance and hesitance as its main character, Graham, is "a guy who is just closed down from what he is expected to engage in,"[44] does seemingly draw a comparison between the two films. However, Norton's description is so woolly that it could equally refer to any number of outcast protagonists throughout American film history, including the 1930s and 1940s hardboiled noir detectives, the loner frontiersmen of revisionist westerns, or Joaquin Phoenix's Arthur Fleck in *Joker* (2019).

As in the case of Norton's evocation, often the fervor with which genealogical connections are championed is not matched with sufficient analysis or explanation. Rather, the American New Wave and its hallmark films are deployed as shorthand for culturally vital auteurist cinema that sits in contrast to Hollywood's humdrum commercial fare. It is a means to signify that a film, or filmmaker, *matters*. I strongly suspect that courting such elevation was Tarantino's intention. Encouraging a parallel between his own milieu and an era touted as Hollywood's most politically, socially, and authorially important can surely be attributed to Tarantino's self-mythologizing project.[45] What is Mr. Brown's (played by Tarantino) opening "Like a Virgin" monologue in *Reservoir Dogs* other than an announcement of himself as a new auteur? Tarantino's unabashed pursuit of auteur status has not been in vain—indeed, the tale of his rise "from an unemployed actor-writer working in a video store to the hottest American filmmaker"[46] has been widely taken up as lore in the American film cultural imaginary.

That Tarantino is the most celebrated filmmaker of the Sundance-Miramax era is indisputable. As Newman writes, "If the American independent cinema of the Sundance-Miramax era has produced a masterpiece, it is *Pulp Fiction* (1994). Tarantino's opus topped many critics' best of the 1990s lists and was crowned by *Entertainment Weekly* in 2008 as the #1 classic of the past twenty-five years."[47] It is illuminating that, although he has been an industry heavyweight for well over three decades, Tarantino continues to court the image of the youthful renegade working against Hollywood's systems in the mold of the American New Wave auteur, despite the fact that many New Wave auteurs went on to become major Hollywood players themselves. *Once Upon a Time … in Hollywood* demonstrates that his fealty to the era that spawned the maverick auteur figure has certainly not dwindled. Both the hang-out style of the film—where the periodized Hollywood setting allows fictional characters to rub shoulders with versions of

Sharon Tate, Mama Cass, Bruce Lee, Steve McQueen, and the Manson Family—and its narrative trajectory reflect the New Wave auteur myth.

In an early scene, Rick Dalton (Leonardo DiCaprio), an actor from a once-popular television western, and his long-running stunt double, Cliff Booth (Brad Pitt), discuss Rick's waning career. "No matter what I do, I'm always going to be the horse's ass that got 'Bounty Law' cancelled because I wanted some fucking rinky dink movie career," stutters Rick. In line with Hollywood's goal-oriented narrative conventions, this statement establishes protagonist motivation, a function made explicit moments later when Rick sights his new neighbors—the beautiful Sharon Tate (Margot Robbie) and her elfin director husband, Roman Polanski (Rafal Zawierucha)—for the first time. His self-pity swiftly shifts to awe:

> Holy shit … that was Polanski. That was Roman Polanski! … Here I am, flat on my ass, and who have I got living next to me? The director of *Rosemary's fucking Baby*, that's who! Polanski's the hottest director in town right now, probably the whole fucking world, and he's my next-door fucking neighbor! Shit … who knows what could happen … I could be one pool party away from starring in a Polanski movie!

Rick's enthusiastic optimism and the audience's presumed knowledge that on August 8, 1969, members of the Manson family murdered Tate among others at that very residence drive the film's dramatic tension and serve as a diversion from Rick's ultimately traditional protagonist arc. In this Sergio Leone-inspired fairy-tale version of events, the would-be murderers bungle their home invasion and are subsequently brutally slain by Cliff, and Tate extends a neighborly invitation to a shaken Rick to "come up for a drink." Thus, it is implied that Rick may well transcend into movie stardom by association with Polanski, the New Wave's most controversial figure—considered either as a convicted rapist or, as he is introduced, the world's "hottest director." Yet, it is the hard bodied, violent Cliff—a man cast in the Western loner mold—whose actions save Tate, and 1969 Hollywood. And so, the story goes. … Once upon a time, maverick men saved Hollywood, just as they had done America.

Mavericks and Renegades

Throughout this chapter, I have made the claim that the maverick auteur figure is the primary genealogical link between the New Wave myth and the narrativization of the Sundance-Miramax era as "a canon of important and meaningfully American art works—indeed, a new cinematic American Renaissance."[48] There is a familiarity in titles such as *Cinema of Outsiders, Rebels on the Backlot, The Sundance Kids: How the Mavericks Took Back Hollywood*, and, most obviously, *Charlie Kaufman and Hollywood's Merry Band of Pranksters, Fabulists and Dreamers: An Excursion into the American New Wave*. In these titles, the recurrent use of terms such as "mavericks" or "pranksters" identifies pivotal filmmakers as a loose collective who resist Hollywood convention in the same individualist fashion as their New Wave predecessors.

Five Easy Pieces' famous diner scene personifies this individualism. Bobby (Jack Nicholson) orders a customized omelet, only to be told that his request cannot be fulfilled—not because it is impossible but rather because it contravenes the diner's arbitrary "no substitutions" policy. Bobby reacts with vitriol, a sentiment shared by his female activist hitchhiking companions. However, when one of these women (played by Helena Kallianiotes) attempts to make a stand, Bobby orders her to "shut up." To obtain a side of wheat toast, Bobby orders a chicken salad sandwich then, coldly, requests the female server "hold" each ingredient—the chicken, he "want[s] [her] to hold between her knees." When Bobby is evicted for his endeavor to outsmart the system, he violently swipes at the table in response, sending glasses and cutlery flying. Despite failing in his mission, Bobby is congratulated for being "very clever" by the woman he had aggressively silenced. This illuminates a key feature of the American New Wave type of protagonist and the myth's overarching politics: challenges to the system are the sovereign domain of white intellectual male individuals, who are admired and thanked by those whose voices they silence or drown out in the process.

American New Wave protagonists were "unmotivated heroes" in Thomas Elsaesser's terms—individuals that rejected American social mores of progression and action as incongruous with their generation's reality.[49] Importantly, the form of individualist refusal to engage with a failing society embodied in these protagonists coalesces with the auteurist narratives attributed to their filmmakers. As Elsaesser writes, "European influence, film school training, a re-evaluation of American directors, and expressive style give body to the idea of the *auteur*, understood as the personality manifesting itself in a film or oeuvre through the singular, authentic 'voice.'"[50] Unlike the classical Hollywood auteur, marked by the ability to make manifest a personal style and vision *within* Hollywood's system and its constraints, the American New

Wave auteur was a romantic artist—"[he] set himself off *against* the system." The gendered language here is illuminating; in its reinforcement of masculinist auteurism, celebration of individualism, and the rhetoric of the maverick whose rebellious disposition allows him to forge a new world of liberty and possibility, it echoes the mythological image of the American frontiersman, in Richard Slotkin's formation.[51] As such, like Ethan Edwards before them, both the New Wave protagonists' and auteurs' positions as staunch male loners imbue them with the authority to question the state of the nation. The individualist ideology instilled in the type of auteur figure associated with the American New Wave is what makes the era—and not just its films—such a deeply American fantasy.[52]

The narrative of the Sundance-Miramax indies mobilizes this discourse as a method of elevation to mythology. Chris Cooling outlines this strategy explicitly, writing that the Sundance discourse

> not only engages with the myth of American independence but also is nostalgic for media representations of this mythology, specifically the 1960s/70s "New Hollywood" declaring itself, on some level, aesthetically independent from an increasingly ineffectual studio system … As a result the discourse effectively conflates the desire for a greater sophistication in film with a desire for a greater complexity to American self-interrogation.[53]

As I stated at the outset of this chapter, indie and independent cinema discourse encourages—either actively or passively—elitism through critically positioning its artifacts as a more sophisticated film culture than what is (supposedly) offered by Hollywood. However, as Cooling suggests, the mechanism for the Sundance-Miramax era's elevation within the indie elitist repertoire is predicated on identifying a band of auteurs, who, like those from the American New Wave, create politically and culturally introspective films and as such can be considered as a nationally important "new wave." Given this courted inheritance, it is perhaps predictable that the Sundance-Miramax era indie discourse has come to celebrate similar white, masculinist cinema. As feminist scholars such as Claire Perkins, Cynthia Baron, and Claire Molloy have adeptly explained, the heightened stylistic approach of the Sundance-Miramax filmmakers readily lends their work to being marketed along the same auteurist lines that have historically marginalized women and people of color.[54] Perkins writes:

> The marginalization of female directors in and through the industrial and critical discourse of US indie cinema is effected most powerfully in the maverick myth that cultivates star auteurs such as Quentin Tarantino, Wes Anderson, and

Charlie Kaufman … these male directors are the "rebels on the backlot" who "take back Hollywood." They are credited with the transformation of commercial filmmaking into a better, more artistic type of popular fare. This reception evokes the Hollywood renaissance era of 1967–75, whose male mavericks … have been similarly cast as forging an adventurous new cinema.[55]

It is incumbent on film scholars and critics to interrogate how the narrativization of these "nationally important cinemas" not only reiterates the frontiersman myth but, in doing so, encourages a culturally colonizing effect in that this formulation privileges a certain set of stylistic and thematic practices associated with white male filmmakers over other forms of American independent cinema—and cinema per se.

What Should We Do with the American New Wave Now?

There is a danger that my criticisms of the American New Wave myth will be mistaken for a call to dismiss the era's key films from scholarly and critical debate. Let me be very clear, this is neither my aim nor personal desire. I do not intend to lambast avid viewers as personally committed to maintaining the patriarchal or racist hierarchies preserved in the era's mythology. I do not object to the legitimacy of American New Wave films or the filmmakers as sites of appreciation or fandom. It is, of course, possible to love something critically. I too am a fan of many canonical American New Wave films. I have seen *The Graduate* upward of twenty times and on each viewing, I relish its amusing ironic dialogue, the narrative functions of Simon and Garfunkel's iconic soundtrack, and the subtle editing that slides between overt and covert character subjectivity—and yet, I find its rampant sexism abhorrent every single time.

Rather than dismiss these films, my aim is to probe the discursive and critical frameworks used to signify the ongoing importance of the American New Wave myth and its use as a benchmark in American film culture. I argue that there has been a misdiagnosis of what is "deeply American" about American New Wave cinema: a celebration of its purported challenges to the status quo rather than its reiteration of exclusively white masculine narratives that are taken to speak for the nation. This strategy repeats and reasserts the very inequalities that the American New Wave myth is credited as challenging. It is revealing that scholarship that seeks to address the gendered and racial demarcations of the New Wave and indie cinema tends to be published in "retrospectives," "revisitations," or "reassessments"—the current volume included. That this collection seeks to reassess the American New Wave and recover films and filmmakers not previously acknowledged as part of its canon highlights the exclusivity of the New Wave's formulation and speaks loudly of its legacy. The work and representation of women and people of color are integral to these acts of recovery and reassessment. That these demographics are subsequently "reinserted" into this *important* era only reinforces that they were written out in the first place. Thus, when the American New Wave is reductively evoked as a lionizing mechanism for more contemporary filmmakers, or groups of filmmakers, it has a culturally colonizing effect—both in terms of American national identity and film culture discourses. Of course, it would be ridiculous to claim the American New Wave should never function comparatively. Indeed, comparisons can be productive—however, they must be justified. That is to say, it simply behooves us to remain alert to *what it is* we are talking about when we invoke the American New Wave and alive to how such invocations operate critically.

Notes

1 Geoff King, "Introduction: What Indie Isn't ... Mapping the Indie Field," in *A Companion to American Indie Film*, ed. Geoff King (Malden, MA: Wiley-Blackwell, 2016), 1.

2 Michael Z. Newman, *Indie: An American Film Culture* (New York: Columbia University Press, 2011), 1–46.

3 Ibid., 2.

4 Kim Wilkins, *American Eccentric Cinema* (New York: Bloomsbury, 2019), 24–30. See also Geoff King, *Indiewood, USA: Where Hollywood Meets Independent Cinema* (London: I.B. Tauris, 2009); and Rona Murray, *Studying American Independent Cinema* (New York: Auteur, 2011).

5 Janet Staiger, "Independent of What? Sorting Out Differences from Hollywood," in *A Companion to American Indie Film*, 16.

6 See Linda Badley, Claire Perkins, and Michele Schreiber's magnificent collection *Indie Reframed: Women's Filmmaking and Contemporary American Independent Cinema* (Edinburgh: Edinburgh University Press, 2016) and chapters by Yannis

Tzioumakis and Andy Stubbs in Kim Wilkins and Wyatt Moss-Wellington, eds., *ReFocus: The Films of Spike Jonze* (Edinburgh: Edinburgh University Press, 2019).

7   For a detailed account of mini-majors and specialty divisions, see Alisa Perren's *Indie, Inc.*, and Yannis Tzioumakis, *Hollywood's Indies: Classics Divisions, Specialty Labels and the American Film Market* (Edinburgh: Edinburgh University Press, 2012).

8   Rob Stone makes a similar assertion in *The Cinema of Richard Linklater: Walk, Don't Run* (New York: Columbia University Press, 2018), 5.

9   Nick Heffernan, "The Last Movie and the Critique of Imperialism," *Film International* 4, no. 3 (2006): 12.

10   Julie Levinson, *The American Success Myth on Film* (New York: Palgrave Macmillan, 2012), 3.

11   See, for instance, Peter Biskind, *Easy Riders, Raging Bulls: How the Sex-Drugs-and-Rock'n'Roll Generation Saved Hollywood* (New York: Simon & Schuster, 1998); Jonathan Demme and Richard LaGravenese's *A Decade under the Influence* (2003); Mark Harris, *Pictures at a Revolution: Five Movies and the Birth of the New Hollywood* (New York: Penguin Press, 2008).

12   Susan Wloszczyna, " 'Easy Riders, Raging Bulls' Author Peter Biskind Looks Back at the New Hollywood" (July 18, 2014), https://www.indiewire.com/2014/07/easy-riders-raging-bulls-author-peter-biskind-looks-back-at-the-new-hollywood-191482/, accessed July 4, 2019.

13   This strategy is not distinct to Biskind, indeed it is employed by other popular accounts, such as Kenneth Bowser's documentary adaptation of *Easy Riders* (2003), *Decade under the Influence* (2003), and Harris', *Pictures at a Revolution.*

14   Richard Maltby, *Hollywood Cinema* (Malden, MA: Wiley-Blackwell, 2003), 18.

15   David Thomson, "Dream Factory," *The Guardian* (February 23, 2008), https://www.theguardian.com/film/2008/feb/23/film (accessed December 17, 2019), but see also Tino Balio's valuable *United Artists, Volume 1, 1919–1950 The Company Built by the Stars* (Madison: University of Wisconsin Press, 2009); and *United Artists: The Company That Changed the Film Industry* (Madison: University of Wisconsin Press, 1987).

16   Thomas Elsaesser, "American Auteur Cinema: The Last—or First—Picture Show?" in *The Last Great American Picture Show: New Hollywood Cinema in the 1970s*, ed. Thomas Elsaesser, Noel King, and Alexander Horwath (Amsterdam: Amsterdam University Press, 2004), 37–8.

17   David A Cook, *Lost Illusions: American Cinema in the Shadow of Watergate and Vietnam, 1970–1979* (Berkeley: University of California Press, 2002); and Robin Wood, *Hollywood from Vietnam to Reagan* (New York: Columbia University Press, 1986).

18 Noel King, " 'The Last Good Time We Ever Had': Remembering the New
    Hollywood Cinema," in *The Last Great American Picture Show*, 32–3.

19 David Thomson, "The Decade When Movies Mattered," in *The Last Great
    American Picture Show*, 82.

20 King, " 'The Last Good Time We Ever Had,' " 33.

21 Jonathan Kirshner and Jon Lewis, eds., *When the Movies Mattered: The New
    Hollywood Revisited* (Ithaca, NY: Cornell University Press, 2019), 7.

22 Ibid.

23 Sean Martin, *New Waves in Cinema* (Harpenden, UK: Kamera Books,
    2013), 11–15.

24 Nicholas Godfrey, *The Limits of Auteurism: Case Studies in the Critically
    Constructed New Hollywood* (New Brunswick, NJ: Rutgers University Press,
    2018), 5.

25 For example, Geoff King's *New Hollywood Cinema: An Introduction* (London: I.B.
    Tauris, 2002) for a breakdown of the contestation of the term "New Hollywood."

26 Godfrey, *The Limits of Auteurism*, 217.

27 Yannis Tzioumakis and Peter Krämer issue a similar warning about "[overstating]
    the unique qualities of the late 1960s and early 1970s in American (film) history"
    or "mistak[ing] the part for the whole." See their "Introduction" in their *The
    Hollywood Renaissance: Revisiting American Cinema's Most Celebrated Era*
    (London: Bloomsbury, 2018), xv–xvii.

28 Godfrey, *Limits of Auteurism*, 17.

29 See, for example, Todd Berliner, *Hollywood Incoherent: Narration in Seventies
    Cinema* (Austin: University of Texas Press, 2010); John Hellmann, "The New
    Hollywood Cinema and After," in *The Cambridge History of Postmodern Literature*,
    ed. Brian McHale and Len Platt (New York: Cambridge University Press, 2016),
    214–29.

30 Godfrey, *The Limits of Auteurism*, 217.

31 Tzioumakis and Krämer, "Introduction," xix.

32 Molly Haskell, "The Mad Housewives of the Neo-Woman's film: The Age of
    Ambivalence Revisited," in *When the Movies Mattered*, 19.

33 Lewis and Kirshner, *When the Movies Mattered*, xix.

34 Cook, *Lost Illusions*, 197, 362.

35 Aaron Hunter, "Designing Authorship: Polly Platt's Contributions to the Early
    Films of Peter Bogdanovich," *SCMS*, Atlanta, 2016. Bérénice Reynaud, "For
    Wanda," in *The Last Great American Picture Show*; and Alexandra Heller-Nicholas
    and Dean Brandum, *Refocus the Films of Elaine May* (Edinburgh: Edinburgh
    University Press, 2019).

36   Charlene Regester, "A Matter of Race and Gender: *Lady Sings the Blues* (1972) and the Hollywood Renaissance Canon," in *The Hollywood Renaissance*, 186.

37   Adilifu Nama, *Race on the QT: Blackness and the Films of Quentin Tarantino* (Austin: University of Texas Press, 2015), 4.

38   Maitland McDonagh is among those who include Van Peebles in the canon; however, it is noteworthy that her work is concerned with exploitation films and marginalization. See her "The Exploitation Generation, Or: How Marginal Movies Came in from the Cold," in *The Last Great American Picture Show*, 108.

39   See Claire Perkins, "Beyond Indiewood: The Everyday Ethics of Nicole Holofcener." *Camera Obscura: Feminism, Culture, and Media Studies* 29, no. 1 (2014): 137–59.

40   King, "'The Last Good Time We Ever Had,'" 32.

41   Ibid.

42   Perren, *Indie, Inc.*

43   James Mottram, *The Sundance Kids: How the Mavericks Took Back Hollywood* (London: Faber & Faber, 2006), xv.

44   Quoted in Peter Biskind, *Down and Dirty Pictures: Miramax, Sundance and the rise of Independent Film* (London: Bloomsbury, 2016), 41.

45   See David Roche, *Quentin Tarantino: Poetics and Politics of Cinematic Metafiction* (Jackson: University Press of Mississippi, 2018).

46   Emanuel Levy, *Cinema of Outsiders: The Rise of American Independent Film* (New York: New York University Press, 1999), 16.

47   Perren, *Indie Inc.*, 182.

48   Chris Cooling, *Declarations of Independence: Film and the American Mythology*, PhD dissertation USC, 2007, 240.

49   Thomas Elsaesser, "The Pathos of Failure: American Films in the 1970s: Notes on the Unmotivated Hero," in *The Last Great American Picture Show*, 279–92.

50   Elsaesser, "American Auteur Cinema," 46.

51   Richard Slotkin, *Regeneration through Violence: The Mythology of the American Frontier, 1600–1860* (Middletown, CT: Wesleyan University Press, 1973).

52   Kathleen A. McHugh, "Miranda July and the New Twenty-First-Century Indie," in *Indie Reframed*, 239.

53   Cooling, *Declarations of Independence*, 33.

54   Perkins, "Beyond Indiewood"; Cynthia Baron, "Not Just Indie: A Look at Films by Dee Rees, Ava DuVernay and Kasi Lemmons," in *Indie Reframed*, 204–20, Claire Molloy, "Indie Cinema and the Neoliberal Commodification of Creative Labor: Rethinking the Indie Sensibility of Christopher Nolan," in *A Companion to American Indie Film*, ed. Geoff King (Malden, MA: Wiley-Blackwell, 2017), 368–88.

55   Perkins, "Beyond Indiewood," 140.

12

Afterword: New Wave, New Hollywood, New Research

Peter Krämer

The "American New Wave," the "Hollywood Renaissance," the "New Hollywood"—
in often ambiguous and, in the case of "New Hollywood," even contradictory ways,
these terms have guided a tremendous amount of scholarly and journalistic writing
about American cinema of the late 1960s and the 1970s.[1] Indeed, partly inspired by
the fiftieth anniversaries of many key films of the late 1960s, the last few years have
seen the publication of, and work toward, a series of high-profile essay collections
on this topic (including the present volume): *The Hollywood Renaissance: Revisiting
American Cinema's Most Celebrated Era*, edited by myself and Yannis Tzioumakis,
published by Bloomsbury Academic in 2018; *When Movies Mattered: The New
Hollywood Revisited*, edited by Jonathan Kirshner and Jon Lewis, published
by Cornell University Press in 2019; *The Other Hollywood Renaissance*, a 2020
collection edited by Dominic Lennard, R. Barton Palmer, and Murray Pomerance
for Edinburgh University Press; and *Women and New Hollywood*, a collection based
on a 2018 conference, currently being put together by Aaron Hunter and Martha
Shearer for Rutgers University Press. There also is Vincent LoBrutto's monograph
The Seventies: The Decade That Changed American Film Forever (forthcoming from
Rowman & Littlefield).

In addition, the years since 2018 have seen the publication of a range of
monographs to do with, for example, key film cycles of the American New Wave/
Hollywood Renaissance/New Hollywood and their critical reception; with some
of the key filmmakers and production companies of the American New Wave;

with poetics and the systematic and detailed analysis of exemplary films such as *Electra Glide in Blue* (1973), *The Parallax View* (1974), and *Carrie* (1976).[2] During this short time, there have also been academic volumes and books addressed to a general audience on individual filmmakers closely associated with the American New Wave such as Robert Altman, Peter Bogdanovich, William Friedkin, John Milius, Mike Nichols, Paul Schrader, and Martin Scorsese; actors such as Robert De Niro; and films such as *Rosemary's Baby* (1968), *2001: A Space Odyssey* (1968), *Easy Rider* (1969), *The Wild Bunch* (1969), *Midnight Cowboy* (1969), *A Clockwork Orange* (1971), *American Graffiti* (1973), *Chinatown* (1974), *Annie Hall* (1977), and *The Deer Hunter* (1978).[3] Also, since 2018, many books have been published about Woody Allen, Stanley Kubrick, Terrence Malick, and Steven Spielberg, four filmmakers who were, for a while, associated with the American New Wave.[4]

As is already indicated by these examples, the main focus of writing about the American New Wave has traditionally been on a relatively small corpus of theatrically released features from the late 1960s and 1970s, most of them financed and distributed by the major Hollywood studios and most of them directed (and also in most cases written and produced) by white males, especially those in their thirties and forties, with typical protagonists being white males as well, albeit on average about a decade younger.[5]

In the same way that the meanings of the labels American New Wave or Hollywood Renaissance or New Hollywood have varied and changed over time, so has the group of films that has been discussed most extensively under this rubric, although there is also a lot of continuity and consistency. Writers and editors (and here I certainly have to include myself) rarely give a detailed explanation for why certain films and filmmakers are included or excluded, instead relying on in places rather vague claims about their distinctiveness (with a particular emphasis on how the films and filmmakers included can be claimed to be stylistically, formally, and thematically innovative and challenging) or simply working with the established canon, with minor additions and subtractions at the margins of a core group of films.[6]

There are some obvious observations to be made about this state of affairs. First of all, there is the simple fact that however the American New Wave corpus is defined, it makes up only a small fraction of the hundreds of American-produced films shown in American cinemas in the late 1960s and the 1970s,[7] and yet, confusingly, the American New Wave is often taken to stand in for all of American cinema during this period, as if this small fraction somehow represented the totality of films or as if American New Wave films were the only ones from this period worth writing about. But clearly the American New Wave is not in any straightforward way representative of the American film industry's overall output, nor would anyone, on reflection, claim that there is nothing worth saying about the hundreds of films from these years which are not usually discussed as part of the American New Wave. This is especially true if one looks beyond the films that belong to a broadly defined mainstream cinema and the art-house sector into experimental, avant-garde, and underground films or outright exploitation and hardcore pornography presented in (often specialized) movie theaters.

It is not the case that the majority of mainstream releases that are excluded from the American New Wave or all these other forms of theatrically exhibited films are not written about at all. There is a substantial literature on American cinema of the 1960s and 1970s that might mention, even highlight, the American New Wave corpus but also discusses hundreds of other films.[8] One area of special scholarly interest—with or without reference to the American New Wave—is the late 1960s and 1970s films made by and/or for and/or about African Americans.[9] There is also a growing literature on female filmmakers and female stars of the 1960s and 1970s.[10] Then there is a considerable amount of writing about experimental, avant-garde, and underground film[11] and about exploitation and pornography of the period.[12] So the problem is not that all these types of film are neglected by scholars, it is just that they are not discussed under the rubric American New Wave—despite the fact that many productions of these types were certainly innovative in their respective fields (whereby porn features such as *Deep Throat* (1972) were also shown in mainstream movie theaters and had a considerable cultural impact).

In response to this state of affairs, one might simply accept (and also state very clearly in each new piece of writing) that ongoing scholarship on the American New Wave is concerned with a tiny fraction of American film production of the late 1960s and 1970s. One could also argue that, given the often rather vague, or merely implied, characteristics used to delineate the corpus under investigation, it is important to work toward a more precise and explicit set of criteria and then to examine whether some films and filmmakers usually excluded from the canon do in fact fit the criteria and therefore should be dealt with as part of the American New Wave (but also whether certain films and filmmakers in the canon do *not* fit them, and therefore should be excluded).

Or, more drastically, one could conclude that enough is enough: Too much time and energy has been spent for several decades on the small corpus of films in this rubric (even if it is occasionally enlarged a little bit). One might go as far as demanding that, as film scholars, we should shift our efforts elsewhere. This last point is not likely to be accepted; after all, academic writing about film noir and Alfred Hitchcock (to name but two, admittedly rather extreme, examples) has been going on, at a high level of productivity, for many decades (and, to move outside the discipline of Film Studies, on Shakespeare for centuries). Indeed, the very fact that much has already been written is part of the very justification for writing even more. And, as this volume clearly shows, there *is* so much more to be said about the American New Wave.

To begin with, the films of the American New Wave are usually discussed in terms of their directors, providing a striking example of the traditional focus of Film Studies on single authors (or "auteurs"), which despite decades-long theoretical debates and, in recent years, much revisionist, empirical research on actual film production has proven to be surprisingly resilient.[13] So there is a lot of work to be done on the production histories of films from the American New Wave canon,[14] dealing, for example, with key creative personnel other than directors (see especially the chapters by Aaron Hunter and Oliver Gruner in this volume) and also other labor; and within the traditional framework of director-based studies, the American New Wave corpus can be expanded to include more women and African Americans (see especially the chapters by Hunter, Aimee Mollaghan, and Aimee Dixon Anthony). The emerging trend toward studying the role of production personnel other than directors in the American New Wave ties in with recent, general developments in Film Studies to do with so-called Production Studies,[15] with Producer Studies[16] as well as with ongoing research on, for example, actors, scriptwriters, and editors.[17]

Building on long-standing scholarly interest in the central role played by Jews in Hollywood,[18] it is also important to examine the American New Wave, which foregrounded ethnicity (mainly Jewish American and Italian American, both on the screen and among personnel) as one of its distinctive features, in this regard (see especially the chapter by Vincent Brook; Jewishness is also discussed, to a lesser extent, in Emilio Audissino's chapter). A certain tension may arise here when discussing the fact that, both on-screen and behind the camera, African Americans were severely underrepresented in the American New Wave (and in 1960s and 1970s Hollywood more generally), while Jewish Americans were massively overrepresented.[19] Arguments for increased participation of African

Americans in Hollywood imply that the participation of those racial/ethnic groups who are overrepresented would have to be reduced. More generally, it has been argued that ethnic self-assertion (by Jewish Americans, Italian Americans, Irish Americans, etc.), especially in the 1970s, was in many ways a defensive response to the civil rights movement and African American radicalism, aiming to justify and thus protect "white" privilege.[20]

This, together with the extreme marginalization of women (on-screen, in the production process, and also in the audience),[21] poses a challenge to the positive critical bias of scholarly work on the American New Wave. To put it bluntly, by and large scholars proceed from the assumption that the American New Wave was a good thing and then focus on demonstrating the aesthetic or political qualities of individual films or groups of films.[22] Connecting with an older tradition that was highly critical of the American New Wave, it is very reasonable to expect that the opposite case will be put forward as well (see especially the chapters by Fjoralba Miraka and Kim Wilkins), but also that certain films, which may have a problematic relationship with the American New Wave (due to their apparently reactionary politics and/or aesthetics or their genre), are being reexamined (see the chapters by Cary Edwards and Audissino).

More generally, there is an ongoing need to critically reflect on the very idea of an American New Wave[23] as part of a broader history of American film criticism (both journalistic and academic) and of the discipline of Film Studies.[24] There have been some attempts to examine how and why the idea that there was something historically new in late 1960s cinema took shape, how it evolved over time, and how it has exerted considerable influence not only on film writing but also on filmmaking (see especially the chapters by Mollaghan, Wilkins, and Karen Ritzenhoff and Hannah D'Orso). More such work is needed.

There is also a shortage of detailed, empirical analyses of the connections between the films and filmmakers of the American New Wave and the filmmaking traditions that preceded and ran in parallel with it.[25] These include not only classical Hollywood cinema (see especially Miraka's chapter) and European art cinema, including the French Nouvelle Vague from which the American New Wave takes its name (see especially Audissino's chapter), but also, among many others, African American filmmaking traditions (see Anthony's chapter), experimental cinema, exploitation cinema, documentary filmmaking, underground cinema, and various television formats. To what extent did the people making American New Wave films explicitly talk about such traditions, what direct contact with the films and filmmakers in these traditions did they have (here one might want to consider the role of art-house cinemas, repertory cinemas, film festivals and film schools),[26] which specific thematic, formal, and stylistic elements did they appropriate, and to what extent was this appropriation recognized as such by critics and general audiences at the time?[27]

These questions are connected to two further lines of inquiry, which have not received sufficient attention. The first is the systematic formal, stylistic, and thematic analysis not just of individual films but of the whole American New Wave canon,[28] which can then be compared with other types of film (e.g., classical Hollywood cinema and European art cinema).[29] Among many promising areas of research are sound design and stylistic issues to do with the presentation of violence and sex.[30]

The second line of inquiry concerns the initial critical reception of, and contemporary media discourses about, American New Wave films.[31] While Reception Studies has made major inroads into Film Studies in recent decades,[32] there have been surprisingly few studies along these lines of individual American New Wave films (do see, however, the discussion of reception in several contributions to this volume, for example in Edwards's chapter).[33] What appears to be missing altogether is extensive studies of the process of reputation building (for films and filmmakers), which, among other things, examine the role of both journalistic and scholarly writing, of rereleases and television broadcasts, of retrospectives and the programming of repertory cinemas.[34] Closely connected to this are much-needed explorations of the teaching of American cinema of the 1960s and 1970s at universities and the role of the American New Wave within it (and within textbooks). Finally, it might be worth comparing the critical standing of American New Wave films with that of other types of film. There are, I think, many surprises to be had when examining the *Sight & Sound* surveys of international critics and filmmakers regarding the world's "greatest films" ever, the American Film Institute's list of the 100 "greatest American" movies of all time or similar polls: for example, Hollywood cinema of the 1950s may well outshine the much celebrated American New Wave canon.

In these ways, it is possible to explore the success of American New Wave films with critics, film industry peers, scholars, and teachers. It stands to reason that historians should also investigate their success at the box office, especially given the fact that most of these films had substantial, and in a few cases such as *The Godfather* (1972) and *The Exorcist* (1973) extremely big (far above average), budgets. More generally, a comprehensive account of the American New Wave should include a business perspective, dealing with film finance, with the operations of production companies and distributors, with marketing strategies, and the financial returns from theatrical releases as well as other sources of income. While there is a vast literature both in Film Studies and in other disciplines on all of these topics,[35] including studies focusing on the 1960s and 1970s,[36] this work rarely explores the specific circumstances of the financing, production, marketing, and release of individual American New Wave films.[37] Many American New Wave films feature prominently in studies of major production trends and hit patterns in the United States due to their outstanding box-office success,[38] but there are few systematic studies of the majority of films that did not do so well at the box office and often lost money for their financiers, distributors, and producers.[39] Such financial studies could in turn be connected to the examination of film cycles, in terms of both textual analysis and financial performance.[40]

Next comes the question in which movie theaters American New Wave films were shown during their original theatrical release, where they were presented later on (in cinemas, on television, video, DVD, streaming services, etc.), and who watched American New Wave films in these different arenas. What were the demographic profiles of these audiences, the circumstances of their viewings, and their responses to the films?[41] Such queries tie in with the major inroads that the study of film exhibition and audiences has made in Film Studies in recent decades.[42]

The enormous scholarly effort that could be involved here becomes even more obvious when one considers that all this research on the marketing, exhibition, critical reception, and audiences of American New Wave films, on reputation building and teaching should ideally cover not only the United States but other countries as well, in many of which these films had a considerable impact. So it seems that, despite the extraordinarily large number of publications on the American New Wave/Hollywood Renaissance/New Hollywood in recent years, and indeed in recent decades, there is, as the saying goes, more work to be done.

At the beginning of this afterword, I mentioned that the term "New Hollywood" has been widely used in contradictory ways. In fact, in some contexts it refers to what is otherwise called the American New Wave or Hollywood Renaissance, and in others to what is usually argued to have come afterward, with the success of *Jaws* (1975) and *Star Wars* (1977) signaling, it is argued, a return to dominance of more traditional forms of film entertainment and the marginalization of the challenging and innovative auteur cinema of the late 1960s and early to mid-1970s. While I would certainly agree that mainstream

American cinema underwent significant changes in the late 1960s and then again in the late 1970s,[43] I have never found the frequently cited opposition of "auteur cinema" and "blockbuster entertainment" very useful to capture these changes. After all, the two most celebrated films of the New Hollywood of the period from the late 1960s to the mid-1970s—*2001: A Space Odyssey* and *The Godfather*—were superexpensive, heavily marketed, and enormously successful blockbusters. In addition, George Lucas and Steven Spielberg, the two most commercially successful filmmakers of the late 1970s and early 1980s, did not only belong to the so-called film school generation but also managed to assert a high degree of control over their filmmaking, to pursue particular themes (including very personal ones) across their films of this period, to receive, both then and later, a lot of critical recognition (not least because in the context of their times both *Star Wars* and *Close Encounters of the Third Kind* (1977) were widely perceived to be highly unusual and indeed risky productions), and to achieve more name recognition than almost all other filmmakers. Surely, we would have to characterize them as auteurs. Thus, in my view, more clarification is needed about whether the American New Wave or Hollywood Renaissance really came to an end, and, if it did, when and why—which is connected to the question raised earlier about the so far rather vague criteria being used to determine whether a particular film or filmmaker belongs to the American New Wave/Hollywood Renaissance in the first place.

Importantly, the question of when, how, and why the American New Wave/Hollywood Renaissance began—which can conveniently be answered with reference to a famous *Time* magazine cover story from December 1967 announcing the arrival of a "renaissance" in American mainstream cinema[44]— also needs further attention. Most specifically, it is obvious that changes in the American film industry's self-regulation of content (and, connected with this, also of style) through the Motion Picture Association of America played an important part in making this renaissance possible. Crucially, Hollywood gave up its traditional aim that all its releases should, in principle, be suitable for all age groups and also largely avoid controversy (especially where municipal and state censorship boards or powerful pressure groups might get involved).[45]

In many scholarly accounts of this fundamental shift, much emphasis has been put on the replacement of the long-standing Production Code with age-specific ratings in 1968.[46] But as 1967 is usually identified, not least by *Time* magazine, as the single most transformative year—most notably in relation to the hugely controversial release, and belated box-office success, of *Bonnie and*

Clyde, with its exceptionally graphic depiction of violence, and the almost record-breaking box-office returns for *The Graduate*, which features a transgressive sexual relationship and nudity—developments in 1966 must have prepared the ground.[47]

Indeed, there is some literature on changes to the Production Code, especially the introduction of the "suggested for mature audiences" label in September 1966, which allowed producers and distributors to depart from the stipulations of the Code and thus opened the door for, among many other things, explorations of sexuality and violence that had not previously been possible in mainstream cinema in the United States.[48] However, not much research has been carried out on how this new label was actually understood and deployed by the Production Code Administration in its decision-making, by distributors and exhibitors in the advertising and publicity they organized, and by cinemagoers making decisions about which films to see.[49] I want to end my afterword with this very specific suggestion for future research on the American New Wave/Hollywood Renaissance/New Hollywood.

Notes

1   I have previously surveyed this literature in Peter Krämer, "Post-classical Hollywood," in *The Oxford Guide to Film Studies*, ed. John Hill and Pamela Church Gibson (Oxford: Oxford University Press, 1998), 296–305; Peter Krämer, *The New Hollywood: From Bonnie and Clyde to Star Wars* (London: Wallflower, 2005), 1–3; and Peter Krämer and Yannis Tzioumakis, "Introduction," in *The Hollywood Renaissance: Revisiting American Cinema's Most Celebrated Era*, ed. Peter Krämer and Yannis Tzioumakis (New York: Bloomsbury Academic, 2018), xiii–xxvii. As will soon become obvious in this chapter, the literature on the films and filmmakers of the American New Wave/Hollywood Renaissance/New Hollywood is truly vast. I will mostly confine myself to references to English-language books, and even these references are highly selective, as are my references to particular English-language book chapters or journal essays, because a comprehensive survey would have to deal with hundreds of titles. I should also note that in the light of this overwhelming number, I have often stuck with the literature I have become most familiar with over the years, including my own publications, although I have also tried to capture the full range of writing about this topic.

2   Nicholas Godfrey, *The Limits of Auteurism: Case Studies in the Critically Constructed New Hollywood* (New Brunswick, NJ: Rutgers University Press, 2018); Jeff Menne,

Post-Fordist Cinema: Hollywood Auteurs and the Corporate Counterculture
(New York: Columbia University Press, 2019); and Hauke Lehmann, *Affect Poetics of the New Hollywood: Suspense, Paranoia, and Melancholy* (Berlin: de Gruyter, 2020). See also Chris Horn, *The Lost Decade: The Fortunes and Films of the "Hollywood Renaissance Auteur" in the 1980s* (PhD diss., University of Leicester, 2020), https:// leicester.figshare.com/articles/thesis/The_Lost_Decade_The_Fortunes_and_Films_ of_the_Hollywood_Renaissance_Auteur_in_the_1980s/12771071/1.

3   In chronological order: Catherine O'Brien, *Martin Scorsese's Divine Comedy: Movies and Religion* (New York: Bloomsbury Academic, 2018); Ash Carter and Sam Kashner, *Life Isn't Everything: Mike Nichols, as Remembered by 150 of His Closest Friends* (New York: Henry Holt, 2019); Alfio Leotta, *The Cinema of John Milius* (Lanham, MD: Lexington Books, 2019); W. K. Stratton, *The Wild Bunch: Sam Peckinpah, a Revolution in Hollywood, and the Making of a Legendary Film* (New York: Bloomsbury, 2019); Alison Castle, ed., *Stanley Kubrick's A Clockwork Orange: Behind the Scenes Book and DVD* (Cologne: Taschen, 2019); Christopher Lane, ed., *William Friedkin: Interviews* (Jackson: University Press of Mississippi, 2020); Michelle E. Moore and Brian Brems, eds., *ReFocus: The Films of Paul Schrader* (Edinburgh: Edinburgh University Press, 2020); Eric San Juan, *The Films of Martin Scorsese: Gangsters, Greed, and Guilt* (New York: Rowman & Littlefield, 2020); Peter Tonguette, *Picturing Peter Bogdanovich: My Conversations with the New Hollywood Director* (Lexington: University Press of Kentucky, 2020); Michael Newton, *Rosemary's Baby* (London: British Film Institute, 2020); Steven Bingen, *Easy Rider: 50 Years Looking for America* (Lanham, MD: Rowman & Littlefield, 2020); Sam Wasson, *The Big Goodbye: Chinatown and the Last Years of Hollywood* (New York: Flatiron Books, 2020); Jay Glennie, *One Shot: The Making of The Deer Hunter* (Chelmsford: Coattail, 2020); Adam Ganz and Stephen Price, *Robert De Niro at Work: From Screenplay to Screen Performance* (Basingstoke: Palgrave Macmillan, 2020); Mark Minett, *Robert Altman and the Elaboration of Hollywood Storytelling* (New York: Oxford University Press, 2021); Mark Harris, *Mike Nichols: A Life* (New York: Penguin, 2021); Glenn Frankel, *Shooting Midnight Cowboy: Art, Sex, Loneliness, and the Making of a Dark Classic* (New York: Farrar, Straus and Giroux, 2021); Peter Krämer, *American Graffiti: George Lucas, the New Hollywood and the Baby Boom Generation* (London: Routledge, forthcoming); and Jonathan Ellis and Ana-Maria Sanchez-Arce, eds., *Remembering Annie Hall* (New York: Bloomsbury Academic, forthcoming). In addition, one might want to include Christopher Frayling, *Once Upon a Time in the West: Shooting a Masterpiece* (London: Reel Art Press, 2019). There is no space here to list all the recent books on *2001: A Space Odyssey* but, for obvious reasons, I would like to give the following volume as an

example: Peter Krämer, *2001: A Space Odyssey*, 2nd ed. (London: British Film Institute, 2020).

4   There are too many titles to list them all here, but see the following examples: Thomas S. Hischak, *The Woody Allen Encyclopedia* (Lanham, MD: Rowman & Littlefield, 2018); Nathan Abrams, *Stanley Kubrick: New York Jewish Intellectual* (New Brunswick, NJ: Rutgers University Press, 2018); Adam Barkman and Antonio Sanna, eds., *A Critical Companion to Steven Spielberg* (Lanham, MD: Lexington Books, 2019); and Joshua Sikora, ed., *A Critical Companion to Terrence Malick* (Lanham, MD: Lexington Books, 2020).

5   Cf. Krämer and Tzioumakis, "Introduction," xviii–xix.

6   For example, when putting together *The Hollywood Renaissance*, Yannis Tzioumakis and I decided mostly to stick to the established canon but also to broaden it by including two films that can certainly be considered innovative but are not usually discussed in this context: *Funny Girl* (1968) and *Lady Sings the Blues* (1972); Krämer and Tzioumakis, "Introduction," xxi–xxii.

7   Cf. Joel Finler, *The Hollywood Story* (London: Octopus, 1988), 280. This book is very useful for all kinds of information about the American film industry as a whole (number of cinemas, number of releases, profits and losses, etc.) and about specific studios (personnel, production trends, budgets, hits and flops, etc.).

8   See, for example, the relevant volumes/sections in the two major multivolume histories of American cinema, namely Cynthia Lucia, Roy Grundmann, and Art Simon, eds., *The Wiley-Blackwell History of American Film Volume III: 1946–1975*; *Volume IV: 1976 to the Present* (Malden, MA: Wiley-Blackwell, 2012); and Paul Monaco, *The Sixties, 1960–1969* (New York: Scribner's, 1999) as well as David A. Cook, *Lost Illusions: American Cinema in the Shadow of Watergate and Vietnam, 1970–1979* (New York: Scribner's, 2000)—these are volumes 8 and 9 in Scribner's *History of the American Cinema*.

9   In addition to coverage in Wiley-Blackwell's and Scribner's multivolume histories, see, for example, the following recent publications: Christopher Sieving, *Soul Searching: Black-Themed Cinema from the March on Washington to the Rise of Blaxploitation* (Middletown, CT: Wesleyan University Press, 2011); Allyson Nadia Field, Jan-Christopher Horak, and Jacqueline Nayuma Stewart, eds., *L.A. Rebellion: Creating a New Black Cinema* (Berkeley: University of California Press, 2015); Novotny Lawrence and Gerald R. Butters, Jr., eds., *Beyond Blaxploitation* (Detroit: Wayne State University Press, 2016); and Eithne Quinn, *A Piece of the Action: Race and Labor in Post-Civil Rights Hollywood* (New York: Columbia University Press, 2020).

10 See, for example, Maya Montanez Smukler, *Liberating Hollywood: Women Directors and the Feminist Reform of 1970s American Cinema* (New Brunswick, NJ: Rutgers

University Press, 2019); and Aaron Hunter and Martha Shearer, eds., *Women and New Hollywood* (New Brunswick, NJ: Rutgers University Press, forthcoming). Also see the extensive literature on Barbra Streisand (e.g., Neal Gabler, *Barbra Streisand: Redefining Beauty, Femininity, and Power* [New Haven, CT: Yale University Press, 2016]) and Jane Fonda; I have referenced some of the rich Fonda literature, much of which relates to the 1960s and 1970s, in Peter Krämer, "When 'Hanoi Jane' Conquered Hollywood: Jane Fonda's Films and Activism, 1977–1981," in *The New Film History: Sources, Methods, Approaches*, ed. James Chapman, Mark Glancy, and Sue Harper (Basingstoke: Palgrave Macmillan, 2007), 104–16.

11   See, for example, David E. James's classic study *Allegories of Cinema: American Film in the Sixties* (Princeton, NJ: Princeton University Press, 1989) as well as, more recently, Juan R. Suarez, *Bike Boys, Drag Queens, and Superstars: Avant-Garde, Mass Culture, and Gay Identities in the 1960s Underground Cinema* (Bloomington: Indiana University Press, 1997); and Ara Osterweil, *Flesh Cinema: The Corporeal Turn in American Avant-Garde Film* (Manchester: Manchester University Press, 2014).

12   See, for example, Jon Lewis, *Hollywood v. Hard Core: How the Struggle over Censorship Saved the Modern Film Industry* (New York: New York University Press, 2002); Eric Schaefer, ed., *Sex Scene: Media and the Sexual Revolution* (Durham, NC: Duke University Press, 2014); and Elena Garfinkel, *Lewd Looks: American Sexploitation Cinema in the 1960s* (Minneapolis: University of Minnesota Press, 2017).

13   For recent publications on Hollywood authorship and "auteurism" with a focus on the 1970s, see, for example, Aaron Hunter, *Authoring Hal Ashby: The Myth of the New Hollywood Auteur* (New York: Bloomsbury Academic, 2016); Godfrey, *The Limits of Auteurism*; and Menne, *Post-Fordist Cinema*. For more general, recent discussions of film authorship, see David A. Gerstner and Janet Staiger, eds., *Authorship and Film* (New York: Routledge, 2003); C. Paul Sellors, *Film Authorship: Auteurs and Other Myths* (New York: Columbia University Press, 2010); and Barrett Hodsdon, *The Elusive Auteur: The Question of Film Authorship throughout the Age of Cinema* (Jefferson, NC: McFarland, 2017).

14   To be fair, there are numerous accounts of the complex production histories of particular films in the large number of filmmaker, actor, and producer biographies and memoirs, and the equally large number of volumes on individual movies. One might say, though, that these accounts tend to revolve around the agency of "auteurs" and are often engaged in a largely descriptive, narrative reconstruction of a film's production and addressed to general readers, rather than developing analytical arguments in the context of specific academic debates. Whether the distinction I am making here is really meaningful can, however, only be

determined through a systematic comparison of different kinds of publications. To indicate how big a job this would be, I just want to list a few books that are centrally concerned with the making of one particular film: Jerome Agel, ed., *The Making of 2001* (New York: New American Library, 1970); Arthur C. Clarke, *The Lost Worlds of 2001* (London: Sidgwick and Jackson, 1972); Piers Bizony, *2001: Filming the Future* (London: Aurum Press, 2000); Stephanie Schwam, ed., *The Making of 2001: A Space Odyssey* (New York: The Modern Library, 2010); Adam K. Johnson, *2001: The Lost Science* (Charlotte, NC: Griffin Media, 2012); Christopher Frayling, *The 2001 File: Harry Lange and the Design of the Landmark Science Fiction Film* (London: Reel Art Press, 2015); Adam K. Johnson, *2001: The Lost Science. Volume 2* (Berkeley, CA: Apogee, 2016); Piers Bizony, *The Making of Stanley Kubrick's 2001: A Space Odyssey* (Cologne: Taschen, 2016); Michael Benson, *Space Odyssey: Stanley Kubrick, Arthur C. Clarke, and the Making of a Masterpiece* (New York: Simon and Schuster, 2018); Alison Castle, ed., *Stanley Kubrick's 2001: A Space Odyssey: Behind the Scenes Book and DVD* (Cologne: Taschen, 2019); Filippo Ulivieri and Simone Odino, *2001 Between Kubrick and Clarke: The Genesis, Making and Authorship of a Masterpiece* (independently published, 2019); and Krämer, *2001: A Space Odyssey.*

15   See, for example, John T. Caldwell, *Production Culture: Industrial Reflexivity and Critical Practice in Film and Television* (Durham, NC: Duke University Press, 2008); Vicki Mayer, Miranda J. Banks, and John T. Caldwell, eds., *Production Studies: Cultural Studies of Media Industries* (New York: Routledge, 2009); and Miranda Banks, Bridget Conor, and Vicki Mayer, eds., *Production Studies, The Sequel! Cultural Studies of Global Media Industries* (New York: Routledge, 2016). In this context, it is also worth pointing to studies of labor relations and unionization in the film industry; see, for example, Michael Nelson, "Toward a Worker's History of the U.S. Film Industry," in *The Critical Communications Review. Volume I: Labor, the Working Class and the Media*, ed. Vincent Mosco and Janet Wasko (Norwood: Ablex, 1983), 47–83; David F. Prindle, *The Politics of Glamour: Ideology and Democracy in the Screen Actors Guild* (Madison: University of Wisconsin Press, 1988); Virginia Wright Wexman, *Hollywood's Artists: The Directors Guild of America and the Construction of Authorship* (New York: Columbia University Press, 2020); and, with a focus on African Americans in the 1960s and 1970s, Quinn, *A Piece of the Action*. For general reference, also see the rapidly growing literature on creative labor and creative industries, for example, Alan McKinley and Chris Smith, eds., *Creative Labour: Working in the Creative Industries* (Basingstoke: Palgrave Macmillan, 2009); and David Hesmondhalgh and Sarah Baker, *Creative Labour: Media Work in Three Cultural Industries* (London: Routledge, 2011).

16 See, for example, Andrew Spicer, A. T. McKenna, and Christopher Meir, eds., *Beyond the Bottom Line: The Producer in Film and Television Studies* (New York: Bloomsbury, 2014). It is worth mentioning that a shift of emphasis away from directors to producers and writers also facilitates the consideration of film projects that were not actually realized. See, for example, James Fenwick, Kieran Foster, and David Eldridge, eds., *Shadow Cinema: The Historical and Production Contexts of Unmade Films* (New York: Bloomsbury Academic, 2021). Of all the filmmakers associated with the American New Wave, the unrealized projects of (writer-producer-director) Stanley Kubrick have received the most attention; for a recent survey of these projects and the extensive literature about them, see Peter Krämer and Filippo Ulivieri, "Kubrick's Unrealized Projects," in *The Bloomsbury Companion to Stanley Kubrick*, ed. Nathan Abrams and Ian Q. Hunter (New York: Bloomsbury, 2021), 327–36.

17 Most notably, there is Rutgers University Press's "Behind the Silver Screen" book series on the histories of individual filmmaking professions, ranging from art direction to costume design, each volume including a section on "The Auteur Renaissance, 1968–1980" (https://www.rutgersuniversitypress.org/series/behind-the-silver-screen/list). Also see, for example, Tom Stempel, *Framework: A History of Screenwriting in the American Film*, 3rd ed. (Syracuse: Syracuse University Press, 2000); Bridget Conor, *Screenwriting: Creative Labor and Professional Practice* (London: Routledge, 2014); Miranda J. Banks, *The Writers: A History of American Screenwriters and Their Guild* (New Brunswick, NJ: Rutgers University Press, 2016); and the work of the Screenwriting Research Network (https://screenwritingresearch.com/); plus the following books on editing (with numerous references to 1960s and 1970s Hollywood): Michael Ondaatje, *The Conversations: Walter Murch and the Art of Editing Film* (New York: Knopf, 2002); and Roy Perkins and Martin Stollery, *British Film Editors: The Heart of the Movie* (London: British Film Institute, 2004). Recent book-length studies on actors and on editing in the American New Wave include Daniel Smith-Rowsey, *Star Actors in the Hollywood Renaissance: Representing Rough Rebels* (Basingstoke: Palgrave Macmillan, 2013); and Alexis Leigh Carreiro, *Script-to-Screen: Film Editing and Collaborative Authorship During the Hollywood Renaissance* (PhD diss., University of Texas at Austin, 2010).

18 See, for example, Neal Gabler, *An Empire of Their Own: How the Jews Invented Hollywood* (New York: Crown, 1988); and Steven Alan Carr, *Hollywood and Anti-Semitism: A Cultural History Up to World War II* (Cambridge: Cambridge University Press, 2001).

19 See the demographic profile of the Hollywood elite (resulting from a 1982 survey) in Stephen Powers, David J. Rothman, and Stanley Rothman, *Hollywood's*

America: Social and Political Themes in Motion Pictures (Boulder, CO: Westview, 1996), 79.

20 See Matthew Frye Jacobson, *Whiteness of a Different Color: European Immigrants and the Alchemy of Race* (Cambridge, MA: Harvard University Press, 1998); Michael Omi and Howard Winant, *Racial Formation in the United States*, 3rd ed. (New York: Routledge, 2015); and Quinn, *A Piece of the Action.*

21 See, for example, Krämer, "When 'Hanoi Jane' Conquered Hollywood," 105–6; Peter Krämer, "A Powerful Cinema-Going Force? Hollywood and Female Audiences since the 1960s," in *Identifying Hollywood's Audiences: Cultural Identity and the Movies*, ed. Melvyn Stokes and Richard Maltby (London: British Film Institute, 1999), 96–7; and Peter Krämer, "From the Margins towards the Centre: Women in 1970s and 1980s Hollywood, Part 1—General Trends," Women's Film and Television History Network (UK/Ireland) blog, October 27, 2014, https://womensfilmandtelevisionhistory.wordpress.com/2014/10/27/from-the-margins-towards-the-centre/. Also see Krämer, *The New Hollywood*, 38–66.

22 For a rare, strong dissenting voice, see James Bernardoni, *The New Hollywood: What the Movies Did with the New Freedom of the Seventies* (Jefferson, NC: McFarland, 1991).

23 See Krämer, "Post-Classical Hollywood," 296–305; Krämer and Tzioumakis, "Introduction," xv–xvi.

24 See, for example, Greg Taylor, *Artists in the Audience: Cults, Camp, and American Film Criticism* (Princeton, NJ: Princeton University Press, 1999); Raymond J. Haberski Jr., *It's Only a Movie! Films and Critics in American Culture* (Lexington: University Press of Kentucky, 2001); Raymond J. Haberski Jr., *Freedom to Offend: How New York Remade Movie Culture* (Lexington: University Press of Kentucky, 2007); Shyon Baumann, *Hollywood Highbrow: From Entertainment to Art* (Princeton, NJ: Princeton University Press, 2007); and Jerry Roberts, *The Complete History of American Film Criticism* (Santa Monica: Santa Monica Press, 2010). Also see Lee Grieveson and Haidee Wasson, eds., *Inventing Film Studies* (Durham, NC: Duke University Press, 2008).

25 No doubt, studies of individual filmmakers frequently discuss filmmaking traditions and other factors influencing their work, but these, it would seem, rarely become the focus of sustained analysis.

26 On art-house cinemas, see, for example, Barbara Wilinsky, *Sure Seaters: The Emergence of Art House Cinema* (Minneapolis: University of Minnesota Press, 2001); and Tino Balio, *The Foreign Film Renaissance on American Screens, 1946–1973* (Madison: University of Wisconsin Press, 2010). On repertory cinemas: Ben Davis, *Repertory Movie Theaters of New York: Havens for Revivals, Indies, and the Avant-Garde, 1960–1994* (Jefferson, NC: McFarland, 2017). On film festivals: Cindy

Hing-Yuk Wong, *Film Festivals: Culture, Power, and the Global Screen* (New Brunswick, NJ: Rutgers University Press, 2011). And on film schools: Michael Zryd, "Experimental Film and the Development of Film Study in America," in *Inventing Film Studies*, ed. Lee Grieveson and Haidee Wasson (Durham, NC: Duke University Press, 2008), 182–216; and Duncan Petrie and Rod Stoneman, *Educating Film-Makers: Past, Present and Future* (Bristol: Intellect, 2014).

27 Although not all of these questions can easily be answered, there are a fair number of exploratory studies including several chapters to do with the influence of European art cinema, documentary, exploitation, avant-garde, and underground films that Yannis Tzioumakis and I collected in *The Hollywood Renaissance*. I have briefly discussed the special importance of television in the careers of key filmmakers in *The New Hollywood*, 84–5.

28 Perhaps the most important work along these lines is Todd Berliner, *Hollywood Incoherent: Narration in Seventies Cinema* (Austin: University of Texas Press, 2010). Also see Lehmann, *Affect Poetics of the New Hollywood*.

29 One model for such systematic and comparative studies is the work of David Bordwell, especially *Narration in the Fiction Film* (Madison: University of Wisconsin Press, 1985). For discussions of late 1960s and 1970s Hollywood, see David Bordwell, Janet Staiger, and Kristin Thompson, *The Classical Hollywood Cinema: Film Style & Mode of Production to 1960* (London: Routledge & Kegan Paul, 1985), 367–77; and the numerous references to this period in David Bordwell, *The Way Hollywood Tells It: Story and Style in Modern Movies* (Berkeley: University of California Press, 2006).

30 See especially Jay Beck, *Designing Sound: Audiovisual Aesthetics in 1970s American Cinema* (New Brunswick, NJ: Rutgers University Press, 2016); Stephen Prince, *Savage Cinema: Sam Peckinpah and the Rise of Ultraviolent Movies* (London: Athlone, 1998); Stephen Prince, *Classical Film Violence: Designing and Regulating Brutality in Hollywood Cinema, 1930–1968* (New Brunswick, NJ: Rutgers University Press, 2003); Richard Barrios, *Screened Out: Playing Gay in Hollywood from Edison to Stonewall* (New York: Routledge, 2003); Linda Williams, *Screening Sex* (Durham, NC: Duke University Press, 2008), 68–180; Tom Pollard, *Sex and Violence: The Hollywood Censorship Wars* (New York: Routledge, 2009); and Aubrey Malone, *Censoring Hollywood: Sex and Violence in Film and on the Cutting Room Floor* (Jefferson, NC: McFarland, 2011). As these titles indicate, style and content were heavily influenced by changing industry self-regulation and censorship. More about this at the end of this chapter.

31 For general debates about the American New Wave, see Krämer, "Post-classical Hollywood," 295–305.

32 See especially Janet Staiger, *Interpreting Film: Studies in the Historical Reception of American Cinem*a (Princeton, NJ: Princeton University Press, 1992); Barbara Klinger, *Melodrama and Meaning: History, Culture and the Films of Douglas Sirk* (Bloomington: Indiana University Press, 1994); and Janet Staiger, *Perverse Spectators: The Practices of Film Reception* (New York: New York University Press, 2000).

33 One publication that was far ahead of its time stands out: Charles Barr, "*Straw Dogs, A Clockwork Orange* and the Critics," *Screen* 13, no. 2 (Summer 1972): 17–31. Later examples include J. Hoberman, "'A Test for the Individual Viewer': *Bonnie and Clyde*'s Violent Reception," in *Why We Watch: The Attractions of Violent Entertainment*, ed. Jeffrey H. Goldstein (New York: Oxford University Press, 1998), 116–45; Janet Staiger, "The Cultural Productions of *A Clockwork Orange*," in *Stanley Kubrick's A Clockwork Orange*, ed. Stuart Y. McDougal (Cambridge: Cambridge University Press, 2003), 37–60; R. Barton Palmer, "*2001*: The Critical Reception and the Generation Gap," in *Stanley Kubrick's 2001: A Space Odyssey: New Essays*, ed. Robert Kolker (Oxford: Oxford University Press, 2006), 13–28; Peter Krämer, *A Clockwork Orange* (Basingstoke: Palgrave Macmillan, 2011), 91–107; Peter Krämer, "'The Ugly Tide of Today's Teenage Violence': Revisiting the *Clockwork Orange* Controversy in the UK," in *Moral Panics, Social Fears and the Media: Historical Perspectives*, ed. Sian Nicholas and Tom O'Malley (London: Routledge, 2013), 210–29; Peter Krämer, "'A Film Specially Suitable for Children': The Marketing and Reception of *2001: A Space Odyssey* (1968)," in *Family Films in Global Cinema: The World Beyond Disney*, ed. Noel Brown and Bruce Babington (London: I.B. Tauris, 2015), 37–52; Seth Friedman, "Beyond the Infinite Interpretations: The Reception of *2001: A Space Odyssey* and the Reframing of Stanley Kubrick's Authorial Reputation," *Film History* 32, no. 1 (2020): 72–105; Peter Krämer, "The Story of Woody & Diane: Stars and Hit Patterns in the New Hollywood," in *Remembering Annie Hall*; and Krämer, *American Graffiti*. Also see Godfrey, *The Limits of Auteurism*. There is, I think, a good case to be made that *Close Encounters of the Third Kind* (1977) very much belongs to the American New Wave; see, for example, Julie Turnock, *Plastic Reality: Special Effects, Technology, and the Emergence of 1970s Blockbuster Aesthetics* (New York: Columbia University Press, 2015), 105–45, 179–200. I have also tried to make that case, and examined the film's critical reception, in Peter Krämer, "Spiritual Science Fiction for the Whole Family: Spielberg, *Close Encounters of the Third Kind* and 1970s Hollywood," in *Steven Spielberg, Hollywood Wunderkind & Humanist*, ed. David Roche (Montpellier: Press universitaires de la Méditerranée, 2018), 35–49. I think there is also a case to be made for *Jaws* (1975), *Star Wars* (1977), and *Grease* (1978) to belong to the American New Wave (on *Star Wars* see Turnock, *Plastic Reality*,

105–78). It may therefore be worth pointing out the following publications which deal, among other things, with the reception of these films: Peter Krämer, " 'It's Aimed at Kids—the Kid in Everybody': George Lucas, *Star Wars* and Children's Entertainment," *Scope: An Online Journal of Film Studies*, December 2001, http://www.nottingham.ac.uk/scope/documents/2001/december-2001/kramer.pdf; Peter Krämer, "The Impact of *Star Wars*," *Pure Movies*, March 16, 2014, http://www.puremovies.co.uk/columns/the-impact-of-star-wars/; Peter Krämer, " 'An Easy Winner': The Marketing, Reception and Success of *Grease*," in *"Grease is the Word": Exploring a Cultural Phenomenon*, ed. Oliver Gruner and Peter Krämer (London: Anthem, 2020), 145–63; Ian Hunter and Matthew Melia, eds., *The Jaws Book: New Perspectives on the Classic Summer Blockbuster* (New York: Bloomsbury, 2020); and Miles Booy, *Interpreting Star Wars: Reading a Modern Film Franchise* (New York: Bloomsbury, 2021).

34   As a useful source for determining the initial development of a film's reputation, the following book provides lists of all kinds of industry and critical awards as well as the results of various surveys of industry people, critics, and audiences: Cobbett S. Steinberg, *Film Facts* (New York: Facts on Film, 1980).

35   The above-mentioned multivolume histories of American cinema by Wiley-Blackwell and Scribner's offer extensive accounts of the American film industry, in particular its overall organization, the main production and distribution companies, key production trends, and financial results. On film finance, see especially Janet Wasko, *Movies and Money: Financing the American Film Industry* (Westport, CT: Praeger, 1982), with some material on the 1960s and 1970s. On film distribution, see Suzanne Mary Donahue, *Film Distribution: The Changing Marketplace* (Ann Arbor, MI: UMI Research Press, 1992) and John W. Cones, *The Feature Film Distribution Deal* (Carbondale: Southern Illinois University Press, 1997), these books having varying degrees of relevance for understanding the 1960s and 1970s. Film marketing has received considerable attention in Film Studies—and also in Business Studies—in recent decades but very rarely with regard to the American New Wave or 1960s and 1970s Hollywood in general. See, for example, Justin Wyatt, *High Concept: Movies and Marketing in Hollywood* (Austin: University of Texas Press, 1994); Tiiu Lukk, *Movie Marketing: Opening the Picture and Giving It Legs* (Hollywood: Silman-James Press, 1997); Thomas Austin, *Hollywood, Hype and Audiences: Selling and Watching Popular Film in the 1990s* (Manchester: Manchester University Press, 2002); Paul Grainge, *Brand Hollywood: Selling Entertainment in a Global Media Age* (London: Routledge, 2008); Robert Marich, *Marketing to Moviegoers: A Handbook of Strategies and Tactics*, 3rd ed. (Carbondale: Southern Illinois University Press, 2013); and Finola Kerrigan, *Film Marketing*, 2nd ed. (London: Routledge, 2017).

36 For case studies of key production companies of the American New Wave, see, for example, Menne, *Post-Fordist Cinema*; and for a recent study of an individual producer involved in several key American New Wave films, see A. T. McKenna, *Showman of the Screen: Joseph E. Levine and His Revolutions in Film Promotion* (Lexington: University Press of Kentucky, 2016).

37 In my research on the films of Stanley Kubrick and on 1970s Hollywood, I have tried to place particular films within ongoing production trends, and I have also analyzed their marketing and release patterns. See, for example, Krämer, *2001: A Space Odyssey*, 32–40, 90–2; Krämer, *A Clockwork Orange*, 74–6, 87–94; Krämer, "'A film specially suitable for children'"; Krämer, "'An easy winner'"; Krämer, "The Story of Woody & Diane"; and Krämer, *American Graffiti*. Also see Olen J. Earnest, "*Star Wars*: A Case Study in Motion Picture Marketing," *Current Research in Film* 1 (1985): 1–18; Frederick Wasser, "Four-Walling Exhibition: Regional Resistance to the Hollywood Film Industry," *Cinema Journal* 34, no. 2 (Winter 1995): 51–65; Friedman, "Beyond the Infinite Interpretations"; and Hunter and Melia, *The Jaws Book*.

38 See, for example, the relevant chapters in Steve Neale and Sheldon Hall, *Epics, Spectacles and Blockbusters: A Hollywood History* (Detroit: Wayne State University Press, 2010); and James Russell and Jim Whalley, *Hollywood and the Baby Boom: A Social History* (New York: Bloomsbury Academic, 2018). Also see Krämer, *The New Hollywood*.

39 See, for example, Godfrey, *The Limits of Auteurism*; Russell and Whalley, *Hollywood and the Baby Boom*, 106–15.

40 For recent work on film cycles, including chapters on the 1960s and 1970s, see, for example, Amanda Ann Klein, *American Film Cycles: Reframing Genres, Screening Social Problems, and Defining Subcultures* (Austin: University of Texas Press, 2011); Richard Nowell, *Blood Money: A History of the First Teen Slasher Cycle* (New York: Continuum, 2011); Peter Stanfield, *Hoodlum Movies: Seriality and the Outlaw Biker Film Cycle, 1966–1972* (New Brunswick, NJ: Rutgers University Press, 2018); and Zoe Wallin, *Classical Hollywood Film Cycles* (New York: Routledge, 2019). For books dealing specifically with American New Wave cycles, see, for example, Stephen Paul Miller, *The Seventies Now: Cultural as Surveillance* (Durham, NC: Duke University Press, 1999); and Godfrey, *The Limits of Auteurism*.

41 See, for example, Peter Krämer, "'Dear Mr. Kubrick': Audience Responses to *2001: A Space Odyssey* in the Late 1960s," *Participations: Journal of Audience and Reception Studies* 6, no. 2 (November 2009), http://www.participations. org/Volume%206/Issue%202/kramernew.pdf; Peter Krämer, "'Movies That Make People Sick': Audience Responses to Stanley Kubrick's *A Clockwork Orange* in 1971/72," *Participations: Journal of Audience and Reception Studies* 8,

no. 2 (November 2011): 416–30, http://www.participations.org/Volume%206/
Issue%202/3g%20Kramer.pdf. The literature on *Star Wars* audiences is, of course,
very substantial; I only want to mention one title here: Will Brooker, *Using the
Force: Creativity, Community and Star Wars Fans* (New York: Continuum, 2002).
Also see the many references to the audiences of American New Wave films in Tom
Stempel, *American Audiences on Movies and Moviegoing* (Lexington: University
Press of Kentucky, 2001); and in Russell and Whalley, *Hollywood and the
Baby Boom.*

42 See, for example, the many monographs and edited collections published
by Martin Barker, Richard Butsch, and Richard Maltby, and the work of the
HoMER (History of Moviegoing, Exhibition and Reception) network (http://
homernetwork.org/). Also see the following two recent publications: Gerald R.
Butters, Jr., *From Sweetback to Super Fly: Race and Film Audiences in Chicago's
Loop* (Columbia: University of Missouri Press, 2015) which includes a chapter
on *The Exorcist*; and William Paul, *When Movies Were Theater: Architecture,
Exhibition, and the Evolution of American Film* (New York: Columbia University
Press, 2016)—unfortunately, this historical study ends in the late 1960s. For a
study of the 1960s and 1970s, see Gary R. Edgerton, *American Film Exhibition
and an Analysis of the Motion Picture Industry's Market Structure, 1963–1980*
(New York: Routledge, 2014).

43 See, for example, Krämer, *The New Hollywood*. Also see Krämer, "Post-classical
Hollywood"; Krämer and Tzioumakis, "Introduction"; and a recent essay, in which
I revisit some of the early academic writing about Hollywood cinema of the late
1960s and 1970s: Peter Krämer, "'She Was the First': The Place of *Jaws* in American
Film History," in *The Jaws Book*, 19–32.

44 Stefan Kanfer, "The Shock of Freedom in Films," *Time*, December 9, 1967, reprinted
in Arthur McClure, ed., *The Movies: An American Idiom* (Rutherford: Fairleigh
Dickinson University Press, 1971), 322–33.

45 On the Production Code and other forms of regulation and censorship, see,
for example, Matthew Bernstein, ed., *Controlling Hollywood: Censorship and
Regulation in the Studio Era* (London: Athlone, 2000); Leonard J. Leff and Jerold
L. Simmons, *The Dame in the Kimono: Hollywood, Censorship, and the Production
Code*, 2nd ed. (Lexington: University Press of Kentucky, 2001); Prince, *Classical
Hollywood Violence*; Francis G. Couvares, ed., *Movie Censorship and American
Culture*, 2nd ed. (Amherst: University of Massachusetts Press, 2006); Ellen C. Scott,
*Cinema Civil Rights: Regulation, Repression, and Race in the Classical Hollywood
Era* (New Brunswick, NJ: Rutgers University Press, 2015); and Sheri Shinen Biesen,
Film Censorship: Regulating America's Screen (New York: Columbia University
Press, 2018).

46 See both the references in the previous endnote and, for example, Jack Vizzard, *See No Evil: Life Inside a Hollywood Censor* (New York: Simon and Schuster, 1970); Stephen Farber, *The Movie Rating Game* (Washington, DC: Public Affairs Press, 1972); Frank Walsh, *Sin and Censorship: The Catholic Church and the Motion Picture Industry* (New Haven, CT: Yale University Press, 1996); Prince, *Savage Cinema*; Gregory D. Black, *The Catholic Crusade Against the Movies, 1940–1975* (Cambridge: Cambridge University Press, 1998); Lewis, *Hollywood v. Hardcore*; Steven Vaughn, *Freedom and Entertainment: Rating the Movies in an Age of New Media* (Cambridge: Cambridge University Press, 2006); Kevin Sandler, *The Naked Truth: Why Hollywood Doesn't Make X-Rated Movies* (New Brunswick, NJ: Rutgers University Press, 2007); Laura Wittern-Keller, *Freedom of the Screen: Legal Challenges to State Censorship, 1915–1981* (Lexington: University Press of Kentucky, 2008); Pollard, *Sex and Violence*; Malone, *Censoring Hollywood*; and Henry Thompson, *Freedom from Choice: The Persistence of Censorship in Post-1968 Hollywood* (PhD diss., University of Manchester, 2011).

47 On the importance of *Bonnie and Clyde* and *The Graduate* and of 1967 as a transformative year, see, for example, Krämer, *The New Hollywood*, esp. 1, 6–8.

48 The Production Code changes in 1966 and the "suggested for mature audiences" label are usually mentioned in the above-referenced literature, but mostly only in passing.

49 A rare exception is Justin Wyatt, "Bridging Commerce and Classification through the American Art Film: The Case of *Who's Afraid of Virginia Woolf* (1966)," in *The Hollywood Renaissance*, 11–12.

Contributors

Nathan Abrams is Professor in Film and codirector for the Centre for Film, Television and Screen Studies at Bangor University in Wales. He lectures, writes, and broadcasts widely (in English and Welsh) on British and American popular culture, history, film, and intellectual culture. He is the founding coeditor of *Jewish Film and New Media: An International Journal*, as well as the author of *The New Jew in Film: Exploring Jewishness and Judaism in Contemporary Cinema*, *Stanley Kubrick: New York Jewish Intellectual*, *Eyes Wide Shut: Stanley Kubrick and the Making of His Final Film* (with Robert Kolker), and *The Bloomsbury Companion to Stanley Kubrick* (with IQ Hunter).

Aimee Dixon Anthony A fourth-generation native of Washington, DC, Aimee Dixon Anthony is a graduate of the Rhode Island School of Design, Maryland Institute College of Art and Columbia University. Born into a home of politicians she chose the world of the arts, starting her career in fashion eventually to become a filmmaker. Her first short film, *Vivian: A Period Piece* (2002), won several awards and was a finalist in the BETJ Best in Shorts national competition. While she continues to make women-centric films that focus primarily on her hometown, Aimee recently began work to support the start-up Institute of Politics Policy and History at the University of the District of Columbia (IPPH) along with former DC Mayor Sharon Pratt. Aimee currently is a Ph.D. candidate in cultural studies at George Mason University with a dissertation focus on African American women filmmakers in early cinema. Aimee has contributed to the Women Film Pioneers Project database as well as a chapter on her earlier research on African American women filmmakers of early cinema in *Silent Women: Pioneers of Early Cinema* (2016).

Emilio Audissino is Senior Lecturer in Media and Audiovisual Production at Linnaeus University, Sweden. He holds one Ph.D. in the history of visual and performing arts and one Ph.D. in film studies. His areas of specialism are Hollywood and Italian cinema, and his research interests are film history; audiovisual production; screenwriting; stylistic and formalist film and media analysis; comedy; horror; and sound and music in cinema. He is the author of *John Williams's Film Music* (2014, second edition 2021), the first book-length study in English on the composer, and *Film/Music Analysis: A Film Studies Approach* (2017), a method for audiovisual analysis that blends Neoformalism and Gestalt Psychology.

He is currently coediting (with Emile Wennekes) a handbook about music in comedy cinema. He has written about the cinema of Zucker-Abrahams-Zucker for *JewThink!* (https://www.jewthink.org/2020/11/04/its-shirley-something-to-remember-airplane-40-years-later) and for the collection of essays *Moments in Television: Substance/Style* (2021), contributing an analysis of the ZAZ TV show *Police Squad!*. www.emilioaudissino.eu

Vincent Brook has a Ph.D. in film and television from the University of California, Los Angeles (UCLA). He has been a regular lecturer at UCLA, the University of Southern California (USC), and California State University, Los Angeles. In addition to dozens of journal and anthology articles, he has authored or edited ten books, most dealing with Jewish issues in American film and television, including *Something Ain't Kosher Here: The Rise of the "Jewish" Sitcom* (2003), *You Should See Yourself: Jewish Identity in Postmodern American Culture* (2006), *Driven to Darkness: Jewish Émigré Directors and the Rise of Film Noir* (2009), and *From Shtetl to Stardom: Jews and Hollywood* (2017, coeditor). He also has written *Land of Smoke and Mirrors: A Cultural History of Los Angeles* (2013) and cowritten two short histories on his home town of Silver Lake, *Silver Lake Chronicles* (2014) and *Silver Lake Bohemia* (2016). His latest effort, *All About Eva: A Holocaust-Related Memoir, with a Hollywood Twist* (2021), recounts his German-Jewish parents' experiences in Nazi Germany and as refugees to the United States in the late 1930s and 1940s.

Hannah D'Orso is a film major with a minor in digital media and journalism at the University of Hartford. She is pursuing a career in sports journalism and postproduction.

Cary Edwards is a lecturer in film and media in Boston, Lincolnshire. He has written for *Bright Lights Film, Horror Homeroom* and *Revenant: Critical and Creative Studies of the Supernatural* on a range of topics including folk horror and on the incompatibility of Ayn Rand and Superman. Cary completed his Ph.D. in film and media at the University of Lincoln in 2018 and is currently putting the finishing touches to his book *The Vigilante Thriller: Violence, Spectatorship and Identification in American Cinema, 1970–76*. He can often be found guesting on podcasts explaining why Timothy Dalton was the best James Bond.

Gregory Frame is a lecturer in film studies and codirector for the Centre for Film, Television and Screen Studies at Bangor University, Wales. He is the author of *The American President in Film and Television: Myth, Politics and Representation*. He has published articles about the politics of American film and television in *Journal of American Studies, New Review of Film and Television Studies*, and *Journal of Popular Film and Television*, among others.

He is developing a monograph that explores the ways in which American film and television handled the 2008/9 financial crisis and subsequent recession.

Oliver Gruner is a senior lecturer in visual culture at the University of Portsmouth. His research explores historical representation in visual media, screenwriting, and the portrayal of the 1960s and 1970s in the United States. He is the author of *Screening the Sixties: Hollywood Cinema and the Politics of Memory* (2016) and coeditor (with Peter Krämer) of *Grease Is the Word: Exploring a Cultural Phenomenon* (2019). His work has been published in the *Historical Journal of Film, Radio and Television*, *Rethinking History*, and *The Poster* as well as various edited collections. He recently received a fellowship from the Harry Ransom Center, Austin, Texas, to undertake archival research into Hollywood screenwriters of the 1960s and 1970s and plans to develop this research into a monograph on the subject.

Aaron Hunter lectures in the Department of Film at Trinity College Dublin. His writing has appeared in *Alphaville* and *Journal of Film and Video*. Publications include *Authoring Hal Ashby: The Myth of the New Hollywood Auteur* (2016) and *Being There and the Evolution of a Screenplay* (2021). Forthcoming works include a monograph on production designer Polly Platt (2021) and a collection, coedited with Martha Shearer, on Women and New Hollywood (2022).

Peter Krämer is a senior research fellow in cinema and TV in the Leicester Media School at De Montfort University (Leicester, UK). He also is a senior fellow in the School of Art, Media and American Studies at the University of East Anglia (Norwich, UK) as well as a regular guest lecturer at Masaryk University (Brno, Czech Republic) and at the University of Television and Film Munich (Germany). He is the author or editor of eleven academic books, including the BFI Film Classic on *2001: A Space Odyssey* (2nd ed., 2020), *The New Hollywood: From Bonnie and Clyde to Star Wars* (2005), *"Grease is the Word": Exploring a Cultural Phenomenon* (jointly edited with Oliver Gruner, 2020) and *The Hollywood Renaissance: Revisiting American Cinema's Most Celebrated Era* (jointly edited with Yannis Tzioumakis, 2018).

Fjoralba Miraka is a research student and Ph.D. candidate at Roehampton University with a research focus on *Women, Movie Brats and Sexual Politics in the era of Hollywood Renaissance*. She is also a film critic for the online magazine Sbunker (https://sbunker.net/autori/fjoralba.miraka). She holds an MA in American Literature and Culture and a BA in English Language and Philology, both from Aristotle University of Thessaloniki, Greece. In 2018 she received the

Arthur Smith Memorial Scholarship, awarded by the Fran Trust, for her participation in the *Women and New Hollywood* conference, Maynooth University, Ireland, where she presented her paper "Gender, Genre, and Class Politics in Barbara Loden's Wanda (1970)." The paper was published in *MAI: Feminism & Visual Culture* in 2019. In 2020 her entry on the history of feminist film theory was published in the first *International Encyclopaedia of Gender, Media, and Communication* by Wiley Blackwell. She has translated part of the memoirs of Albania's first woman director, Xhanfize Keko, for the film *Beni Walks on His Own*, which was published in 2020. Currently she is working on translations of the director's memoirs on the film *Spoiled Mimoza* to be published in 2022.

Aimee Mollaghan is the subject lead for film at Queen's University, Belfast. Prior to this she was a senior lecturer in media, film and television at Edge Hill University. Her current research is concerned with exploring music, sound, and soundscape across disciplinary boundaries. She is the author of the monograph *The Visual Music Film* (2015). Her current research interests focus on the relationship between music/sound and the moving image and on landscape and sound in cinema. She continues to publish in both areas.

Karen A. Ritzenhoff is a professor in the Department of Communication at Central Connecticut State University (United States). She is affiliated with the Women, Gender, and Sexuality Studies Program and cinema studies. In 2019 her coedited book (with Clémentine Tholas and Janis Goldie) titled *New Perspectives on the War Film* was published. She is also publishing another coedited book in 2021 titled *Mediated Terrorism in the 21st Century* (with Elena Caoduro and Karen Randell). In 2019, Ritzenhoff completed a coedited collection of essays with Janis Goldie entitled *The Handmaid's Tale: Teaching Dystopia, Feminism, and Resistance across Disciplines and Borders*. Another book project is *Black Panther: Afro-Futurism, Gender, Identity and the Re-Making of Blackness*. Dr. Renée White is coediting this volume.

Kim Wilkins is a postdoctoral research fellow in screen cultures at the University of Oslo where she researches German and American screen media. She is the author of *American Eccentric Cinema* (2019), coeditor of *Refocus: The Films of Spike Jonze* with Wyatt Moss-Wellington (2019), and *Refocus: The Films of Richard Linklater* with Timotheus Vermeulen (forthcoming, 2022). She has published essays on American indie cinema in *New Review of Film and Television Studies*, *Film Criticism*, *Sydney Studies in English*, *Texas Studies in Literature and Language* and in Peter Kunze's *The Films of Wes*

Anderson: Critical Essays on an Indiewood Icon (2014). She has an essay on Noah Baumbach, literary filmmaking, and neoliberal creativity forthcoming in *Textual Practice* (2022). Her writing on contemporary television has appeared in a collection on *Westworld* (2019) and in forthcoming editions of *Screen* and *Cinephile* (both 2021).

Index

8½ 72, 74
20th Century Fox 45
2001: A Space Odyssey 59, 69, 222, 228

Abel-Bey, Gay 147
À bout de souffle 83, 89, 90
Abrahams, Jim 14, 82 *see also* ZAZ
    (Zucker, Abrahams, and Zucker)
Abrams, Nathan 61, 68, 69, 70
Adventures of Robin Hood, The 131
aesthetics 7–9, 15, 17, 25
    debates 5
    documentary-style aesthetic 66
    and landscapes 167, 169
    of phenomenological realism 26–7
    unplanned aesthetic 41
    unplanned realist aesthetic 46
African Americans 223, 224
    culture 144
    filmmakers 11, 142
    performers 210
    radicalism 225
African American women
    in early cinema 150–1
    filmmakers 15–16, 141–9, 155–6
ahistoricism 9
Aina, Shirikiana 147
Airplane! 79, 81, 84, 85, 87, 90, 92, 99n50
Airport 41, 87
Albee, Edward 75
Aldrich, Robert 3, 87
Alexander, George 149
Alex in Wonderland 60, 74
Alice Doesn't Live Here Anymore 27
Alice's Restaurant 59, 61, 62, 64, 67
Allen, Dede 67, 74, 80, 106
Allen, Woody 6, 8, 14, 59, 61, 65, 66, 67,
    71–3, 74, 75, 79, 80, 84, 93, 130, 222
Allison, Deborah 42, 43
All Quiet on the Western Front 25
All the President's Men 4, 28, 60

Alonzo, John 104, 114
Alphaville 83, 94
Altman, Robert 6, 60, 74, 101, 182, 208, 222
ambiguities 39–40, 43, 45, 48, 55, 163,
    171–4, 221
American Graffiti 222
American Honey 164, 169, 170, 171,
    172, 177n24
American Jewish activists and artists 61
Anderson, P. T. 211
Anderson, Wes 202, 203, 211, 215
Andrew, Dudley 44, 142
Angels in America 65
animated shorts 82
Annie Hall 59, 71–2, 80, 222
Anspach, Susan 74
Apocalypse Now 6, 24, 28
Apprenticeship of Duddy Kravitz, The 75
Arkin, Alan 59
Arnold, Andrea 16, 162, 163, 164, 165, 166,
    168, 169, 170, 171, 172, 175, 176n5
Artful Dodger, The 125, 128
artistic motivation 93, 94
Ashby, Hal 60, 122, 135, 136, 204
auteurism/auteurs 3, 4, 6, 8–10, 13, 14, 21,
    27, 39, 40, 42, 55, 69, 83, 84, 96, 101,
    102–3, 130, 197n3, 203, 206, 212, 227,
    228, 232n14
    Cahiers auteur 102–3
    change and development over
        time 103–4
    components of 102–3
    conceptual changes 102
    criticism 102
    gender difference 102
    indie-auteurs 203, 211
    and Jewishness 12
    male centric auteurism 15
    maverick auteurs 134, 212, 213–16
    and mise-en-scène analysis 104
    myth 213

oeuvres 208
popular auteurism 130
production designers 116
and racism 208–9
as romantic artists 215
scenarios driven by 41
sexism 209
visual consistency 102
white male auteurists 8, 12
authorship 5, 15, 28, 55, 104, 108, 115, 122, 135, 208
Avery, Brian 64
Avildsen, John G. 4, 134
Awakening of Jacob, The 71

back-projection 89–90
Badlands 161, 162
Bad News Bears, The 108, 114–16
Bainbridge, Caroline 180
Baker, Lenny 74
Bakshi, Ralph 60, 75
Balio, Tino 81
Ballenger, Melvonna 147
Bananas 59, 93
Bancroft, Anne 30
Bande à part 83, 89
Banks, Miranda 130
Baron, Cynthia 215
Barry Lyndon 69
Bartlett, Hall 87
Bartók, Béla 71
Basinger, Jeanine 23
Bates, Sandy 72
Baumbach, Noah 202
Beard, Henry N. 82
Beatty, Ned 113
Beatty, Warren 62
Beck, Glenn 68
Bedknobs and Broomsticks 208
Beetz, Zazie 186
Beguiled, The 54
Belmondo, Jean-Paul 90
Benjamin, Richard 59, 71
Benny Hill Show, The 80
Benton, Robert 24
Beyoncé 149
Beyond the Valley of the Dolls 75
Big Sleep, The 33

Biloxi Blues 65
Bingelli, Elizabeth 154
Bird Cage, The 65
Birth of a Nation, The 143, 157n9
Biskind, Peter 105, 204, 218n13
Bisset, Jacqueline 113
Black, Karen 163
Black Caesar 75
Black Lives Matter 192, 193–4
Blaxploitation 9, 75
Blazing Saddles 60, 74, 79
Blow Out 6
Blue, Carroll Parrott 147
Blume in Love 60, 74
Boas, Franz 152, 153
Bob & Carol & Ted & Alice 60, 74, 124
Bogart, Humphrey 71, 90
Bogdanovich, Peter 60, 75, 101, 105, 108, 109, 110, 116, 118n20, 119n33, 144, 204, 208, 209, 222
Bonnie and Clyde 1, 2, 3, 5, 18, 46, 59, 61, 62, 63, 67, 83, 106, 107–8, 162, 174, 228–9
Boorman, John 3
Bordwell, David 83, 84, 94, 198n18
Bored of the Rings 82
Bound for Glory 107
Bourdieu, Pierre 202
Bowser, Kenneth 218n13
Bozzuffi, Marcel 45
Brando, Marlon 24
Bravo, Enrique "Ricky" 41
Breslin, Jimmy 123
Bresson, Robert 183
Brightsweet, Stormé 147
Brody, Richard 161, 165
Brooks, Albert 59
Brooks, James L. 101, 109
Brooks, Mel 8, 59, 71, 73, 74, 79, 80, 85, 93, 130
Brooks, Xan 63
Brown, Clarence 153
Buccaneers, The 131
Buckland, Warren 67
Bud Yorkin Productions 108
Burgess, Anthony 69
Burstein, Robert 25
Buscombe, Edward 47

Butch Cassidy and the Sundance Kid 92
Bye Bye Braverman 66

Caesar, Sid 74
Cahiers auteur 102–3
Cahiers du Cinema 102
Canby, Vincent 44
Cannon, Dyan 74
Capitalism and Freedom 5
Capricorn One 70
Carnal Knowledge 59, 65
Carney, Raymond 165
Carrie 222
Carter, Jimmy 3
cartoons 82
Cass, Mama 213
Cassavetes, John 60, 74, 165
Catch 22 59, 65
CBS Television Network Productions 48
Cervantes, Miguel de 125
Chanan, Michael 147
Chartoff, Robert 123
Chase, Chevy 85
Chayefsky, Paddy 67
Childers, William 125, 129
Chinatown 13, 33–4, 60, 75, 104, 107, 108, 222
Christian, Barbara 156
Chudnow, Dick 81
Cimino, Michael 2, 24, 28
cine-literate audience 44
cinéma de papa 88, 90
Cinema Novo 206
cinematography/cinematographers 8, 41, 103–4, 106, 108, 166, 170–1
cinema-verité techniques 40
cinephilia 73, 79, 82–4
Cissé, Souleymane 147
civil rights movement 11, 24, 53, 126, 146, 162, 192, 210, 225
classical Hollywood 21, 23–4, 25, 27, 40, 41, 65, 71, 90, 106, 132, 145, 202, 214, 226
classic binary 50
Cléo de 5 à 7 168
Clift, Montgomery 24
Clockwork Orange, A 59, 69, 222
Close Encounters of the Third Kind 228

Closer 6
Clouse, Robert 87
Cocks, Geoffrey 70, 71
Coen brothers 203
Cohen, Larry 75
Columbia Pictures 10
comedy 79, 86
    comedian-comedies 84–5, 93
    silent-cinema comedy 82
    of stylistic excess 93–6
comic-based movies 86, 87, 181
Coming Home 121, 125, 131, 135
compositional motivation 93, 96
continuity 89, 222
continuity editing 199n18
Conversation, The 28
Coogan's Bluff 47
Cook, David 3, 21, 137
Cooling, Chris 215
Coonskin 60
Coppola, Francis Ford 6, 23, 24, 28, 60, 74, 96, 130, 144, 181, 204
Coppola, Sofia 211
Corliss, Richard 102, 130
Corman, Harvey 74
Corman, Roger 105, 108, 110, 111
Cosgrove, Dennis 164
Costa-Gavras 41
counterculture movement 17, 40, 43, 53–4, 62, 122–3, 126, 127, 162, 203
Crawford, Joan 25
Cripps, Thomas 150
critical reactions 39, 44–5, 47, 55 *see also* fascistic reaction; throwback
Crosby, Bing 80, 84
Cullen, Brett 187
cultural cachet 202
cultural consciousness 10, 13

Daniel 66
Danny Kaye Show, The 75
Dash, Julie 16, 142–5, 147, 148–50, 152, 155–6
Dassin, Jules 65
Dauber, Jeremy 73
Daughters of the Dust 143, 145, 149, 155
Davis, Zeinabu Irene 25, 147

Day of the Dolphin, The 65
Day of the Locust, The 121, 122, 129, 130, 131, 132, 134–5
Dead Men Don't Wear Plaid 79
Dean, James 24
Debord, Guy 168
Decade under the Influence 218n13
decay 133–4
Deconstructing Harry 73
deconstruction 79, 81, 82, 87, 89–91
Deep Throat 223
Deer Hunter, The 24, 28, 222
De Niro, Robert 24, 34, 60, 180, 187, 222
De Palma, Brian 6, 23, 24, 28, 60, 74
Dern, Bruce 135
De Sica, Vittorio 165
Desser, David 66, 73
Deutscher, Isaac 73
Diamonds are Forever 208
Diary of a Mad Housewife 60
Diary of an African Nun, The 148
Diary of Anne Frank, The 67
DiCaprio, Leonardo 213
digitalization, impact of 207
Direct Cinema movement 165, 166
Directors Guild of America 10, 130
Dirty Dozen, The 3, 87
Dirty Harry 8, 13, 39–48, 51, 52, 54–5
Dixon, Thomas 143
Dmytryk, Edward 33, 67
Doane, Mary Ann 23
Dog Day Afternoon 59, 66, 67
Dollars (trilogy) 47
Donaldson, Lisa 164
Don Quixote 125, 126, 128
Double Indemnity 25, 31
Dowd, Nancy 135
Drew, Robert 166
Drew Associates 166
Dreyfus, Richard 59, 71
Dr. Strangelove 70
Dr. Strangelove: How I Learned to Stop Worrying and Love the Bomb 59, 68
DuBois, W.E.B. 151, 159n39
Dullea, Keir 69
Dunaway, Faye 33, 62, 106
Duncan, James 164
Duncan, Nancy 164

Duras, Marguerite 161
Duvall, Shelley 70
DuVernay, Ava 149

Eastman, Carole 175n5
Eastwood, Clint 14, 40, 42, 44, 46, 47, 48, 53, 54, 55, 58n52
Easy Rider 83, 124, 127, 161, 162, 168, 170, 173, 174, 209, 222
Ebiri, Bilge 181
Edmund, Larry 108
Electra Glide in Blue 222
elitism 8, 215
Ellis, John 57n37
Elsaesser, Thomas 25, 26, 165, 205, 214
Enter the Dragon 87
Epps, Garrett 44
Erens, Patricia 72
ethnicity 5, 63, 66, 224 *see also* Jews/Jewishness
Ethno-Communications Program 146, 148
ethno-religious tribute 72
European cinema 1, 155
    art cinema 6, 14, 72, 74, 225, 226
    New Wave 106
    realism 155, 163, 166
Everything You Always Wanted to Know about Sex 79
Exorcist, The 60, 226
exploitation 21, 45, 220n38, 223, 225
Eyes Wide Shut 7

Fail Safe 68
Farrelly Bros., The 81
Fascinating Mrs Fraser, The 23
fascistic reaction 39
Feiffer, Jules 65, 68
Feldman, Marty 74
female directors *see also* African American women
female filmmakers 223
    marginalization of 215
female movies
    road movies 161–75
female stars 23, 223
Feminine Mystique, The 31
feminism 10, 23, 30, 102, 162, 215
femme fatale 13, 29–35

Fessenden, Larry 164
Fiddler on the Roof 208
Field, Allyson Nadia 11, 147
film noir 22, 25, 29–35, 63, 65–6, 182–3,
    184, 224
Film Studies 9, 11, 22, 224, 225,
    226, 227
financial studies 226–7
Finch, Peter 68
Fincher, David 211
finger gun motif 188, 190
Finler, Joel 231n9
Fisher, Carrie 65
Five Easy Pieces 60, 161, 162, 163, 164, 172,
    174, 175n5, 209, 214
Flame and the Arrow, The 123
flash-cutting technique 67
Fleshler, Glenn 188
Floyd, George 192, 193
folklore 72, 148, 152
Fonda, Jane 31, 135
Fosse, Bob 60
Foster, Jodie 34, 186
Foster, Norman 25
Foster, William 150
Four Friends 61, 63–4
Four Women 148
Frankenheimer, John 58n53, 74
Frayling, Christopher 47
Frazier, Jacqueline 147
French Connection, The 13, 28, 39–40, 41,
    43–4, 45, 46, 47, 48–51, 54, 55, 60, 210
French Connection, The, II 58n53
French New Wave/*nouvelle vague* 2, 14, 41,
    54, 62, 66, 68, 74, 79, 81, 82–83, 84,
    91, 92, 94, 147, 206, 225
Friedan, Betty 31
Friedkin, William 13, 39, 41, 46, 60, 222
Friedman, Lester 66, 73
Friedman, Milton 5
Fritz the Cat 60, 75
Frodon, Jean-Michel 83
Front, The 71, 72
frontier mythology 173
Full Metal Jacket 7
Funny Girl 231n6
Funny Lady 60
future research 229

Gable, Clark 71
Gabriel, Teshome 147
Gaines, Jane 150
Gang 125
gangster films 25, 27, 63, 83, 127, 132, 179
Gang That Couldn't Shoot Straight, The 122,
    123, 124, 128, 132, 134
Garbo Talks 66
Gelbart, Larry 74
gender 9, 10, 12–13, 17, 22 *see also* women
    demarcations 217
    in melodrama 27
    and public space limitations 28
generic transformation 47, 48
genre codes 21, 40–1
genre revisionism 21, 33, 35, 36, 80,
    84, 85, 96
genres 21–4, 27, 29
Gibson, Gloria 156
Giffith, D. W. 23
Gilman, Sander 73
Girgus, Sam 73
Gist, Eloyce King Patrick 156
Giuliani, Rudy 192, 199n25
Godard, Jean-Luc 14–15, 81, 82–4, 88, 89,
    90, 91, 92, 93, 94, 95, 96
Godfather, The (I and II) 28, 104, 210,
    226, 228
Godfrey, Nicholas 206, 207, 208
Gomez, Sara 147
Gosford Park 7
Gould, Elliott 59, 71, 74
Graduate, The 1, 3, 5, 13, 18, 30–1, 59, 62,
    64, 65, 83, 211, 212, 216, 229
Grant, Cary 71
Gran Torino 58n52
Graves, Peter 85
Greenfield, Pierre 53
Griffith, D. W. 23, 143, 157n9
Grodin, Charles 59, 71
Groening, Matt 81, 109
Guffey, Burnett 106, 107, 117n12
Guthrie, Arlo 62
Gutiérrez Alea, Tomas 147

Hackman, Gene 40, 41, 46, 63
Haller, Michael 107
Hang 'Em High 47

Hangover, The (trilogy) 181
Hanson, Helen 29
Harlan, Veit 69
Harlem Renaissance, the 141, 151–4
Harold and Maude 107
Harper, Graeme 167
Harris, Leonard 187, 218n13
Harvard Lampoon 82
Haskell, Molly 9, 209
Hawks, Howard 25
Heartburn 65
Heaven's Gate 2, 6
Heavy Traffic 60
Heffernan, Nick 204
Heim, Allen 67
Heller, Joseph 65
Hellman, Jerome 122–3, 128, 133, 135
Hellman, Monte 75, 161
Hell Up in Harlem 75
Hellzapoppin' 97n16
Hendershot, Heather 182, 183
Henry, Buck 65
Hepburn, Katherine 25
Herndon, Samantha 118n27
Hester Street 75
Higgins, Michael 163
High Anxiety 74, 80, 85, 86, 93
Higson, Andrew 165, 166, 167, 169
Hill, Benny 80
Hill, Derek 211
Hill, George Roy 60, 92
Hill, Walter 113
Hiller, Arthur 41
Hitchcock, Alfred 69, 80, 90, 224
Hoberman, J. 4, 182
Hodge, Bob 57
Hoffman, Dustin 24, 30, 59, 63, 64, 65, 71, 123
Hollywood Heroines 29
Holmes, Maori Karmael 148
Honeymoon Kid, The 60, 75
hooks, bell 149
Hope, Bob 80, 84
Hopper, Dennis 83, 161, 204
Horak, Jan-Christopher 11, 147
Horsley, Jake 48
Houston, Drusilla Dunjee 143
Hughes, Langston 151, 152

Hunter, Aaron 122, 208, 221
Hurst, Fannie 153
Hurston, Zora Neale 16, 141–5, 151–6
Huston, John 33
Hutcheon, Linda 86, 199n23

identity politics 63, 66
ideology 14, 21–2, 29, 40, 41, 44, 47, 48, 54, 55, 165, 208
illusions 26, 31, 72, 131–5
Illusions 137, 148
Imitation of Life 153
indie cinema 201–3, 211, 215, 217
individualist ideology/individualism 203, 204, 214–15
intensification of Hollywood's traditional practices 79, 87–9, 90, 96
Interiors 67, 72
international crisis 133–4
intertextuality 82–4
Invasion of the Body Snatchers 42, 43
Irishman, The 179
irreverence 81, 84, 88, 96
Italian Americans 60, 224, 225
Italian neorealism 26, 147, 206
Ivanhoe 123

Jacobs, Diane 60
James, David E. 146
Jaws 3, 4, 227
Jewish Americans 224
Jewish angst 66
Jewish Enlightenment *(haskalah)* 61
Jewish humor 73, 82
Jewish New Wave 59, 60, 70
  directors 59
  film noir 63, 65–6
  liberal political and avant-garde artistic aspects 61
  noir attributes 63
Jews/Jewishness 60, 224
  Ashkenazi Jews 12
  and auteurism 12, 14
  Central European Jews 70
  insider/outsider complex 73
  Jewish actors 59, 74
  Jewish identity 69
  religious practice and belief 60, 69

secular Jewish activism 67
Johnson, Ben 105
Johnson, George 150
Johnson, James Weldon 152
Johnson, Noble 150
Joker 17, 179–82, 184, 185, 188–96, 198,
    199n24, 212
Jones, Robert C. 135
Jonze, Spike 211
Journey Into Fear 25
Judgment at Nuremberg 67
Juggler, The 67
Jules et Jim 74
jump cuts 15, 83, 89, 96, 106
Just Tell Me What You Want 66

Kael, Pauline 44, 102, 130, 161
Kahn, Madeline 59, 74
Kallianiotes, Helena 214
Kaminsky, Stuart M. 42
Kane, Carol 59
Kanin, Michael 130
Karina, Anna 91
Karloff, Boris 111, 112
Kaufman, Charlie 216
Kazan, Elia 65, 161
Kellner, Douglas 28
Kennedy, Robert 126
Kenney, Douglas C. 82
Kentucky Fried Movie, The 81, 87
Kentucky Fried Theater, 81
Keogh, Riley 172
King, Geoff 3, 106, 201
King, Noel 205, 206, 210, 211
King, Stephen 70
King Jr., Martin Luther 126
King of Comedy, The 17, 180, 187,
    194, 195
King of Marvin Gardens, The 60
Kirshner, Jonathan 3, 4, 5, 6, 7, 9, 10, 12,
    142, 182, 195–6, 206, 207, 209, 221
Kiss of Death 132
Klein, Philip 110
Klinger, Barbara 168, 171
Klute 13, 31–2, 33, 60
Kolker, Robert 96, 106, 208
Kotcheff, Ted 75
Kovács, Laszló 104, 111, 112, 117n2

Krämer, Peter 2, 3, 5, 6, 7, 8, 9, 12, 17, 18,
    197n3, 208, 219n27, 221
Kramer, Stanley 66, 67
Kramer vs Kramer 24, 30
Krassner, Paul 68
Krutnik, Frank 84
Kubrick, Stanley 7, 14, 59, 61, 68–71,
    222, 234n16
Kurtzman, Harvey 68
Kushner, Tony 65

Laderman, David 162
Lady Sings the Blues 231n6
Lancaster, Bill 114
Landis, John 81
landscapes 16, 164–71, 174, 211
Lane, Sasha 164
Lange, Dorothea 16, 166
L.A. Rebellion 11, 16, 142, 144, 146–7, 150,
    151, 156
Larkin, Alile Sharon 147
Last Picture Show, The 60, 75, 105, 107, 114,
    118n20, 208
Lathrop, Philip 113
LeBeouf, Shia 172
Lee, Bruce 172, 213
Lehrer, Tom 68
Le Mépris 83, 90, 92
Lemonade 149
Lennard, Dominic 221
Leone, Sergio 46–7, 213
Leopard's Spots, The 143
LeRoy, Mervyn 25
Les Quatre Cents Coup 91, 171
Lester, Richard 60
Levinson, Julie 204
Lewis, Jerry 80, 84, 187
Lewis, Jon 3, 4, 5, 6, 7, 9, 10, 12, 142, 181,
    182, 195–6, 198n15, 206, 207, 209, 221
Liberating Hollywood 10
Linklater, Richard 203, 211
Little Big Man 59, 61, 63, 67
Little Caesar 25
Lloyd, Danny 70
Loach, Ken 166
LoBrutto, Vincent 221
location 107, 114, 182
    choices 43

scouting 104, 105, 107
shooting 41, 83, 104
Locke, Alaine 152
Loden, Barbara 8, 9, 16, 142, 162, 163,
    165, 166, 168, 169, 171, 172, 176n5,
    177n24, 209
Lolita 59, 68
Lord of the Rings, The 60, 82
Losey, Joseph 65
Love and Death 59, 71
Lovell, Alan 42, 43
Love Story 41
Lucas, George 4, 144, 182, 228
Lucas, Marcia 105
Lumet, Sidney 4, 14, 59, 61, 65–8, 74, 107,
    134, 199n22

Maas, Peter 125
MacFarlane, Seth 81
Mad (magazine) 68, 82
Made in U.S.A 83, 94
Makarah, O. Funmilayo 147
male psyche 22, 25, 29, 33, 35, 209
Malick, Terence 7, 161, 222
Malpaso Company 42
Maltby, Richard 204
Maltese Falcon, The 33
Man, Glenn 33
Mancini, Henry 113
Manhattan 59, 72
Man of La Mancha 125
Manson Family, the 213
Man with No Name (trilogy) 46
Marchand, Corrine 168
marketing 45, 46, 227
Marshall, Frank 113, 116, 119n33
Martin, Dean 60, 80, 84, 89
Marx Brothers 97n16
masculine ideal 24–5, 123
M*A*S*H 124, 125
Mason, Charlotte Osgood 145, 153
master-scene script 128, 130
Matthau, Walter 114
maverick auteurs 134, 212, 213–16
May, Elaine 21, 29, 60, 64, 65, 75, 165, 209
Mayshark, Jesse Fox 211
Mazursky, Paul 60, 73, 74, 75
M'Baye, Babacar 152

McCabe and Mrs. Miller 207, 208
McCullough, Barbara 147
McDonagh, Maitland 220n38
McKay, Claude 152
McKee, Lonette 148
McQueen, Steve 213
Mean Streets 27, 28, 179, 180
media jokes 81
Medium Cool 60, 75
Meek's Cutoff 164, 167, 170, 171, 173
Mellencamp, Patricia 148, 149
melodrama 13, 22–9, 35, 83
    of action 25
    classical melodrama 25, 26, 27
    domestic melodrama 28
    male melodrama 27–8
    New Melodrama 24
    of passion 25, 27
    postclassical melodrama 25
    and realism 26
    stylized mise-en-scène 26, 27–8, 196
Menne, Jeff 5, 6
Meyer, Russ 75
Micheaux, Oscar 150
Mickey One 59, 61
Midnight Cowboy 60, 75, 121–2, 123, 124,
    128, 129, 135, 207, 222
Midnight Special, The 81
Mikey and Nicky 60
Milestone, Lewis 25
Milius, John 74, 222
minority cinemas 146
Miracle Worker, The 30
Miramax *see* Sundance–Miramax era
Mission: Impossible 6, 85
Missouri Breaks, The 61, 63, 67
mockeries 80, 81, 84, 93, 94, 95
Molloy, Claire 215
Monaco, Paul 67
Monkees 75
Monty Python's Flying Circus 80
Moore, Robin 41–2, 56n13
moral ambiguities 39–40, 43, 45, 48, 55
moral structures 47–8
Moses, Man of the Mountain 152
Mostel, Zero 59, 74
Motion Picture Association of America 228
Mottram, James 176n5, 211

movie theaters 227
M Squad 87
Mules and Men 152
multiple authorship 122
Mulvey, Laura 23
Murder My Sweet 33
Murray, Bill 85
Music for Strings, Percussion and Celesta 71
myth 204–8
 "deeply American" 203, 207, 208, 210, 215, 216
 overarching politics 214
 and Sundance–Miramax era, link between 213–14
 tensions behind 208–10

Nabokov, Vladimir 68
Naked Gun, The (trilogy) 81, 92
Nama, Adilifu 210
narrative images 45–6
naturalism 41–2
Neale, Steve 84
Nelson, Ralph 47
neo-noir 31, 33, 34, 63, 66, 192
neorealism 26, 66, 147, 206
Netflix 116, 119n33, 179, 207
Network 4, 59, 67–8
Neve, Brian 65
New German Cinema 206
New Leaf, A 60
Newman, Michael 201, 202, 211, 212
New Yorker, The 44
New York Jewish intellectualism 69
New York Times, The 44
Next Stop Greenwich Village 60, 74
Nichols, Mike 1, 5, 6, 14, 59, 61, 64–5, 66, 67, 75, 83, 96, 222
Nicholson, Jack 24, 33, 70, 163, 214
Nielsen, Leslie 85
Night Moves 59, 61, 63, 67
Nixon, Richard 4, 45, 81, 162, 180, 182, 183, 192, 195
nonsensical accumulation 86, 87, 93, 96
Norton, Edward 212

Oats, Warren 113
Obsession 24
O'Kelly, Tim 111

Once Upon a Time … in Hollywood 17, 204, 212–13
O'Neal, Tatum 112, 115
O'Neal, Ryan 112
Osteen, Sam 67
Other Side of the Wind, The 116, 119n33
Owl and the Pussycat, The 60

Pacino, Al 24–5, 60
Paint Your Wagon 42
Pakula, Alan J. 4, 13, 60, 83
Palance, Jack 90
Palmer, R. Barton 33, 221
Panic in Needle Park 60, 75
Paper Moon 60, 105, 107, 112, 113, 114
Parallax View, The 28, 60, 83, 222
parametric narration 94–5, 96
Paramount 87, 104, 105, 108, 109
parody/spoof genre 14, 31, 48, 73–4, 79–80, 82, 84, 86–7, 93, 94, 96
Pawnbroker, The 59, 66, 67
Payne, Alexander 211
Peckinpah, Sam 60, 80
Penderecki, Krzysztof 71
Penn, Arthur 1, 14, 30, 46, 59, 61–4, 67, 74, 83, 96, 107, 162
periodization 5–7, 17, 212
peritexts 91–2, 99n50
Perkins, Claire 215
Perry, Frank 60
Pesci, Joe 60
Petrie, Graham 102
Petulia 60
Phillips, Todd 179–82, 186, 190–6, 199
Phoenix, Joaquin 180, 212
Pictures at a Revolution 218n13
Picture Show 116
Pillow Talk 107
Pitt, Brad 213
Platt, Polly 15, 101–2, 104–5, 107, 108–15, 116, 118n21, 209
Player, The 7
Play It Again, Sam 60, 72
Play It as It Lays 60
Play Misty for Me 54
Play Time 95
Point Blank 3
Polanski, Roman 13, 33, 60, 75, 213

Police Squad 81, 87, 89, 92, 93, 94, 99n50
political positions 17, 44–5, 203
Pollack, Sydney 60
Polonsky, Abraham 65
Pomerance, Murray 221
populism 2, 207
pornography 223
Post, Ted 47
Postcards from the Edge 65
Post-Fordist Cinema 5
postmodernism 22, 25, 28
post-Sarris auteurists 103
pranksters 214
Presley, Elvis 87
Price, Steven 127, 128, 130
Primary Colors 65
Producers, The 60, 74
Production Code 1, 5, 40, 62, 68,
    182, 228–9
production design/production designers
    15, 101, 103, 104, 106–8, 109–10, 114,
    115, 119
Production Studies 224
Proferes, Nicholas 165, 166
Proud Boys, The 193
Psycho 90
psychogeography 167–8
psychological realism 175
Public Enemy, The 25
Pulp Fiction 212

Queen Sugar 149

race/racism 9, 11–12, 14–15, 17, 210,
    217, 225 *see also* African Americans;
    African American women
Rachel and the Stranger 123
Rafelson, Bob 60, 161
Rafelson, Toby 105
Raging Bulls 105, 204
Rapf, Joanna E. 131
Rappaport, Michael 165
Rawhide 48
Rawlings, Marjorie Kinnan 153
Rayner, Jonathan 167
Reagan, Ronald 3
realism 106, 107, 155, 163, 165, 166
    classical realism 26–7

construction of narrative spaces in 167
of extravaganza 26
phenomenological realism 26–7
of phenomenological realism 26–7
psychological realism 175
surface realism 165, 166, 175
unplanned realist aesthetic 46
Realist (magazine) 68
realistic motivation 93
realist melodrama 26, 27
Reception Studies 226
Redford, Robert 65
Redmond, Sean 180
Regester, Charlene 210
Reichardt, Kelly 16, 162, 163, 164, 165,
    166, 168, 169, 170, 171, 172, 175,
    176n5, 177n24
Reiner, Carl 59, 74, 79, 101
Renoir, Jean 165
reputation building 226
Reservoir Dogs 211, 212
Rey, Fernando 40
Reynaud, Bérénice 161
rhetoric versus practice paradox 103
Richardson, Tony 166
Ritchie, Michael 101, 114, 119n35
Ritt, Martin 66, 71, 74
River of Grass 164, 171, 172, 176n5
road movies 161–2, 174–5
    ambiguity and dispossession 171–4
    context 162–4
    and landscapes 164–71
Robbie, Margot 213
Robeson, Eslanda Goode 143, 154
Robeson, Paul 143
Robinson, Andy 40
Rocha, Glauber 147
Rocky 4
Rohmer, Eric 82
Roizman, Owen 41, 104
romance, decline in 28
Room 237 70
Rosemary's Baby 75, 222
Rosenblum, Ralph 67, 71
Ross, Herbert 60, 72
Rossen, Robert 65
Rosson, Richard 25
Running on Empty 66

Rush, Richard 60, 74
Rushmore 211
Russell, David O. 211
Ryan, Michael 28

Salt, Waldo 15, 121–35
Sarafian, Richard C. 161
Sarris, Andrew 5, 9, 44, 102, 103, 144
Scarecrow 60, 161, 162, 174
Scarface 25
Schatzberg, Jeffrey 60, 75, 161
Scheider, Roy 41
Schickel, Richard 44
Schlesinger, John 60, 75, 123, 128, 129, 130, 133, 135
Schrader, Paul 222
Schulman, Bruce 127
Scorsese, Martin 4, 6, 17, 23, 27, 28, 60, 74, 96, 103, 144, 179–84, 186, 188, 191, 192, 194, 195, 196, 198n15, 222
screenwriters/screenwriting 15, 121, 127–34
script-led style 42
Search, The 67
Seaton, George 41, 87
Seberg, Jean 90
Segal, George 59, 71, 74, 81
self-reflexivity 40, 41, 47, 54, 58n52, 72, 83, 87
Sellers, Peter 68
Sembène, Ousmane 147
Seraph on the Sewanee 153–4
Serpico 59, 66, 67, 121, 122, 125, 126, 127, 129, 131, 134, 135, 199n22
sex, lies and videotape 202, 212
Shampoo 107
Shandling, Garry 65
Shearer, Martha 221
Shepherd, Cybill 34, 118n20, 189
Shiel, Mark 40
Shining, The 59, 69, 70, 78
Shohat, Ella 142
Shopworn Angel, The 131
Short Cuts 7
Siegel, Don 8, 13, 39, 42–3, 47, 53, 54, 55
Silent Movie 74
Silkwood 6, 65
Silver, Micklin 65, 75

Simmon, Scott 23
Simon, Danny 74
Simon, Neil 65, 74
Simone, Nina 148
Sirk, Douglas 153
Situationist International 167–8
Sleeper 59
Slotkin, Richard 215
Smart-Grosvenor, Vertamae 149
Smith, Murray 58
Smukler, Maya Montañez 10, 208
social tradition in American film 65–6
Soderbergh, Steven 202, 203, 211
Soldier Blue 47
Sorcerer, The 60
source lighting 41
Spaghetti western 47
spectator's subject position 45–8
Spielberg, Steven 3, 6, 60, 144, 182, 222, 228
Stahl, Francis E. 117n9
Stahl, John M. 153
Staiger, Janet 202
Stam, Robert 142
Stanley Kubrick: New York Jewish Intellectual 61
Stanwyck, Barbara 25, 31
Stardust Memories 72, 73
Star Is Born, A 109
Star Wars 4, 227, 228
Stempel, Tom 130
Sterile Cuckoo, The 60
Sterritt, David 83
Stevens, George 67
Stewart, Jacqueline Najuma 11, 147
Stewart, James 24
Stranger Among Us, A 66
Straw Dogs 209
Streep, Meryl 30
Streisand, Barbra 59, 112
structure of sympathy 58n48
Stucker, Stephen 98n30
Studio System 40
style-centered approach 15, 16
stylistic difference 41
stylistic excess 93–6
stylistic techniques 41
subject positions 48–54

Sugarland Express, The 60
Sundance-Miramax era indies 17, 202, 203, 211, 212, 214, 215
superhero movies 179, 180–1, 182, 196
surface realism 165, 166, 175
surrealism 61–2, 81–2, 91
Sutherland, Donald 32
Sweet Sweetback's Baadasssss Song 210
Sylbert, Richard 104, 107, 108, 116
Symmons, Tom 133

Take the Money and Run 59, 67, 71, 72, 80
Tarantino, Quentin 17, 203, 211, 212, 215
Taras Bulba 131
Targets 105, 110–11, 114
Tashiro, Charles 104
Tate, Sharon 213
Tati, Jacques 95
Taubin, Amy 183, 184
Tavoularis, Dean 104, 106, 107, 108, 116
Taxi Driver 4, 13, 17, 27, 34–5, 180, 182–6, 188–92, 194, 195, 196
Taylor, Charles 75
Taylor, Clyde 147
Taylor, Elyseo 147
Terms of Endearment 109
Tesich, Steve 64
textual understandings 45–8
Thackeray, William Makepeace 69
Their Eyes Were Watching God 152
They Shoot Horses, Don't They? 60
Thief Who Came to Dinner, The 108, 113
Thin Red Line, The 7
Third Cinema 11, 16, 147
Thompson, Kristin 84, 95, 198n18
Thomson, David 205, 206
Tightrope 58n52
Time magazine 3, 5
Tolkin, Mel 74
Top Secret! 81, 82, 87, 91, 95, 99n50
transtextual motivation 93, 94
Tree of Life, The 7
Tripp, David 57
Truffaut, Francois 74, 82, 91, 102, 171
Trump, Donald 13, 180, 192, 193, 194, 195, 199n24
Tuggle, Richard 58n52
Twelve Angry Men 67

Two-Lane Blacktop 75, 161, 173
Tzioumakis, Yannis 2, 3, 5, 7, 8, 9, 12, 197n3, 208, 219n27, 221

Une femme est une femme 83, 89, 92, 94
Une femme mariée 83–4
Unforgiven 58n52
United Artists 123, 205
Unmarried Woman, An 60
Untouchables, The 6
Ustinov, Peter 123

Valley of the Prehistoric Women 105
Vanishing Point 161, 162, 168, 173
Van Peebles, Melvin 210, 220n38
Varda, Agnès 168
vérité mode of cinema 40, 165–6
Vietnam War 4, 63, 124, 125, 135, 180, 192, 195
Village Voice, The 44
Vivre sa vie 83, 90–1
Vixen! 75
Voight, Jon 123, 132, 135
Von Sternberg, Joseph 23

Walker, Alice 148, 152
Walker, Madame C.J. 143
Wanda 8, 16, 161–75, 209–10
Warner Bros. 10, 46, 99n50, 105, 106, 109, 112, 196
Washington, Booker T. 159n39
Wasson, Craig 63
Watergate scandal 180
Wayans Bros., The 81
Wayne, John 24, 47, 71
Way We Were, The 60
Webb, Lawrence 40–1, 65, 107
Weill, Claudia 9, 142
Welles, Orson 25, 65, 116, 119n33
Wellman, William A. 25
Wendy and Lucy 164, 169, 170, 171, 172
West, Nathanael 129, 131, 132
westerns 47–8
Wexler, Haskell 60, 75, 104
Wexler, Norman 135
What Planet Are You From? 65
What's Up, Doc? 105, 112, 113, 116

White Anglo-Saxon Protestants (WASPs) 12, 64–5
Whitehead, J. W. 64
white male-centric period 141
Who's Afraid of Virginia Woolf? 5, 75
Who's That Knocking at My Door 28
Widmark, Richard 132
Wild Angels, The 105
Wild Bunch, The 222
Wilder, Billy 25, 31
Wilder, Gene 25, 59, 74
Wilkinson, Alissa 181
Williams, Linda 22
Williams, Michelle 164, 171
Willie and Phil 60, 74
Willis, Gordon 104, 117n2
Winfrey, Oprah 149
Winkler, Irwin 123
Winters, Shelley 74
Witches of Eastwick, The 109
Wizards 60
Wolf at the Door, The: Stanley Kubrick, History, and the Holocaust 70
women 224

her-stories 145–6
in melodrama 22–3, 27
in New Hollywood 29–35
women's film 23–5, 27–8, 142
Wood, Robin 40
Woodstock 124
Working Girl 6

Yang, Jeff 199n24
Yearling, The 153
Young Frankenstein 60, 74, 79
Your Show of Shows 75

Z 41
Zawierucha, Rafal 213
ZAZ (Zucker, Abrahams, and Zucker) 14, 79–81, 84–8, 90–4, 96
Zero Hour! 87
Zinnemann, Fred 66, 67
Zsigmond, Vilmos 104, 117n2
Zucker, David 14, 84, 87 *see also* ZAZ (Zucker, Abrahams, and Zucker)
Zucker, Jerry 14, 82, 86 *see also* ZAZ (Zucker, Abrahams, and Zucker)

CPSIA information can be obtained
at www.ICGtesting.com
Printed in the USA
LVHW050436150523
746989LV00008B/399